ICON OF EVIL

ICON OF EVIL

Hitler's Mufti and the Rise of Radical Islam

David G. Dalin and John F. Rothmann

Random House New York

Published in the United States by Random House,
an imprint of The Random House Publishing Group,
a division of Random House, Inc., New York.

RANDOM HOUSE and colophon are registered
trademarks of Random House, Inc.

LIBRARY OF CONGRESS CATALOGING-IN-PUBLICATION DATA

Dalin, David G.
Icon of evil: Hitler's mufti and the rise of radical Islam /
David G. Dalin and John F. Rothmann.
p. cm.
Includes bibliographical references and index.
ISBN 978-1-4000-6653-7
1. Husayni, Amin, 1893–1974.   2. Palestine—History—1917–1948.
3. Mandates—Palestine.   4. World War, 1939–1945.
5. Arab-Israeli conflict.   I. Rothmann, John F.   II. Title.
DS125.3.H79D35 2008   956.94'04092—dc22 [B]   2007045131

Printed in the United States of America on acid-free paper

www.atrandom.com

9 8 7 6 5 4 3 2 1

First Edition

Book design by Laurie Jewell

*To my mother, Bella Dalin, and my brother and sister-in-law,
Ralph and Hedy Dalin, with love and appreciation for their
continuing support and encouragement.*

— DAVID G. DALIN

*To Ellen Tuchman Rothmann, my wonderful wife,
with all of my thanks and love, and with deep appreciation
for everything you do every day to make our lives complete.*

—JOHN F. ROTHMANN

Preface

We have been thinking about writing this book for forty years. The genesis of this volume dates from our shared experience in Israel. On August 14, 1968, we visited Yad Vashem, the Holocaust memorial and museum in Jerusalem. We came to Israel that summer as college students, participating in a study program at the Hebrew University in Jerusalem directed by Professor Yonah Alexander. As we walked through the somber setting of Yad Vashem, we came upon an enlarged photograph of two men, Adolf Hitler and Haj Amin al-Husseini, the grand mufti of Jerusalem. We were immediately struck by the same question: What was the story behind that photo? Ever since that August day in Jerusalem forty years ago, we have pursued the story of the mufti with relentless determination, devoting innumerable hours to researching his life and times.

On a very personal note, we are delighted to report that this book was completed without a moment of disagreement or dissension. Working on this book together has deepened our friendship of more than forty years.

Contents

Preface | *vii*

Chapter 1: Rendezvous with Destiny | *3*

Chapter 2: The Genesis of Modern Jihad | *7*

Chapter 3: Partners in Genocide | *39*

Chapter 4: The Mufti's Reflection | *66*

Chapter 5: The Mufti's Return to the Middle East | *79*

Chapter 6: Mandate for Hate | *107*

Chapter 7: The Mufti's Legacy | *128*

Acknowledgments | *145*

Chronology of the Mufti's Life | *149*

Appendix: Correspondence and Documents | *153*

Notes | *173*

Bibliography | *199*

Index | *213*

ICON OF EVIL

Chapter 1

Rendezvous with Destiny

Shortly after noon on November 28, 1941, just nine days before the Japanese attack on Pearl Harbor, Haj Amin al-Husseini, the grand mufti of Jerusalem, left his luxurious mansion on Berlin's fashionable Klopstock Street and was driven to the Wilhelmstrasse, the historic street on which were located most of the German government ministries. The mufti and the führer were scheduled to meet at Adolf Hitler's private office in the Reich Chancellery.

The meeting had been scheduled for the afternoon, to accommodate Hitler's well-known penchant for working through the night and sleeping through much of the late morning. After a short drive down the elegant Wilhelmstrasse, imperial Berlin's old center of power,[1] the large government Mercedes arrived at the corner of Voss-Strasse, in front of the Reich Chancellery, the opulent seat of Hitler's government. It is plausible to assume that as the mufti's driver turned south from Unter den Linden, which had been one of the main areas of Jewish shops in Berlin, he may have mentioned to al-Husseini, a recently arrived visitor to the German capital, that before Hitler's assumption of power in 1933, the land under the new Reich Chancellery had belonged to the Jewish department store magnate Georg Wertheim. Wertheim had been coerced into donating his Berlin property to the new Nazi regime.

As he was escorted down a long, marble-floored corridor, al-Husseini was suitably impressed by the monumental grandeur of one of the architectural wonders of the Third Reich, perhaps the greatest achievement of Hitler's favorite architect, Albert Speer. When the führer had commissioned Speer to design and build the new Reich Chancellery in 1938, he had commented that the old building, which dated from Bismarck's tenure in the 1870s, was "fit for a soap company"[2] and was not suitable as headquarters of the German Reich. Speer was to create an edifice of "imperial majesty,"[3] an imposing building with grand halls and salons. Al-Husseini was driven through the Court of Honor, the building's main entrance, ascended an outside staircase, and approached the visitors' elaborately ornate reception room, immediately adjacent to Hitler's personal office. As the mufti neared the reception room, he passed through a round room with domed ceiling and a gallery 480 feet long, the exquisitely furnished mirrored gallery that Hitler had praised as surpassing the famous Hall of Mirrors at the Palace of Versailles. It boasted a length of nearly 1,200 feet, and its floor and walls were lined with dark red marble. Hitler's immensely spacious private office and study, measuring nearly 4,500 square feet, was located immediately to its side.[4]

Following his arrival in Berlin three weeks earlier, rapturous crowds had hailed the mufti as the führer of the Arab world. The week before his meeting with Hitler, al-Husseini had been honored at a reception given by the Islamische Zentralinstitut,[5] a German-Islamic institute recently established in Berlin. As the mufti was driven down the Wil-helmstrasse, adoring crowds of Palestinian Arab expatriates lined the streets to cheer and pay homage to their revered leader, the *Grossmufti von Jerusalem.*

Hitler regarded the mufti with both deference and respect. With the possible exception of King Ibn Saud of Saudi Arabia, al-Husseini was the most eminent and influential Islamic leader in the Middle East. The mufti, unlike Ibn Saud, was a trusted supporter of Hitler's Germany, a man upon whom the Nazis could always rely.

The mufti began by thanking the führer for the great honor he had bestowed by receiving him. In his effort to both flatter his host and so-licit his patronage and support, the mufti told Hitler that he "wished to seize the opportunity to convey to the Fuhrer of the Greater German Reich, admired by the entire Arab world, his thanks for the sympathy he had always shown for the Arab and especially the Palestinian cause. . . . The Arab countries were firmly convinced that Germany would win the war and that the Arab cause would then prosper." The Arabs, the mufti assured his host, "were Germany's natural friends because they had the same enemies as had Germany, namely the English, the Jews and the Communists. They were therefore prepared to cooperate with Germany with all their hearts and stood ready to participate in the war, not only negatively by the commission of acts of sabotage and the insti-gation of revolutions, but also positively by the formation of an Arab Legion. The Arabs could be more useful to Germany as allies than might be apparent at first glance, both for geographical reasons and because of the suffering inflicted upon them by the English and the Jews."[6]

The mufti's objectives were far-reaching. He wanted to terminate Jewish immigration to Palestine, but he also hoped to help lead a holy war of Islam in alliance with Germany, a jihad that would result in the extermination of the Jews.[7]

As al-Husseini would write in his memoirs: "Our fundamental con-dition for cooperating with Germany was a free hand to eradicate every last Jew from Palestine and the Arab world. I asked Hitler for an explicit undertaking to allow us to solve the Jewish problem in a manner befitting our national and racial aspirations and according to the scientific methods innovated by Germany in the handling of its Jews. The answer I got was: 'The Jews are yours.' "[8]

To the mufti's delight, the führer responded with a strong and unequivocal reaffirmation of his anti-Jewish position and of his support for the radical Arab cause, assuring the mufti that he was fully committed to pursuing a war of extermination against the Jews and to actively opposing the creation of a Jewish national home in Palestine. As the mufti would recount after their meeting, Hitler had assured him that "Germany was resolved, step by step, to ask one European nation after the other to solve its Jewish problem, and at the proper time direct a similar appeal to non-European nations as well. Germany's objectives would then be solely the destruction of the Jewish element residing in the Arab sphere under the protection of British power [in Palestine]."[9] In that hour, the führer assured al-Husseini, the mufti would become the most powerful leader in the Arab world.

For the forty-six-year-old mufti, this meeting with the führer was his rendezvous with destiny. Haj Amin al-Husseini had been preparing for this moment for much of his adult life. He had gone to the Reich Chancellery to convince Adolf Hitler of his total dedication to the Nazi goal of exterminating the Jews. The führer had instantly embraced him, eagerly welcoming al-Husseini as his ally and collaborator.

At the conclusion of their ninety-five-minute meeting, the mufti could reflect with great satisfaction on what he had achieved: Only three weeks after his arrival in Berlin on November 7, the mufti's dream of a more formal alliance between radical Islam and Hitler's Germany had become a reality.

As the mufti stood up to leave, he and the führer embraced and shook hands. It was a handshake, each believed, that would change the world.

Chapter 2

The Genesis of Modern Jihad:
Haj Amin al-Husseini, Palestinian Nationalism,
and the Birth of Radical Islam

Amin al-Husseini was born in the last decade of the nineteenth century. The year of his birth is given by various sources as 1893, 1895, and 1897, but it is generally agreed that he was born in 1895. He was educated first in Jerusalem, where he attended a Turkish government school, and then in Cairo, at the school of Sheikh Rashid Rida. Here, young al-Husseini was indoctrinated with a virulent anti-Semitism. It was as a teenager that al-Husseini first learned about the Prophet Muhammad's historic antipathy toward the Jews of Medina, who actively opposed the Prophet and rejected his message. As descendants of those who opposed the founder of Islam, and who refused to accept the new faith that he preached, al-Husseini was taught, Jews would forever be condemned by Muslims as infidels who denied the truth of Muhammad's message. This was a lesson that the impressionable al-Husseini would learn well as a student in Cairo, a lesson he would never forget and that would shape his own attitudes toward Jews throughout his life. In 1913, after briefly attending Al-Azhar University in Egypt, he fulfilled the Muslim religious obligation of pilgrimage to Mecca and thereafter added the title "Haj" to his name. From then on, he would be known as Haj Amin al-Husseini.

Al-Husseini never completed his academic studies at Al-Azhar University, a fact that would remain a source of controversy for his Muslim critics over the years. Since he'd dropped out of Al-Azhar without completing a degree, or the course of study necessary for ordination as a Muslim cleric and legal scholar, his Muslim opponents were able to belittle his academic credentials and maintain that he did not have sufficient accreditation to hold the position of mufti and spiritual leader in the Muslim religious community. Throughout his public career, al-Husseini tended to reinvent his own autobiography, claiming credentials and professional experience that he did not in fact possess. Thus, for example, from the outset of his career he would imply that he had been ordained as a Muslim cleric and that while at Al-Azhar he had completed the requisite studies in Sharia (Muslim religious law) to qualify for ordination. Had he done so, he would have been known as Sheikh Amin al-Husseini, a title that properly ordained members of the Muslim clergy were qualified to hold.[1]

With the outbreak of World War I, al-Husseini enlisted in the Turkish army and became an officer. The Ottoman Turkish Empire, in whose army he fought, had allied itself with Germany, joining the Central Powers in its losing war against Great Britain, France, and the United States. History would prove that this was a tragically fateful—and foolish—decision for the once formidable Ottoman Turkish Empire: As British prime minister Herbert Asquith remarked at the time, the Ottoman Empire "in making this decision [to join the Central Powers] was in effect committing suicide and sealing its own doom."[2] In 1918, after Germany and Turkey's defeat, al-Husseini returned to his native Jerusalem, where he worked first as a clerk in the office of the Arab adviser to the British military governor and then as a teacher.

As he began to assume a leadership role in Palestinian Arab public life in the aftermath of World War I, he exhibited political skill beyond his years. He quickly attracted the attention of Jerusalem's young Palestinian Arab nationalists, who began to look to him for advice and leadership. This was advice and leadership that the young al-Husseini, hoping to embark on a political career, was most happy to provide. In Jerusalem, he began to develop a grassroots political organization in the city, mobilizing a coterie of followers and political supporters who shared his virulent hatred of the British and the Jews. A charismatic and spellbinding orator, he mesmerized crowds on the street corners and outside the mosques of his native city and soon attracted a significant political following, expanding and cementing what became a passionately loyal political base that would support him in the years to come. Beginning in 1918, he became a frequent contributor to Arab nationalist journals, writing articles that were violently anti-Jewish.[3] In these essays, he did not hide his all-consuming hatred of the British and the Jews or his fanatical opposition to the creation of a Jewish state in Palestine. Some more moderate Arab nationalists were ready to consider working together with the Jews of Palestine and to accept the idea of a Jewish state. Haj Amin al-Husseini was adamant in rejecting such a moderate, conciliatory approach. To him, any cooperation with the Jews was out of the question.

The roots of al-Husseini's hatred of the Jews were clear and unambiguous. The Jews were the enemy. From his earliest point of awareness, young Amin knew that the Jews were not Muslims. He knew that the Jews were determined to take his homeland. He believed that the Jews were part of a grand conspiracy that would ultimately destroy Islamic civilization. For the mufti, reading *The Protocols of the Elders of Zion* for the first time was a revelation. This was the book that explained his world, that accurately described precisely the events taking place in his beloved homeland, British-occupied Palestine. The British were clearly part of the very conspiracy described in the *Protocols*. British army officers in Jerusalem, fresh from Europe, were reading and widely distributing copies of the *Protocols* among themselves and to the

Arabs of Palestine. If the Jews were to be prevented from succeeding in the nefarious conspiracy outlined in the *Protocols,* someone would have to raise the banner of Islam in jihad against this mortal enemy.

Al-Husseini saw himself as destined to fulfill that heroic role. He was born into one of the most patrician families of Arab Palestine, a family that could trace its lineage directly back to the Prophet Muhammad. During the last decades of the nineteenth century, the Husseinis were part of the political elite of Palestine. Members of the family served in the Turkish Parliament and as regional governors, mayors, and religious leaders. Growing up in turn-of-the-century Jerusalem, then still under Turkish Ottoman rule, the young al-Husseini was heir to a political dynasty that had been ruling Arab Jerusalem since the early 1880s. His father, Sheikh Tahr al-Husseini, had served as mufti of Jerusalem, as had his father, Mustapha al-Husseini, before him. When Amin's father died in 1908, his older brother, Kamal al-Husseini, assumed his position,[4] carrying on a family tradition that al-Husseini himself would later continue. In 1918, immediately after World War I, his cousin Musa Kasim Pasha al-Husseini became mayor of Jerusalem. A shrewd and successful politician who governed the Holy City as if it were his family's personal fiefdom, Musa Kasim Pasha at first ruled with the complete support of the British mandatory government, which after World War I had replaced Ottoman Turkish rule in Palestine. As head of one of the leading Muslim families in the city, he emerged as the preeminent radical Islamic opponent of the British Mandate for Palestine, and of Great Britain's pledge, in its Balfour Declaration of November 2, 1917, to create a Jewish national home in Palestine.

The idea for a British mandatory government in Palestine had initially been established by the Sykes-Picot Agreement, a secret deal that the Allies (chiefly Great Britain and France) had negotiated in 1916 to divide the Ottoman Empire—which included present-day Turkey, Lebanon, Syria, Israel, Saudi Arabia, Yemen, Kuwait, Jordan, Iraq, Bahrain, and the United Arab Emirates—among themselves. The Ottoman Turks had ruled most of these territories for centuries. Carving up the spoils under Sykes-Picot, England tightened its grip on Egypt (already under British rule) and also took control of Palestine, Iraq, several Gulf states, and Transjordan (today's Hashemite Kingdom of Jordan). At the Paris Peace Conference at the conclusion of World War I, the victorious Allies ratified the provisions of Sykes-Picot, stipulating that Palestine would be ruled by the British under a mandatory system. Under the mandate, Great Britain was responsible for all governmental, administrative, and security functions in Palestine. These moves reneged on promises of postwar independence that had been made to various Arab leaders by the flamboyant British representative in the region, T. E. Lawrence—Lawrence of Arabia. In carving up the Ottoman Turkish Empire and establishing its British colonial administration in Palestine and throughout the Arab Middle East, the Allies had shaken the foundations of what had been the established political order in the Arab world.

The Balfour Declaration, which was published as a letter by British foreign secretary Arthur James Balfour to Lord Walter Rothschild, head of the London branch of the great Jewish banking family, was issued shortly before al-Husseini's return to Jerusalem. It was a cataclysmic event for Palestinian Arabs and further shook the foundations of their political order. For the young radical Islamist al-Husseini, it was an act of political betrayal that he would never accept or forgive. It was also the catalyst that led to his emergence as leader of the radical Muslim opposition to the British mandatory government in Palestine, and to his increasingly virulent hatred of both the British and the Jews. The Balfour Declaration had stated, unequivocally, that "His Majesty's Government view with favor the establishment in Palestine of a National Home for the Jewish people, and will use their best endeavors to facilitate the achievement of this objective, it being clearly understood that nothing shall be done which may prejudice the civil and religious rights of the existing non-Jewish communities in Palestine or the rights and political status enjoyed by Jews in any other country." To

Palestinian Arabs, it was a bombshell. After all, they asked, by what right do the British, who have no legal standing in Palestine, have to give what is not theirs to a people who represent a minority of the population in Palestine? Just a little more than five weeks later, the unthinkable happened. British military forces under the command of General Sir Edmund Allenby entered Jerusalem on December 11, 1917, achieving a quick victory over the Ottoman Turkish forces defending the city. The surrender of Jerusalem to the British put the Holy City under the control of non-Muslim authorities for the first time since the Crusades. General Allenby's capture of Jerusalem fired the psyche of the Allies. For Catholics, the holy places that had been lost when Saladin conquered Jerusalem more than eight hundred years earlier were once again under Western, and Christian, rule. General Allenby was elated by his victory, as were the city's Jews. Within two years of Allenby's British conquest of Jerusalem, the emerging British mandatory policy in Palestine would radicalize the Palestinian Arab world that al-Husseini aspired to lead.

On January 8, 1918, the president of the United States, Woodrow Wilson, addressed a joint session of Congress. It was during this speech that Wilson presented what came to be known as "the Fourteen Points," his vision of the principles upon which the postwar world should be constructed. Two of these points were of special significance to the Arabs of Palestine. Article 5 called for "a free, open minded, and absolutely impartial adjustment of all colonial claims, based upon a strict observance of the principle that in determining all such questions of sovereignty the interests of the populations concerned must have equal weight with the equitable claims of the government whose title has been determined." Article 12 stated, in part, "The Turkish portions of the present Ottoman Empire should be assured a secure sovereignty, but the other nationalities which are now under Turkish rule should be assured an undoubted security of life and an absolutely unmolested opportunity to autonomous development. . . ."[5] These two points were viewed by young radical Arab leaders and activists, such as al-Husseini, as calls for an end to British colonialism in the Middle East, as a repudiation of the provisions of the Sykes-Picot Agreement, and as a call for self-determination for Arab populations previously governed by the Ottoman Empire. Haj Amin al-Husseini and other young leaders of the Arab world were more determined than ever to actively fight the British. And so they did.

On April 4 and 5, 1920, during the annual celebration of the Muslim festival of Nebi Musa, celebrating the birth of Moses, the first intifada, or uprising, against British colonialism erupted in Jerusalem. At the Nebi Musa festival, coinciding in that year with the Passover and Easter seasons, al-Husseini provoked the Arabs of Jerusalem to incite anti-Jewish violence in the city. In the Muslim Quarter of Jerusalem, wall posters appeared with the words: "Kill the Jews: There is no punishment for killing Jews."[6] In the Jewish Quarter, rioting Arabs ransacked the Torat Hayim religious seminary and attacked Jewish men, women, and children, killing some and wounding many others. In the two days of rioting, 5 Jews and 4 Arabs were killed, 211 Jews and 21 Arabs were wounded. Two Jewish women were raped. "I regret to say," the British secretary of state for war, Winston Churchill, told the House of Commons at the end of the month, "that about 250 casualties occurred [in Jerusalem], of which nine-tenths were Jewish."[7]

The Jews called the April 1920 riots a pogrom. The Arabs viewed it as a legitimate action against enemies whose political interests were different from their own. The British viewed it as minor disturbance that needed to be avoided in the future.

The riots were the first of many violent radical Islamic uprisings against the Jews of Palestine that would take place over the next eight and more decades, throughout the twentieth century and on into the twenty-first. In personally inciting the violent intifada of 1920, al-

Husseini established a precedent, for the use of violence and terror, that future generations of radical Islamists would emulate in their ongoing wars against the Jews and the West.

The British held al-Husseini personally responsible for the April 1920 riots and sought him out for arrest. According to one account of what followed, two British officers came to the door of the Husseini residence in May 1920 in search of Haj Amin. They were greeted by a young man who informed them that Haj Amin was his brother and that he was not home. When the British officers told him that they had a warrant for Haj Amin's arrest, the young man suggested that if they returned later, they would find him at home. Of course, the young man was Haj Amin al-Husseini, and he promptly fled Jerusalem and escaped across the Jordan River to safety.[8] Not long after that, he was tried in absentia and sentenced to ten years in prison.

Al-Husseini's Appointment as Grand Mufti

On April 24, 1920, at the San Remo Conference of the League of Nations, British prime minister David Lloyd George officially accepted the establishment of a British Mandate for Palestine. Less than three months later, on July 1, 1920, a British civil administration was set up in Palestine, with its headquarters in Jerusalem. Sir Herbert Samuel was appointed by Prime Minister Lloyd George as British Palestine's first high commissioner.

Lloyd George was intentionally offering the appointment to one of England's most prominent Jews, a man who actively supported the Zionist dream of establishing a Jewish state in Palestine. A member of the Anglo-Jewish elite who was related to the Montagus and other eminent Jewish families,[9] Samuel was widely recognized as one of England's most distinguished diplomats and statesmen. The scion of a wealthy Liverpool banking family that had been active in the Jewish community and in British politics, Herbert Samuel had joined David Lloyd George's Liberal Party shortly after completing his university studies at Oxford. First elected to Parliament in 1902, and the first British Jew to be appointed to a seat in a prime minister's cabinet, Samuel served as postmaster general and, subsequently, as home secretary. During his tenure as home secretary, he became a great advocate for women's rights, including the right of a woman to run for Parliament. In addition, during his tenure he helped to contain the political disturbances in Ireland.[10] His friend writer George Bernard Shaw predicted that Samuel would one day become prime minister.[11] Samuel had been knighted by King George V in 1920, shortly before receiving his appointment as high commissioner of Palestine. After his appointment, Samuel was hailed as "the first Jew to rule the land of Israel in 2,000 years."[12]

Many political observers believed at the time that Lloyd George's appointment of Herbert Samuel was an act of political genius.[13] The appointment generated tremendous enthusiasm among the Jews of England and leaders of the Zionist movement. Hebrew "hymns of redemption" were composed in honor of Samuel, who became a hero to Jews throughout the world. Carpets were woven bearing Samuel's image. His picture was hung on the walls of many Jewish homes, often next to that of Theodor Herzl,[14] the founder of political Zionism.

Herbert Samuel's involvement with Zionism had dated at least from the outbreak of World War I in 1914. When in November of that year the Ottoman Empire joined the Central Powers, Samuel formally suggested to the British foreign secretary that a Jewish state be established in Palestine. In March 1915, Samuel, then postmaster general in the British Liberal government of Herbert Asquith, wrote a memorandum formally proposing the establishment of a British protectorate over Palestine[15] that would lead eventually to the establishment of a Jewish state. In proposing that Great Britain establish a mandate over Palestine, Samuel argued persuasively to his parliamentary colleagues that Palestine would form a new and exquisite jewel in the imperial crown of the British Empire.[16] As the first practicing Jew to sit in a British cabinet, moreover, Samuel said he felt that it was right and proper to support the creation of a Jewish state in Palestine. From the opening shots of World War I, he proposed to his cabinet colleagues British support for creation of a Jewish state in Palestine.[17] This proposal—the first of its kind ever made by a British government official—was enthusiastically supported by David Lloyd George and became the inspiration for the Balfour Declaration two years later.

At the time, and in the decade that followed, not all British Jews shared Herbert Samuel's support for Zionism and for the eventual establishment of a Jewish national home in Palestine. Quite the contrary: Many Jewish leaders, especially among the wealthy Anglo-Jewish elite of which Samuel's family was a part, vocally opposed the Balfour Declaration, asserting that the Zionist aims were "inconsistent with British citizenship."[18] Samuel's cousin Edwin Montagu, the prominent Liberal Party politician and newly appointed secretary of state for India, stated his opposition in intensely personal terms: "If you make a statement about Palestine as the National Home for Jews," argued Montagu, "every anti-Semitic organization and newspaper will ask what right a Jewish Englishman, with the status at best of a naturalized foreigner, has to take a foremost part in the government of the British Empire."[19] Montagu's objections, shared by other members of Lloyd George's war cabinet, played a role in delaying the issuance of the government's pro-Zionist Balfour Declaration for several months.[20] Resistance to the Balfour Declaration within the cabinet was overcome when, on October 31, 1917, an overwhelming majority of Lloyd George's war cabinet voted to affirm their support for a Jewish national home in Palestine. Three days later, the Balfour Declaration was issued.[21]

Al-Husseini's vocal and vicious opposition to the Balfour Declaration had been well known to Samuel even before his appointment as high commissioner. That made even more remarkable the most controversial act of Samuel's tenure as high commissioner: his appointment of al-Husseini as grand mufti of Jerusalem. Of the many disputes that arose in Jerusalem during the mandate years, Haj Amin al-Husseini's appointment was one of the most controversial.[22]

The great hopes and expectations that had greeted Samuel's appointment quickly gave way to Jewish anger and resentment. Many Zionist leaders especially regarded Samuel's appointment as an act of inexcusable political naïveté, if not veritable treason to the Zionist cause. While the Zionist movement regarded Herbert Samuel with great respect and reverence when he first arrived in Jerusalem, David Ben-Gurion, the future prime minister of Israel, told the World Zionist Congress in 1921, "But what did he give us? Haj Amin al-Husseini as Mufti of Jerusalem."[23]

At first, to be sure, Samuel had not been well predisposed toward al-Husseini. On July 1, 1920, upon assuming his duties, Samuel felt it was important to demonstrate his fairness and impartiality toward the Arabs of Palestine. As a *Jewish* high commissioner, he felt that this should be one of the first priorities of his new administration. Thus, on July 7 he issued a full amnesty for all Palestinian Arabs who had been sentenced previously by British military courts. Al-Husseini, however, was not granted amnesty immediately. It would take another seven weeks for Sir Herbert, under pressure from the Arabists in the British Foreign Office, to grant a special, individual amnesty to al-Husseini, who then returned to Jerusalem in September and would soon assume a religious and political role in radical Islamic public life with far-reaching consequences.

When the death of al-Husseini's older brother, Kamal al-Husseini, five months later left vacant the position of mufti of Jerusalem, al-Husseini announced his candidacy to succeed him. However, he was one of four candidates to emerge as leading contenders and far from a shoo-in for the vacancy. Moreover, among the Palestinian Arab community in Jerusalem, the appointment of Haj Amin al-Husseini was not unopposed. In fact, the Nashashibi family, the Husseini family's chief rival for leadership of the Palestinian Arab community, staunchly opposed al-Husseini's candidacy. The family rivalries between the Nashashibis and the Husseinis, which dominated Palestinian Arab politics in Jerusalem, went back many years and would persist for several years to come. Their family rivalries and jealousies would extend to the municipality of Jerusalem, formerly headed by a member of the Husseini clan but controlled from 1920 until the mid-1930s by one of the mufti's leading political rivals, Ragheb Bey al-Nashashibi.[24] Just months earlier, in the aftermath of the April 1920 Jerusalem riots, Ragheb Bey al-Nashashibi had been appointed mayor of Jerusalem to succeed Haj Amin al-Husseini's cousin Musa Kasim Pasha al-Husseini, who had been abruptly dismissed from his post by the British. The Nashashibis were so opposed to the candidacy of yet another Husseini as mufti that the new mayor of Jerusalem, Ragheb Bey al-Nashashibi, campaigned actively against Haj Amin's appointment.[25]

In the Muslim elections for mufti that followed, on April 12, 1921, al-Husseini came in a distant fourth, which disqualified him. Existing voting regulations stipulated that the new mufti would be selected by the high commissioner from the top three vote getters. The election results infuriated the passionately anti-Semitic Husseini family, who then mounted a protest campaign, sending petitions and telegrams to the high commissioner's office claiming that the Jews had exerted their sinister influence against Haj Amin al-Husseini's candidacy.[26] Their effort to pressure British officials into invalidating the electoral results was successful: One of the three top vote getters, who happened to be the candidate of the Nashashibi family, was persuaded to step aside, thus allowing al-Husseini to be among the top three candidates. The two other Muslim contenders were more moderate and considerably less virulent in their hatred of both the British and the Jews; al-Husseini was by far the most radical. With his election, radical Islam would prevail over more moderate Islamic voices within the Palestinian Arab community.

Sir Herbert Samuel promptly appointed al-Husseini as the new mufti of Jerusalem, thus assuring the continuation of the Husseini family in its traditional role. With his formal appointment on May 8, 1921, Haj Amin al-Husseini now assumed the religious leadership of Islam's third holiest city. In appointing him, the British hoped to appease the anger and concerns of the most radical Palestinian Arab opponents of British rule in Palestine.

What if Sir Herbert had chosen a candidate other than al-Husseini as mufti of Jerusalem? The top vote getter, and candidate of the Nashashibi family, was Sheikh Husain al-Din Jarallah. He had been compelled to step out of the running owing to pressure brought to bear by the Husseini family. There is little doubt that had Sheikh Husain resisted the pressure and then been appointed mufti, he would have been killed by the followers of Haj Amin al-Husseini. Throughout the years of struggle for the leadership of the Arabs of Palestine, the Husseinis targeted and killed those who opposed their claim to leadership. The fact is that whoever Sir Herbert selected for leadership as mufti would have been driven by radical elements led by Haj Amin al-Husseini to oppose both the British and the Jews. Tragically, it was not al-Husseini who imposed the radical path, but the Arabs of Palestine themselves who demanded the course of action that was to lead to generations of bitterness and conflict.

The New Mufti: A Diminutive Demagogue

Although he was a center of controversy throughout his long and contentious public life, Haj Amin al-Husseini seemed to others to be always mild-mannered and soft-spoken. Twenty-six years old at the time of his appointment as mufti, al-Husseini was described by contemporaries as a short and stocky man who dressed simply but elegantly. He always wore the same black patent-leather shoes and the traditional but imposing mufti's headdress—a large white cloth wrapped, in a turban, around a red tarboosh. He was invariably cloaked in an elegant and precisely tailored long black robe that covered him completely to his ankles. People who met him for the first time were surprised by his gentle, even meek, demeanor.

They were most surprised, perhaps, by his non-Muslim, truly

Western appearance: His most notable features were his fair skin and reddish brown beard, blond hair, and expressive pale blue eyes. He had been clean-shaven as a young man and grew a beard only on the eve of his appointment as mufti, when Sir Herbert Samuel encouraged him to do so, suggesting that a beard would give al-Husseini, who looked much younger than his years, the added gravitas appropriate for someone assuming a position of such political power and responsibility.

Unlike other clerics of varying faiths, the mufti never took a vow of poverty and was not uncomfortable with the accoutrements of power. He had a well-known penchant for expensive haircuts and immaculately manicured fingers. He also had a taste for fine food and luxurious living accommodations that he increasingly indulged over the years during his long travels and sojourns outside of Arab Palestine.

Although diminutive in stature, al-Husseini was a larger-than-life figure who dominated whatever political stage he was acting upon. A charismatic and spellbinding orator, he mesmerized both small groups and large crowds whenever he spoke. Supporters and opponents, friends and foes alike, came away from his talks spellbound by his rhetoric and by the passion of his arguments. From his youth, he was a natural politician, with a gift for remembering names and faces, who knew instinctively how to work a crowd.

Al-Husseini's serene and elegant appearance, together with the courteous manner of one who seemed never to raise his voice in private conversation, gave him more the look of a reserved and otherworldly philosopher or theologian. Yet he was known and feared far and wide for his vicious temper; he was prone to fits of rage that often bordered on the pathological when colleagues or political rivals opposed him. He often ordered the execution of political rivals and opponents within Arab Palestine, including members of the Nashashibi family. As a result, his life was threatened on numerous occasions. Always fearful of assassination, he took extraordinary safety precautions. He never went out without his bulletproof vest, and a loyal contingent of bodyguards accompanied him everywhere.

The Mufti and Ernest Richmond:
A Special Relationship That Changed History

Al-Husseini's appointment as mufti generated both support and opposition. Ernest Richmond, the assistant political secretary of the high commissioner's office in Jerusalem and the high commissioner's adviser on Arab affairs,[27] who was a virulent anti-Semite and a declared enemy of Zionism, actively favored his appointment. Richmond's support for al-Husseini played the decisive role in Samuel's decision.[28] Shortly after his arrival in Jerusalem to assume his post in the high commissioner's office, Richmond had befriended al-Husseini, with whom he shared a fanatical hostility to the Balfour Declaration and to the declared policy of the British government in support of the creation of a Jewish homeland in Palestine.[29] The Zionist movement, and its supporters within the British mandatory government, Richmond wrote, "is dominated and inspired by a spirit that I can only describe as evil,"[30] a sentiment passionately shared by his friend al-Husseini.

Rumors were rife within the British administration in Jerusalem that the relationship between al-Husseini and Richmond was more than a passing friendship. It was rumored that Richmond and al-Husseini were involved in a passionate homosexual relationship. As a result of their relationship, Richmond enthusiastically used his political influence to persuade Sir Herbert Samuel to appoint al-Husseini as mufti. Richmond, who had previously been employed as a minor British government official in Cairo, had been brought to Jerusalem from Egypt by his longtime lover and mentor, Sir Ronald Storrs, the British mandatory governor of Palestine. Richmond and Storrs shared a house in Jerusalem and had earlier shared an apartment in Cairo.[31] In his memoirs, Storrs spoke of Richmond as his "most charming and hospitable friend and companion," who "taught me much for which I can never be grateful enough."[32] In 1921, Richmond prevailed upon Storrs, a close adviser and political confidant of Sir Herbert Samuel, to help him in his effort to have al-Husseini named grand mufti. Richmond's intimate friendship with Storrs,[33] which was well known and widely acknowledged in the Jerusalem of the early 1920s, was crucial to his successful effort to persuade Samuel, who yielded to Richmond's arguments on behalf of al-Husseini's candidacy.[34] Samuel naively followed Richmond and Storrs's recommendation, which resulted in the decision to name al-Husseini as grand mufti.[35] This single political decision was to have far-reaching consequences whose effects are felt to this day.

Other British Middle East policy makers, however, strongly opposed Samuel's decision, viewing it as a foolhardy attempt to appease and placate radical Arab opposition to Zionism and to Great Britain's stated pro-Zionist policy in Palestine. Colonel Richard Meinertzhagen, for example, who served as one of the two chief advisers on Arab affairs to Winston Churchill during Churchill's two-year tenure as colonial secretary of state in charge of British colonial policy in mandatory Palestine, noted in his diary that al-Husseini hated both the British and the Jews and concluded that his appointment "is sheer madness."[36]

Haj Amin al-Husseini was not satisfied to inherit his brother's title of mufti of Jerusalem. His goal was to be the preeminent Islamic religious authority throughout the area of the British Mandate.

Yet even such wide-ranging religious authority was not enough to satisfy his growing political ambitions. Al-Husseini well understood that religious authority alone would not give him the leadership role within the Palestinian Arab community that he believed was his destiny. Political power, and the leverage to wield it, was of equal if not greater importance.

An opportunity soon came his way. In December 1920, the British mandatory government created a new body, the Supreme Muslim Council, whose function was to administer Islamic religious courts, maintain all mosques, Islamic holy shrines, and schools, and appoint or dismiss officials of these institutions. The council, which was composed of five members headed by a president, was put in charge of the

Muslim Religious Trust, the Waqf, which administered an annual budget of one hundred thousand British pounds and was also given responsibility for the administration of all Muslim social services. With the active support of Sir Herbert Samuel and other British Mandate officials, al-Husseini was elected president of the Supreme Muslim Council on May 1, 1922. At its first meeting, the council confirmed al-Husseini's position as both the religious and political leader of the Arab community in Palestine. In a classic demonstration of nepotism, al-Husseini appointed at least twenty-one of his own relatives to lucrative positions with the council. Throughout the 1920s, as president of the Supreme Muslim Council, al-Husseini would greatly enhance and extend his authority.

In assuming the presidency of the council, moreover, al-Husseini claimed that the position was for life, or identical with his tenure as mufti. This claim exacerbated the already existing tensions between the Husseinis and the Nashashibis.

Appeasement

Throughout the 1920s, during the first decade of the British Mandate, the British governing of Palestine was predicated on a policy of appeasement. Immediately after World War I, anti-Zionist British officials such as Ernest Richmond began to urge the government to renounce the Balfour Declaration because of local Arab opposition to the establishment of a Jewish state.[37] Later, after having failed to persuade the British government to renounce the declaration, Richmond and some of his anti-Zionist colleagues in the British Foreign Office argued that the local Arab community could be appeased by the appointment of radical Arab Palestinian leaders, such as al-Husseini, to positions of political authority.[38]

Sir Herbert Samuel approved such measures because he believed in appeasement.[39] No doubt, Sir Herbert reasoned, it made better sense to accommodate the concerns of the Arab majority in Palestine; after all, as more Jews arrived and the demographics changed, British policy could once again be adjusted and redefined. This would give the British time and flexibility to achieve their ultimate aim. Although the British Mandate was in theory temporary, in the end the British wanted a government that would support the empire.

While courteous and urbane even to a fault, Samuel retained a life-long reputation for aloofness and formality that many colleagues and constituents perceived as an icily cold, sometimes distant personality. Throughout his political career, both as a rising member of Parliament and as high commissioner, in an effort to compensate for his apparent lack of personal warmth and effusiveness,[40] he went out of his way to accommodate the policy concerns and viewpoints of his critics and political opponents. Generating goodwill and popular support in this way, however, was achieved at a price.

From the beginning, Samuel's tenure as high commissioner was not entirely popular among pro-Zionist officials in the British government such as Richard Meinertzhagen, who believed passionately in affirming the Balfour Declaration's commitment to creating a Jewish homeland in Palestine. These concerns about Samuel were shared by Chaim Weizmann and other leaders of the Zionist movement, who recognized that when Samuel became British Palestine's first high commissioner in July 1920, he faced growing opposition from the anti-Zionist bureaucrats within his own office, who often tried to undermine or sabotage the policies that he and the Lloyd George government espoused.[41] Like many political appointees before and since, Samuel soon found that his role in formulating and carrying out policy was overshadowed by that of his professional military and civilian subordinates, who were virulently anti-Zionist.[42]

Samuel had always endorsed the aims of the Zionist movement and worked to facilitate its policies.[43] In 1918 and 1919 in particular, as he says in his *Memoirs*, he was "co-operating closely" with the Zionist leaders[44] and even ready, at times, to use his political influence and connections to further their cause. As a British official in Jerusalem, however, his emphasis was on preserving peace and tranquillity in the city, and this required him to seek to pacify the local Arab population[45] and to accommodate even their most intransigent demands and concerns.

After his appointment of al-Husseini, Samuel continued to be a voice for British appeasement of Islamic demands and concerns. In so doing, he unwittingly but unequivocally played into al-Husseini's hands.

In May 1921, shortly after Samuel's appointment of al-Husseini as mufti, a new wave of violent anti-Jewish rioting erupted, instigated by the mufti's propaganda, including a translation in the Palestinian Arab press of the notoriously anti-Semitic *Protocols of the Elders of Zion*.[46] The mufti and his followers were outraged by the fact that since 1918 the Jewish population of Palestine had almost doubled as a result of Jewish immigration, and Tel Aviv had grown from a township of two thousand to a town of thirty thousand.[47] Blaming this on the British, they took to the streets in protest. This new violence began in Jaffa, the ancient Arab port city alongside the new Jewish town of Tel Aviv, and quickly spread to Jerusalem. Within a week, this local dispute grew into a widespread Arab protest against the growing presence of Jews in Palestine and against the British Mandate.[48] Samuel's response to these riots, which left 47 Jews dead and 146 wounded, convinced al-Husseini that violence paid off. Accepting the report of a British commission, which placed the blame for the attacks on Arab anger and resentment over Jewish immigration, Samuel decided to temporarily suspend such immigration.[49] This was the first of several such bans and restrictions that the British government would impose during the 1920s and 1930s. The news of Samuel's announcement, indicating as it did a shift in British policy in Palestine, was hailed as a victory by the mufti and his supporters. Jews, however, reacted with deep indignation to what appeared to them as Samuel's weakness and acquiescence in the face of Arab violence.[50] Arab intimidation seemed to have been tangibly rewarded. In a subsequent speech on June 3, 1921, which Jewish leaders would attack as a further concession to Arab violence,

Samuel tried to reassure the Arab majority in Palestine that their political interests would always be protected and safeguarded.[51]

Well before the end of his tenure as high commissioner, Herbert Samuel would come to be viewed by many Jewish leaders, both in England and in Palestine, as a spokesman for the British policy of appeasement of the mufti and of radical Islam in the Middle East. Neville Chamberlain has long been the enduring symbol of British appeasement in modern times. In fact, more than fifteen years before Chamberlain's appeasement of Hitler at Munich, Sir Herbert Samuel had articulated the disastrous policy that would guide the British government until the outbreak of World War II.

The British policy of appeasement continued well after Samuel's departure as high commissioner in 1925. It was especially apparent in the British response to the murderous riots of 1929—"the second intifada," as it has come to be called—which was the worst outbreak of anti-Jewish violence since the British Mandate had been instituted.

The Mufti, the Western Wall, and the Riots of 1928–1929: The Second Intifada

As al-Husseini's power grew, he made the strategic decision to focus his energies on establishing the absolute dominance of the Waqf in matters involving control of all the holy places—Jewish as well as Muslim—in Jerusalem. In September 1928, a dispute over Jewish religious rights and practices at the Western Wall led to an outbreak of anti-Jewish rioting and violence, planned and instigated by the mufti, that was unprecedented in the history of modern Jerusalem.

Over the centuries, religious quarrels have consistently erupted in Jerusalem, frequently at the Western Wall, a religious site sacred to Jews. One of the holiest sites for Jews, the Wall, known as ha-Kotel ha-Ma'aravi (the Western Wall), is the one surviving remnant of the western exterior supporting wall of the Temple Mount, which was built on the site of the Temple of Solomon and was destroyed by the Romans in 70 CE. Throughout the centuries, Jews have come to this holy site to pray and to mourn the destruction of the First and Second Temples and the lost glory of ancient Israel.

The Wall is also the westernmost supporting wall of the Haram al-Sharif (Noble Sanctuary), Islam's third holiest shrine, a rectangular area enclosing the Al-Aqsa Mosque and the Dome of the Rock. The Al-Aqsa Mosque is the principal mosque in Palestine. The Dome of the Rock is traditionally the site from which the Prophet Muhammad ascended to heaven. For Muslims, the Western Wall was also called al-Buraq, after the name of the Prophet's horse, which he supposedly tethered there before his "Night Journey" described in Sura 17 of the Koran.

Before World War I, in disputes over the Western Wall, the Ottoman Turkish rulers of Palestine often decided in favor of their Muslim core-ligionists.[52] These disputes arose most frequently from Jewish demands to be allowed to bring to the pavement in front of the Wall chairs and benches for the elderly, an ark to house the Torah scrolls containing the Five Books of Moses that were read at worship services, and a screen to divide men from women during prayer. Muslims routinely protested Jewish innovations at the Wall, restricting Jewish worship practices in favor of Jerusalem's Muslim community. The Jews of Jerusalem had to endure these restrictions, which centuries of Muslim-inspired anti-Jewish laws and customs had established, until the aftermath of World War I, when under the new British mandatory government in Palestine and its Jewish high commissioner, Jerusalem's Jewish community grew in size and political power. During the 1920s, the status quo at the Western Wall, which had heretofore always favored the city's Muslim population, was increasingly challenged by Jewish leaders. The city's Palestinian Arabs, inspired by the demagoguery of Haj Amin al-Husseini and his fellow radical Islamists, openly resisted their demands. By the late 1920s, a showdown was inevitable.

It took place on September 23, 1928, on the eve of Yom Kippur, the Jewish Day of Atonement and the holiest day of the Jewish calendar year, when religious Jews set up a screen to divide men from women who came together to pray at the Western Wall. They did this in accordance with traditional Jewish religious worship practice, as a physical division between the sexes was a requirement of Jewish religious law. The city's Muslim religious officials, led by al-Husseini, protested that the screen was an innovation that altered the prevailing status quo at the Wall. As a result of their protests, British policemen were instructed to have the screen forcibly removed.

The British police arrived at the Wall during Yom Kippur worship services on the following day. No Jewish police officer was present, because it was the Day of Atonement. Upon arriving, the police ordered members of the Jewish congregation to remove the screen, which they refused to do. To do so, according to traditional Jewish law, would be a form of work, and the Jewish worshippers at the Wall understandably refused to work on this holiest of Jewish holy days. In the middle of the concluding prayers of Yom Kippur, a British police officer interrupted the worship services and began forcibly to remove the screen. As he did so, members of the congregation, both men and women, resisted. A scuffle ensued, during which an elderly Jewish woman attacked a policeman with her umbrella,[53] and several Jewish worshippers were hurt. The screen was torn and then taken away. Jews around the world protested the action.

The mufti exploited the incident at the Western Wall, transforming a relatively minor dispute into a violent political struggle, instigating a local Islamic war against the city's Jews. Incited by al-Husseini's inflammatory rhetoric, the Muslims of Jerusalem were jubilant that the screen had been taken down. Inspired by the mufti, rumors spread that the real intention of the Jews was ownership not just of the Western Wall, but ultimately of the entire Temple Mount, with the goal of tearing down the Dome of the Rock and the Al-Aqsa Mosque in order to rebuild the Jewish Temple in Jerusalem. Speaking in the name of the Supreme Muslim Council, following the violence, the mufti declared: "The Jews' aim is to take possession of the Mosque of al-Aqsa gradually." At his urging, the Supreme Muslim Council subsequently passed a resolution opposing "the establishment of any right to the Jews in the Holy Burak area."[54]

The anti-Jewish violence of 1929 had been in preparation by the mufti for nearly a year. On October 28, 1928, in a memorandum submitted to the Supreme Muslim Council, al-Husseini falsely claimed that the Jews were planning to take possession of Haram al-Sharif, site of the ancient Jewish Temple, an area sacred to the Muslims that is located a short distance from the Western Wall.[55] At the instigation of the mufti, the city's Muslims changed the cul-de-sac in front of the Wall into a thoroughfare by knocking down an old wall at one end of the area. They also organized noisy Muslim calls for prayer from a nearby rooftop, timed perfectly to disrupt Jewish worship services at the Wall. Nor were these the only anti-Jewish provocations. Even more inflammatory, photographs were fabricated and distributed to the Muslims of Jerusalem displaying the blue-and-white Jewish flag, with the Star of David at its center, flying from the top of the Dome of the Rock.[56] Faked pictures were also widely disseminated among the Arabs of Jerusalem showing the Dome of the Rock in ruins. The caption beneath declared that it had been destroyed by Jewish infidels who were now seeking to rebuild on its site the ancient Jewish Temple.[57]

Discussions continued throughout 1928 and into 1929 about the status of the Western Wall. Clashes broke out periodically in Jerusalem. It was a situation fraught with danger, an explosion waiting to happen. On August 15, 1929, a group of young Jews marched to the Western Wall through the Muslim Quarter of the Old City, carrying the Zionist flag.[58] As they marched they sang "Hatikvah," the Jewish national anthem. They demanded the restoration of Jewish rights at the Western Wall. That same evening, a group of the city's more radical Islamists, calling itself the Protection of the Mosque Al-Aqsa Association, responded in the Arab press, stating, "The Jews at 3:30 on this day, at the Wailing Wall itself, held a severe demonstration against the Moslems. Resentment is great and general. Do what ought to be done of protest and disapproval."[59] On the following day, by way of retaliation, the mufti ordered a counterdemonstration that was held at the Western Wall itself. In mosques throughout Jerusalem, Muslim clerics gave inflammatory sermons, inspiring Arab mobs to march to the Western Wall and to carry on the mufti's holy war against the city's infidel Jews. In leading this violent counterdemonstration, al-Husseini's preachers advised their flock that "he who kills a Jew is assured a place in the next world."[60] The few Jewish worshippers present were forced to flee for their lives, Jewish religious symbols were openly desecrated, and Hebrew prayer books were torn up and burned.[61]

A day later, on August 17, Abraham Mizrachi, a young Jew, accidentally sent a football flying into an Arab garden. While retrieving the ball, he was attacked and stabbed. He died in the hospital three days later. In the days following the Mizrachi boy's murder, tensions rose throughout Jerusalem. Incident followed incident, culminating in the violent events beginning on Friday, August 23, and concluding on Thursday, August 29. A Jewish response to the attack was summarily stopped. The Jews were prevented from entering the Old City of Jerusalem by the British police, and twenty-four of the Jewish youths in the demonstration were injured. Later the same day, after services at mosques in the Old City, hundreds of armed radical Islamist demonstrators, incited by al-Husseini, entered Jerusalem's Jewish Quarter. Jews were assaulted, 133 Jews were killed, and 339 were wounded.

Anti-Jewish violence escalated as the Jews of Jerusalem fell victim to a new intifada, the second in less than a decade. The entire Jewish community in Hebron was forced to flee; 67 Jews were murdered and 60 were wounded, while 116 Arabs lost their lives (most of the Arab casualties were the result of British actions to contain the violence). More than five decades later, Chaim Herzog, who would subsequently become president of Israel, could not erase the horrific memory of the riots he had witnessed as a child. With great emotion, he would later recall the vicious attack on his own eighty-year-old great-grandmother by the Arab rioters in Hebron. Helpless as the mufti-inspired carnage engulfed the Jews of Hebron, she was "cut down by a dagger."[62] Later the same week, the Hebron tragedy was repeated in Safad, where 45 Jews were killed,[63] on the orders of al-Husseini.

News of the 1929 riots in Jerusalem made headlines throughout the world,[64] and the British government in London set up a commission of inquiry to examine the causes of Arab unrest that led to the violence.[65] Despite the politically inspired findings of the Shaw commission, the official commission of inquiry that had been appointed by the British government to investigate the causes of the violence, the mufti's responsibility for the murders and other anti-Jewish crimes that occurred could not be denied. He and he alone precipitated the controversy over the Western Wall. In his testimony before the Shaw commission, the mufti publicly affirmed that Arabic translations of the notorious czarist forgery *The Protocols of the Elders of Zion* had, with his encouragement, been widely distributed throughout Palestine. He was convinced, he declared in his commission testimony, that the *Protocols* provided evidence of a Jewish plot, or conspiracy, in Palestine "to take possession of the Buraq [Wall]" and other Muslim holy sites and "then restore the Temple."[66] The Shaw commission, while rejecting al-Husseini's charges of alleged Jewish plots, exonerated the mufti of responsibility for any of the bloodletting of 1929 by assigning it to the general cause of Arab opposition to increasing Zionist immigration and land purchases.[67] The immediate source of the anti-Jewish violence, the mufti's inflammatory anti-Jewish rhetoric and the mob violence perpetrated by his willing followers, was not mentioned in the Shaw commission report, which seemed to uncritically accept al-Husseini's biased explanation.

To further radical Arab concerns and to assuage Arab opposition to Jewish immigration to Palestine in the future, the Shaw commission recommended greater regulation and curtailment of Jewish immigration and land sales to Jews,[68] a policy proposal that the British Foreign Office in London eagerly adopted. The commission report was followed by the British government's swift adoption of the Passfield

White Paper, which appeased growing Arab fears about increasing Jewish immigration and the Balfour Declaration's promise of a Jewish national home by recommending that all Jewish immigration and settlement in Palestine be suspended.

The Mufti, the Arab Revolt of 1936–1938,
and the Jews of Palestine

In 1936, Haj Amin al-Husseini incited yet another Arab massacre of Jewish settlers in Palestine, one that came to be widely known as "the Arab Revolt." It might also be referred to as "the third intifada."

Between 1933 and 1936, the Jewish population of Palestine increased from 234,967 to 384,078, from just over 20 percent to just under 30 percent.[69] On April 15, 1936, in protest against any further Jewish immigration, Arab leaders in Palestine, inspired by the mufti's rhetoric, began a general strike, calling for the nonpayment of taxes and a nationwide strike of Arab workers and businesses. This strike, the mufti proclaimed, would continue until all Jewish immigration to Palestine was halted. Several days later, the mufti persuaded several Palestinian Arab leaders to establish an Arab Higher Committee for Palestine, with himself as president.[70] The Arab Higher Committee, whose presidency al-Husseini would hold until his death in 1974, would become the political voice of the Arabs of Palestine.

The mufti's call for a general strike led to violence. That same day, Arab rioters attacked a bus, murdering two of its Jewish passengers. In an act of retaliation, the following night, two Arabs were killed by Jews. Within forty-eight hours, Arab gangs were searching for Jews throughout the towns of Jaffa and Tel Aviv, attacking them and setting fire to Jewish-owned shops. In the days that followed, the violence escalated into a murderous rampage.

By midsummer of 1936, the intensity of the fighting mounted as Arab rioters and terrorists attacked Jewish homes, farms, and villages throughout Palestine. A majority of the Arab terrorists were local

Palestinians recruited by the mufti and his agents. Before long, however, Syrian and Iraqi volunteers began arriving in Palestine at the rate of two or three hundred a month.[71] Their leader, Fawzi al-Kawukji, who would become a close friend and political ally of the mufti, played a major role in the Arab Revolt. Like al-Husseini, al-Kawukji had served in the Turkish Ottoman army during World War I; after the war, he accepted a commission as an officer in the Iraqi army, and in 1936 he resigned his Iraqi command to help al-Husseini organize and carry out his Palestinian Arab rebellion.

The first year of the Arab Revolt resulted in a veritable reign of terror against the Jews of Palestine—murder, bomb throwing, looting, torture, night assaults on Jewish homes and farms, and the destruction of cattle and crops. During the summer of 1936, thousands of Jewish-farmed acres were destroyed and fruit orchards cut down in deliberate acts of Arab vandalism. More and more Jews were murdered. Despite denunciations of the violence by the British mandatory government, which tried without success to keep the peace, Jews continued to be killed, resulting in a death toll of 80 by October. British troops killed more than 140 Arabs, while 33 British soldiers died in armed clashes with Arab bands.[72]

Pressure mounted for some resolution. On May 18, 1936, the British House of Commons announced that a royal commission would be set up to investigate the causes of the unrest. Lord Robert Peel, who had served as Great Britain's secretary of state for India, was appointed the commission's chairman, with Sir Horace Rumbold, a former British ambassador to Berlin, as his deputy. When the Peel commission arrived in Palestine on November 11, 1936, exactly eighteen years after the end of World War I, the country was in turmoil. In his testimony before the Peel commission on January 12, 1937, as chief witness for the Palestinian Arab community, Haj Amin al-Husseini reiterated his long-standing demand for the cessation of all Jewish immigration to Palestine and called for the removal of 80 percent of the Jews already in the country (four hundred thousand), to bring their total number back to the level that prevailed prior to World War I (eighty thousand).[73] He also demanded an immediate and complete prohibition against the sale of Arab-owned land to Jews. In response to the Peel commission's subsequent report, the mufti and his Arab Higher Committee unequivocally rejected the commission's recommendation that Palestine be partitioned into two independent states, one Arab and one Jewish. Instead, he called for an end to the British Mandate and the creation of only one state, an independent Arab state, in its place.

During the summer of 1937, after the Arab Higher Committee's rejection of the Peel commission report, full-scale violence was unleashed by Arab terrorist bands in Palestine. After an Arab terrorist assassinated Lewis Andrews, the British district commissioner for the Galilee, the British government finally took decisive action. On September 30, the British outlawed the Arab Higher Committee, stating that the goals of the committee were antithetical to those of the British mandatory government. The mufti and several of the committee's other leaders were banished from Palestine.

Disguised as a woman, al-Husseini escaped by boat to Beirut, Lebanon, on October 15, 1937. Clean-shaven, he wore the plain flowing black dress of an observant Muslim woman, appropriately modest female attire that enveloped his entire body from head to toe. His face was covered by the *niqab* (the traditional full-faced veil allowing only a narrow slit for the eyes), which was worn by all Muslim women who were obedient to Islamic religious tradition. As he fled Beirut by boat in the dead of night, no one suspected his true identity.

The mandatory government forbade the mufti to return to Palestine. After a short stay in Beirut, he moved to Damascus, Syria. During the following two years of his political exile in Syria, he directed the violence and terrorist activity of the Arab Revolt in Palestine, which continued until May 1939. Many of the more moderate Arab leaders of Palestine who had opposed the mufti and his policies were murdered at his command. The tool of political assassination employed by the mufti against his Palestinian Arab political opponents would become a plague in the political life of the Islamic Middle East.

The Mufti, the Founding of the Muslim Brotherhood, and the Rise of Radical Islam

The events of 1929 had elevated the standing of Haj Amin al-Husseini throughout the Islamic world. He was now more than the leader of the Muslims of Palestine; he was also the defender of Jerusalem, the third holiest city of Islam. Al-Husseini had become the most revered defender of Muslim honor in the world. His call for a new world order based on Islam, and for a campaign of jihad against the British, the Jews, and the West, was striking an increasingly responsive chord.

On December 7, 1931, al-Husseini convened the World Islamic Congress in Jerusalem. Attended by 122 delegates representing all of the world's Muslim countries except Turkey, it was convened to articulate the shared grievances of a united Islam against the West. The congress was especially virulent in its condemnation of Zionism and of British colonial government throughout the Muslim world, in Egypt, India, and Palestine. For the first time, with a united voice, the Muslim world was speaking in unison, stating its radical opposition to Western civilization, to both the culture and the politics of what Islam viewed as the secular West. It had a common enemy, Western imperialism and colonialism, as manifest in British colonial government in Muslim India and throughout the Islamic Middle East. As the convener and president of the World Islamic Congress, Haj Amin al-Husseini was now increasingly recognized as the preeminent voice of radical Islam and a new and powerful force on the world political scene.

His stature was further elevated by his emerging leadership role within the Muslim Brotherhood, a radical Islamic religious organization that had been founded in Egypt in 1928. The brotherhood's goal was to create a new world order based on Islam, an objective it still pursues today. Many future leaders of radical Islam, such as Egyptian presidents Gamal Abdel Nasser and Anwar Al Sadat, began their political careers as young activists in the Muslim Brotherhood during the

1930s. Youssef Nada, chairman of Al Taqwa Bank, joined the Muslim Brotherhood during World War II, when he was recruited along with others in the Muslim Brotherhood by German military intelligence agents supervised by the mufti for espionage against the British colonial government in Egypt.[74] Yasser Arafat became active in the Muslim Brotherhood during the early 1950s.

The Muslim Brotherhood had been founded in Cairo by al-Husseini's ideological soul-mate, Hassan al-Banna, a young Egyptian schoolteacher and political organizer who shared al-Husseini's passionate hatred of the British and the Jews. Born into an impoverished Egyptian family in 1906, al-Banna had participated in a protest demonstration against the British at the young age of thirteen. While a college student in Cairo, he was deeply disturbed by the effects of Westernization that he saw there, especially the rise of secularism and the breakdown of traditional moral values, which he came to blame on British colonial rule in his native Egypt. At the age of twenty-two, he founded the Muslim Brotherhood, the first mass-based overtly political movement to oppose the ascendancy of secular and Western ideas and values, and British colonial rule, in the Middle East. By the late 1930s, it had established branches in every Egyptian province. A decade later, it had five hundred thousand active members in Egypt alone and a vast and loyal network of political supporters in Palestine and throughout the Arab Middle East.

The Muslim Brotherhood, a forerunner of Hamas, Hezbollah, and al-Qaeda, was established as a pan-Islamic movement that believed in the virtue of a one-world Islamic utopia and the use of terrorism, when necessary, to achieve its goal. From the brotherhood's inception, jihad (holy war) became one of its central tenets. Members of the brotherhood emphasized the honor and reverence given to those who sacrifice their lives as jihadist martyrs in the name of Islam, proclaiming, "Allah is our objective. The Prophet is our leader. Koran is our law. Jihad is our way. Dying in the name of Allah is our highest hope."[75] Muhammad Sa'id al-'Ashmawy, the distinguished Egyptian jurist and former chief justice of Egypt's High Criminal Court, best described the Muslim

Brotherhood when he referred to its ideology as a "perversion of Islam" and spoke of "the fascistic ideology" that infuses the worldview of the brotherhood, "their total (if not totalitarian) way of life . . . [and] their fantastical reading of the Koran."[76] This is a description that aptly defines the ideology of the mufti as well.

The philosophy of the Muslim Brotherhood was characterized by the doctrine that a universal Islamic reawakening will bring about the establishment of a unified Islamic state throughout the Muslim world. The goal of this radical Islamic reawakening was the reestablishment of pan-Islamic political power and authority as represented by the rule of a caliph, the title bestowed upon the successors of the Prophet Muhammad.[77] Both al-Husseini and al-Banna called for the reestablishment of the caliphate, which had been abolished by the Turkish government in 1924. Of course, each radical Islamic leader thought he should become the new caliph. "We want an Arabian United States with a Caliphate at its head and every Arab state subscribing wholeheartedly to the laws of the Koran," declared al-Banna. "We must return to the Koran. . . . The laws of the Koran are suitable for all men at all times to the end of the world."[78]

Al-Banna's worldview was expressed most clearly in the Muslim Brotherhood's newspaper, *Al-Ikhwan al-Muslimun:* "No justice will be dealt and no peace maintained on earth until the rule of the Koran and the bloc of Islam are established. Moslem unity must be established. Indonesia, Pakistan, Afghanistan, Iran, Iraq, Turkey, Syria, Lebanon, Trans-Jordan, Palestine, Saudi Arabia, Yemen, Egypt, Sudan Tripoli, Tunis, Algeria and Morocco all form one bloc, the Moslem bloc, which God has promised to grant victory, saying: 'We shall grant victory unto the faithful.' But this is impossible to reach other than through the way of Islam."[79] Adhering to the doctrine that only Muslim believers can govern in Islamic lands, al-Banna and his followers in the Muslim Brotherhood vehemently rejected the influence of the secular democratic West and the legitimacy of secular regimes throughout the Middle East.

The rise of radical Islam, and the evolution of its political and reli-

gious worldview, drew further inspiration from the writings of the
Muslim Brotherhood's most influential theoretician, Sayyid Qutb, a
contemporary of al-Banna and al-Husseini. Born in a village in Upper
Egypt in 1906, Qutb studied in Cairo and for several years worked as a
teacher and then as an official in the Egyptian Ministry of Education.[80]
He then embarked on a career as a writer and critic. The writings of
Qutb had a profound ideological influence on the emerging radical
Islamic movement, including its principal leaders—ranging from
al-Husseini and al-Banna in the 1930s to Yasser Arafat, Ayatollah
Khomeini, and Osama bin Laden in later decades—and its principal
terrorist organizations—Hamas, Hezbollah, Islamic Jihad, and al-
Qaeda.[81] Together, al-Husseini, al-Banna, and Qutb constituted the
founding fathers of radical Islam as we know it today.

In perhaps his most important and oft-quoted essay, "Our Struggle
with the Jews," Qutb claims that Jewish "wickedness," "deception," and
"plotting" are what keep "the Muslim world in a state of estrangement
from the teachings of the Qur'an, thereby depriving it of the real
sources of knowledge and power." The true aim of all Jews, he alleges,
is to destroy Islam itself. Indeed, there is no other human group
"whose history reveals the sort of mercilessness, [moral] shirking and
ungratefulness for Divine Guidance as does this one. . . . The Jews perpetrated the worst sins of disobedience [against Allah], behaving in
the most disgustingly aggressive manner and sinning in the ugliest
way. Everywhere the Jews have been they have committed unprecedented abominations. From such creatures who kill, massacre and de-
fame prophets, one can only expect the spilling of human blood and
any dirty means which would further their machinations and evil-
ness."[82]

Chapter 3

Partners in Genocide

Throughout the 1930s, until his departure from Palestine in 1937, Haj Amin al-Husseini continued to incite violence against the Jews of Palestine. At the same time, he began to make overtures to the new Nazi regime in Germany. In late March 1933, shortly after Hitler's accession to power, al-Husseini had approached the German consul general in Jerusalem, Dr. Heinrich Wolff, and offered his support to the new Nazi government in Berlin,[1] an offer he would reiterate to Nazi officials over the next few years. In January 1937, the mufti was quoted by *The New York Times* as to his willingness to ally himself with Hitler because of the common enemy shared by radical Islam and Nazi Germany: "We are fighting Zionism in Palestine, which is supported by the British," stated al-Husseini. "What do we care who backs us, or who we align ourselves with, as long as it helps us to attain our goals. . . . We don't care who we have to align ourselves with." We, Arabs and Germans, "have a common enemy, the British and the Jews."[2] By 1938, after British prime minister Neville Chamberlain's infamous capitulation to Hitler at Munich, al-Husseini's overtures to Germany were officially reciprocated and became the basis of a nascent Islamic-Nazi alliance.

All across the Middle East, during the 1930s, sympathy for Nazi ideas and support for Germany had been spreading. Several of the new Arab political parties founded during the 1930s betrayed shades of the Nazi model. In 1935, when the anti-Jewish Nuremberg Laws were promulgated, telegrams of congratulation to the führer were sent from all over the Islamic world, especially from Morocco and Palestine, where German propaganda had been most active. Between 1933 and 1938, political parties such as the Syrian Popular Party and the Young Egypt Society, which were organized throughout the Arab Middle East, were explicitly anti-Semitic in their ideology and programs. The leader of Syria's Socialist Nationalist Party, Anton Sa'ada, styled himself as the führer of the Syrian nation, and the party's banner even featured the swastika. So, too, the anti-Semitic program of the Young Egypt Society, under the emerging leadership of Gamal Abdel Nasser and Anwar Al Sadat, included vocal support for Nazi ideology, the publication and distribution of anti-Jewish propaganda, and the organization of boycotts against the Jewish community of Egypt.[3] The pro-Nazi sensibility shared by al-Husseini and his collaborators among the new Arab leadership was recounted in an autobiographical memoir by a leader of the pro-German Ba'ath Party in Syria:

We were racists, admiring Nazism, reading its books and the source of its thought, particularly Nietzsche . . . Fichte and H. S. Chamberlain's *Foundations of the Nineteenth Century,* which revolves on race. We were the first to think of translating *Mein Kampf.* Whoever lived during this period in Damascus would appreciate the inclination of the Arab people to Nazism, for Nazism was the power which could serve as its champion, and he who is defeated will by nature love the victor.[4]

Between 1938 and 1941, it was this already emergent predisposition of the Arab people toward Nazism that al-Husseini effectively exploited in shaping the new alliance between the radical Islamic parties and monarchs of the Middle East and Hitler's Nazi regime. King Farouk of Egypt, who was to become a close friend and ally of the mufti, was especially eager to do so. On April 15, 1941, King Farouk sent a secret message to Hitler welcoming a German occupation of his country and offering his support to the Third Reich. This message was conveyed secretly to the führer by Farouk's father-in-law, Zulficar Pasha, the rabidly pro-Nazi Egyptian ambassador in Tehran. On April 30, Pasha, who would be the intermediary for several secret wartime communications between Hitler, the mufti, and the Egyptian king, received a response from Hitler himself, which he personally and promptly conveyed to King Farouk.[5] King Farouk's secret communications and subsequent collaboration with Nazi Germany, fostered and furthered by the mufti, beginning in 1941, form a little-known chapter in the history of the Arab-Nazi German alliance during World War II. In March 1943, at the urging of the mufti and with the approval of the führer, arrangements were made for Farouk to escape from Cairo to Nazi-occupied Europe in the event of an attempt on the Egyptian monarch's life by the British, which the Nazi government thought likely to occur. In a letter to Farouk, the mufti assured the king "that he would be received with all honors due a friendly reigning sovereign" and that he would be given every possible means by the Nazis for continuing the activities of his Egyptian government in exile.[6] In his appreciative response to the German offer of political asylum in the event of a possible British assassination attempt, Farouk noted that he "was still hoping for an Axis victory" and conveyed "his best wishes to the Mufti of Jerusalem and to all those who work with him for the success and victory of the Axis."[7]

Of course, the mufti was making a strategic gamble: that Hitler's armies would prove invincible and that Germany, then at the height of its military power, would succeed in winning the war.

The mufti was not alone in thinking that Hitler would prevail. Throughout much of 1941, it seemed to many, especially among Hitler's friends and allies, that a Nazi victory was on the horizon. Having already annexed Austria, occupied Bohemia and Moravia, and conquered France, Czechoslovakia, Poland, Norway, Holland, Denmark, Belgium, Luxembourg, Yugoslavia, and Greece, Hitler and his Axis allies seemed invincible to many.[8] On June 10, 1940, Benito Mussolini, fulfilling a promise he had made to Hitler aboard a train at the Brenner Pass the previous March, had declared war on England.[9] By the beginning of 1941, Italy's military and naval forces in the Mediterranean were actively enlisted in the Axis war effort.

On June 22, 1941, Germany would launch Operation Barbarossa against its erstwhile ally the Soviet Union. With the Battle of Britain raging and London under continuous German air attack, Field Marshal Erwin Rommel, known as the Desert Fox, was advancing deep inside Egypt. It was only a matter of time, al-Husseini and Hitler's other supporters believed, before Rommel's forces would advance from Cairo to Baghdad, Damascus, and Jerusalem, establishing Nazi hegemony over the entire Middle East. With the United States still not in the war, Great Britain, led by Prime Minister Winston Churchill, stood virtually alone against the Axis onslaught.

Germany's war against the British Empire struck a responsive chord in much of the Islamic world, whose people viewed the war as a meritorious battle against British imperialism.[10] With the exceptions of Ibn Saud of Saudi Arabia and Abdullah of Jordan, no leader of the Islamic Middle East opposed Hitler and supported the Allied cause. Indeed, the widespread support for the Axis cause among Arab leaders prompted the American journalist John Gunther to note, "The greatest contemporary Arab hero is probably Hitler."[11]

In October 1939, a month after Hitler attacked Poland and Britain had declared war on Germany, the mufti moved his base of operations from Jerusalem to Baghdad. In October 1939, he left for Iraq, where he continued his pro-Nazi propaganda activities. In so doing, al-Husseini assumed the role of a loyal Axis ally. By January 1941, al-Husseini had decided to align himself openly with Germany. In a letter to Hitler that the mufti wrote at the end of January, he assured "the great Fuhrer" of the "friendship, sympathy and admiration" of the Arab people and pledged that Arabs everywhere were "prepared to act as is proper against the common enemy and to take their stand with enthusiasm on the side of the Axis and to do their part in the well deserved defeat of the Anglo-Jewish coalition."[12] In thus pledging his allegiance to the Nazi regime, al-Husseini did not shy away from raw adulation: "I am anxious here to reiterate my thanks to your Excellency," he wrote Hitler, "and to assure your Excellency of the sentiments of friendship, of sympathy, and of admiration which the Arab people pledges to your Excellency, great Fuhrer, and to the courageous German people."[13]

On the Road to Berlin, April–November 1941

Al-Husseini next sought to evict the British from Iraq and to replace the country's pro-British regime with a pro-German Iraqi government. In pursuit of this objective, he joined forces with a group of army officers led by the Iraqi lawyer and politician Rashid Ali al-Gaylani, who seized power in a pro-Nazi coup that forced the Iraqi prime minister, the pro-British Nuri Said Pasha, to resign. As part of the cabal, al-Husseini played a role in organizing this coup, which brought to power the strongly pro-German regime of al-Gaylani, who became prime minister of Iraq on April 1, 1941. The goal of the pro-German coup was to give Hitler the oil he needed to enable his armies to conquer the Middle East.

On May 9, 1941, the mufti issued a fatwa proclaiming the Iraqi coup a jihad against the British and the Jews, "the greatest foe of Islam."[14] However, despite some aid to the pro-German Iraqis from Syria, which was still controlled by the pro-Axis French Vichy government, the pro-Nazi Iraqi government of Rashid Ali al-Gaylani and Haj

Amin al-Husseini did not last long. The British moved quickly, sending planes and troops into Baghdad. The rebellion was crushed, and the new pro-German government overthrown, after only one month of fighting. After the coup failed, the mufti incited a pogrom that broke out in Baghdad on June 1–2, 1941, and resulted in the murder of 110 Iraqi Jews[15] and the wounding of several hundred others. Several thousand Jews were made homeless in the pogrom, their property looted.

One of the pro-Nazi plotters in the Iraqi coup of 1941 and a trusted friend and confidant of al-Husseini during his years in Iraq was Saddam Hussein's uncle, General Khairallah Talfah, who would later become Saddam's guardian, mentor, and father-in-law. Talfah would regale his young nephew, entrusted to his care, with exciting stories about the heroic exploits of the mufti and his Nazi collaborators, whom Talfah regarded as heroes.[16] Thus, Saddam Hussein, who as a child learned about the pro-Nazi Iraqi coup of 1941 and the mufti's subsequent wartime efforts on behalf of the Third Reich, grew up in awe of the mufti, whose devotion to the cause of radical Islam he sought to emulate. For the young Saddam Hussein, the mufti's vision of radical Islam was inspirational,[17] and others like Saddam Hussein came to regard the mufti as both hero and mentor.

Al-Husseini sought refuge in neighboring Iran. The mufti arrived in Tehran on June 1, where he was welcomed by the pro-Nazi Shah Reza Pahlavi. From his sanctuary at the Japanese embassy in Tehran, the mufti began to incite anti-Jewish hatred and violence as he had done throughout much of his stay in Baghdad. His well-deserved reputation as an anti-Jewish provocateur preceded him. In response to his anti-Jewish pronouncements and propaganda, a large number of Iranian Jews actually fled from Tehran to Istanbul. They feared the sorts of reprisals that Baghdad's Jews had suffered.

The mufti's safe haven was short-lived. Only four months after his arrival, the shah was forced to abdicate. Great Britain and the Soviet Union landed troops in Iran, arrested pro-government Nazi ministers, and replaced the shah with his young son, who immediately severed diplomatic relations with the Axis powers. The mufti was given sanctuary in the Italian embassy in Tehran, where he hid for several days. Aware that al-Husseini was still in hiding in Tehran, British prime minister Winston Churchill sought to capture him before he fled the Iranian capital. On September 3, 1941, Churchill telegraphed the British minister in Tehran, Sir Reader Bullard: "The fact that the Mufti has escaped from Persian surveillance is much regretted. His capture, dead or alive, is an important object, of which the Persian government should be made to feel the importance."[18] In a subsequent letter to British foreign secretary Anthony Eden, Churchill wrote: "I presume all measures are being taken to prevent his [the mufti's] getting away. Will you please do whatever is possible."[19] With the British in hot pursuit, al-Husseini had to flee once again, this time from Iran, to Turkey, and then to Italy. In the dead of night on October 11, 1941, traveling incognito with his beard shaven, hair dyed, and a counterfeit Italian passport,[20] the mufti was flown to Italy on an Italian air force plane sent by Benito Mussolini.

Upon his arrival in Rome, the red carpet was rolled out by the Italian authorities. Mussolini's Fascist government was generous in its hospitality to its new ally, putting at the mufti's disposal a luxuriously spacious villa in Rome, a full staff of servants and bodyguards, and an official car and escort of policemen on motorcycles. At Mussolini's instruction, all of al-Husseini's living expenses were covered by the government, as were those of his entourage who followed him to Rome.[21]

The highlight of the mufti's Rome visit was a private audience with Mussolini, which took place on October 27, 1941, at Il Duce's office on the first floor of the Palazzo Venetia, the exquisitely ornate Renaissance palace built by Pope Paul II in the fifteenth century and the seat of Mussolini's Fascist government since 1928. It was in this same office, at the Palazzo Venetia, that Mussolini had met with Adolf Hitler during the führer's much heralded state visit to Rome in 1937. As his chauffeured car passed the Roman Colosseum and the Pantheon en route to his destination, the mufti could not help but be impressed by the city's grandeur. The stories about the historic Palazzo Venetia, where Napoleon Bonaparte's government administration had held court at the beginning of the nineteenth century, were legendary. Since Mussolini's assumption of power, lights at the palazzo were left on all night to give the impression that Mussolini and his Fascist regime worked without pause. From the balcony of the Palazzo Venetia, just above his private office, that overlooked the public square below, Mussolini drew huge crowds in his widely publicized speeches to the people of Rome, who were invariably mesmerized by his spellbinding oratory.

Il Duce received al-Husseini warmly, immediately endorsing his claim for an independent Arab government in Palestine and offering the mufti military support to fight the British.[22] Al-Husseini and Mussolini shared a devotion to fascism as well as a passionate hatred for both the British and the Jews. In welcoming his Arab guest, Mussolini affirmed al-Husseini's belief that the Jews had no historical right to establish a state in Palestine.[23] Il Duce shared the mufti's virulent opposition to Zionism. If the Jews want their own state, Mussolini told his delighted guest, "they should establish Tel Aviv in America."[24] He also shared the mufti's hope for the eventual extermination of the Jews. "We have here, in Italy, 45,000 Jews, but none will be left," Mussolini told al-Husseini. "They are our enemies, and there will be no place for them in Europe."[25]

The mufti parted from Mussolini beaming. That night he noted in his diary: "I was very satisfied with my meeting with Mussolini and his statements about Jews and Zionism."[26] When the mufti departed from Rome on November 6, 1941, he had the firm support of one key member of the Axis leadership. Now he was determined to proceed to the next step in his grand design.

Hitler and the Mufti

Upon his arrival in Berlin on November 6, 1941, the mufti was welcomed warmly by the leaders of the Third Reich. As in Italy, he was greeted as a head of state in exile and deferred to as an important ally and political supporter. The mufti's reputation as a high liver, with a taste for fine food and luxurious living, had preceded him. The Nazi government spared no expense in offering him their hospitality, providing al-Husseini with a luxurious home on Berlin's fashionable Klopstock Street, a full staff of servants, a chauffeured Mercedes limousine, and a monthly stipend in excess of $10,000, as well as four other residences and suites in two of Berlin's must luxurious hotels.[27] The mufti was also given a generous monthly food budget, which would enable him to lavishly entertain the many leaders of radical Islam residing in or visiting Nazi Germany, whom the mufti would be able to use in mobilizing further Arab support for the Nazi cause.

Everywhere he went in Berlin, he was greeted by adoring crowds of Palestinian Arab expatriates. When al-Husseini had left Baghdad for Berlin, he had been accompanied by an entourage of Palestinian Arab colleagues, including Rashid Ali al-Gaylani and other leaders of the recently failed German coup in Iraq.[28] Upon establishing his new residency in Germany, al-Husseini paved the way for other pro-Nazi Arab leaders to find a safe haven in the German capital, where they would remain throughout World War II. Berlin soon came to be home to the largest group of Arab leaders outside of the Middle East.

When al-Husseini met with German foreign minister Joachim von Ribbentrop on November 28, part of their agenda was to discuss his forthcoming meeting with Hitler, scheduled for later that day. The mufti had been preparing for this meeting for much of his adult life.

One of the intriguing questions about the führer-mufti meeting is why Hitler agreed to meet, and to ally himself, with the mufti in the first place. Hitler had written about the racial inferiority of the Muslims in *Mein Kampf,* and he had a general contempt for all non-Aryans, including Arabs.[29] Al-Husseini, with his blond hair, red beard, and blue eyes, appears to have been an exception. Hitler even went so far as to accept the mufti as an honorary Aryan.[30] As Hitler would later remark, the mufti "gives one the impression that he is . . . a man with more than one Aryan among his ancestors and one who may well be descended from the best Roman stock."[31] Despite his earlier comments in *Mein Kampf,* the German leader seems to have later developed a new respect for Islam.[32] According to documented private conversations he had with his staff, Hitler expressed admiration for the solidarity of the Muslim people and believed that they could be potentially valuable allies in his war against their common enemies, the British and the Jews.[33] The mufti especially, Hitler felt, would be a useful ally in the Third Reich's effort to eventually conquer and rule the Middle East. Hitler took very seriously the principle of the Aryans' sole right to rule the world.[34] His racial acceptance of the mufti, and his admiration for al-Husseini's political sagacity and shrewdness, enabled the führer to envision a role for al-Husseini as a trusted political ally and future Aryan ruler of a Nazi-controlled Middle East.

For the führer, as for the mufti, in their shared war against the British and the Jews, the enemy of my enemy became an ally and friend. The mufti's long-sought alliance with the Nazis provided him with the opportunity to fight for Palestinian Arab independence from Great Britain and against further Jewish immigration to Palestine, while at the same time helping his new ally to achieve their shared goal of the extermination of *all* Jews. Their passionately shared hatred of their common enemies brought them together, to the detriment of humankind.[35]

By all accounts, al-Husseini's long-hoped-for meeting with the führer went exceedingly well. The mufti and the führer shared much in common. The mufti had found his soul-mate in the German führer and thanked him profusely for his unbending commitment to the radical Islamic cause. Leaving the Reich Chancellery, al-Husseini had been elated and inspired and had been convinced that his destiny was now assured. A partnership had been forged, which if successful would reshape the Middle East. As he reflected, the mufti was well aware of his good fortune, realizing that as a trusted ally and confidant of the führer, he would be able to do much to shape and promote the emerging alliance between radical Islam and Nazism and to mobilize support for Hitler's war against the Jews. In the months ahead, his hopes and dreams were realized.

The Mufti's Relationships with German Leaders

Throughout his years in Germany, al-Husseini enjoyed a close working relationship with several Nazi leaders, including Joachim von Ribbentrop, Heinrich Himmler, and Adolf Eichmann. As Hitler's foreign minister, von Ribbentrop was to become a close ally of al-Husseini. Under his direction the section of the Ministry of Foreign Affairs responsible for "Jewish Affairs," Referat Deutschland, "vigorously defended Nazi anti-semitism abroad and denounced foreign attempts to 'interfere' in German Judenpolitik at home."[36] On November 2, 1943, the twenty-sixth anniversary of the Balfour Declaration, von Ribbentrop sent the mufti a telegram that established beyond any doubt the position of the German government when it came to the Middle East. "I send out my greetings to your Eminence and to those who are today in the capital of the Reich at the gathering under your chairmanship," wrote von Ribbentrop. "Germany is tied to the Arab nation by old bonds of friendship and today more than ever we are allies. The removal of the so-called Jewish National Home, and freeing all Arab lands from oppression and the exploitation of the Western powers is an unalterable part of the policy of the Greater German Reich. May the hour not be distant when the Arab nation shall be able to build its future and establish unity and full independence."[37] In subsequent letters to the German foreign minister, al-Husseini asked von Ribbentrop for his assistance in ensuring that no Jews would be permitted to leave Europe to enter Palestine.[38] Sharing al-Husseini's passionate hatred of the Jews, von Ribbentrop was especially happy to promise to give this type of assistance. Al-Husseini and von Ribbentrop were in complete sympathy with each other's hopes and aspirations. On April 28, 1944, von Ribbentrop established yet another division in the Foreign Ministry. The "Anti-Jewish Action Abroad" was designed to assist in the "physical elimination of Jewry," thus to "deprive the race of its biological reserves." Among those designated to be advisers in this effort to ensure the destruction of the Jews were Haj

Amin al-Husseini and Rashid Ali al-Gaylani.[39] Joachim von Ribbentrop was convicted as a war criminal at the Nuremberg trials, where he was sentenced to death and hanged for his crimes.

Of the major Nazi leaders, Heinrich Himmler was the one with whom al-Husseini collaborated most actively and consistently.[40] The mufti's first official meeting with Himmler, chief of the SS and the Gestapo, took place in March 1943. They quickly became close political confidants and friends. By July 1943, the mufti's relations with Himmler warmed to the point that Himmler dedicated a picture of himself with al-Husseini, "To His Eminence, the Grand Mufti, in Remembrance."[41] This inscribed photo from Himmler would become one of Haj Amin al-Husseini's prized possessions. That their first meeting had been an important one can be inferred from the note of appreciation the mufti sent Himmler: "This memento of our first meeting, which created the basis of our confiding, is of special value to me."[42] In his relations with Nazi leaders, al-Husseini always knew whom to flatter. In this same note, he stated that the picture would always remind him of Himmler "as an understanding, great and energetic man." In October 1943, the mufti sent a letter to Himmler, on the occasion of the Nazi leader's birthday, and used the opportunity to express the wish that "the coming year may make our cooperation even closer and bring our common goals even nearer."[43]

One of the common goals shared by al-Husseini and Himmler, who was the architect and administrator of the Nazis' "Final Solution,"[44] was the extermination of the Jews. In the text of his telegram to the mufti sent on November 2, 1943, which was read at the twenty-sixth anniversary of the Balfour Declaration, Himmler proclaimed the essence of their mutual objectives: "The National Socialist Movement of Greater Germany has, since its beginning, inscribed upon its flag, the battle against world Jewry. It has therefore always pursued with sympathy the battle of the freedom loving Arabs against the Jewish intruders. The recognition of this enemy and the common battle against him provides the firm basis for the natural ties between National Socialist Greater Germany and the freedom loving Moslems in the whole world. With this thought I convey to you, on the anniversary of the un-holy Balfour Declaration, my deepest greetings and wishes for the suc-cess of your battle until final victory."[45]

The mufti's close working relationship and friendship with Adolf Eichmann, as with Heinrich Himmler, is well documented and indis-putable. Following the capture of Eichmann in May 1960, the specula-tion about the relationship between these two men became a subject of active public discussion. In a press conference held at the time of the Eichmann trial, on May 4, 1961, al-Husseini denied any connection with Adolf Eichmann during World War II. Indeed, he claimed at this press conference that he did not even know who Eichmann was until he read about his capture in the newspapers.[46] In fact, the mufti and Eichmann not only knew each other, but collaborated actively in their years of service to the Third Reich. At the Nuremberg trials, Dieter Wisliceny, one of Eichmann's senior deputies, would testify that the mufti "was one of Eichmann's best friends and had constantly incited him to accelerate the extermination measures. I heard him say that, accompanied by Eichmann, he had visited incognito the gas chamber of Auschwitz."[47] On this visit to Auschwitz, al-Husseini reportedly urged the guards in charge of the chambers to be more diligent and ef-ficient in their efforts.[48]

One can only imagine how the mufti must have rejoiced as he toured the Auschwitz death camp complex. What he witnessed was indeed, in his mind, the final solution to his Jewish problem. With a sweeping au-dacity that was almost too bold to grasp, Hitler had determined simply to eliminate his perceived enemies. As he examined the details of the process that led to extermination, al-Husseini realized that he would not have to transport his Jews anywhere. The Jews were concentrated in the Tel Aviv/Jaffa region of Palestine. No railroad cars would be needed for transport. No "selection" would be necessary. No Jew would be needed to work or labor in any way for his Arab state of Palestine. All that the mufti would need would be the technical assistance of his good friends Hein-rich Himmler and Adolf Eichmann to construct factories of death to eliminate the Jews from Palestine once and for all.

As the mufti left Auschwitz to return to Berlin, he could only marvel at Germany's ruthless efficiency in solving its Jewish problem. With a smug certainty, he marveled at his good fortune in living at a time when he was blessed with such a superb ally and friend in the person of Adolf Hitler.

Eichmann and al-Husseini admired each other tremendously. Eichmann, as Dieter Wisliceny recalled in his testimony at Nuremberg, "was very strongly impressed with the Mufti."[49] The mufti, in turn, reciprocated this admiration. When he spoke of Eichmann in the presumed privacy of his diary, al-Husseini observed that he was a "very rare diamond, the best savior of the Arabs."[50]

Hitler's Voice to the Arabs:
The Mufti and Nazi Radio Broadcasts to the Middle East

From the very outset of his stay in Berlin, it became apparent that the Nazis planned to employ al-Husseini as their chief spokesman in the Middle East. Working closely with Joseph Goebbels, the Third Reich's propaganda minister, the mufti organized and planned Nazi propaganda broadcasts throughout the Arab world. Throughout the war, al-Husseini appeared regularly on German radio broadcasts to the Middle East. He began making pro-Axis radio broadcasts from Berlin as early as December 1941.[51] In February 1942, he asked the Japanese to broadcast his Berlin-based radio addresses to Muslim areas in the South Pacific and to India.[52]

From his Arab bureau office in Berlin, the mufti was able to coordinate and broadcast daily radio messages. All the German and Axis radio stations were placed at his disposal, and Arabic radio programs were broadcast daily to every country with a Muslim population.[53] These broadcasts were vital to al-Husseini as a method of maintaining an active, live, audible presence throughout the Muslim world while he resided in Germany. Through these broadcasts, he was able to assert his leadership despite his physical separation from the Middle East and, in so doing, reach out to his extensive Arab constituency to further develop and expand his personal and political network in support of the German war effort.

Many of the mufti's pro-German propaganda broadcasts to the Middle East were directed specifically against the British. Arabs in Syria, Lebanon, Palestine, Iraq, and Egypt were called upon, "in the name of the Koran and for the honour of Islam, to sabotage the oil pipe lines, blow up bridges and roads along British lines of communication, kill British troops, destroy their dumps and supplies, mislead them by false information [and] withhold their support." In these exhortations, the mufti frequently reiterated to his Muslim listeners that they could achieve eternal salvation by rising up and killing the Jewish infidels living in their countries.[54] The mufti addressed a similar but special radio message to the Muslims of India, demanding that they rise up in rebellion against the British raj. Al-Husseini's frequent radio addresses to the Middle East also warned his fellow Arabs to prepare for the moment when the German invasion force would come to liberate them. He, the mufti, would let them know when that moment had arrived.[55]

In several of the mufti's radio broadcasts, he shared his microphone with Rashid Ali al-Gaylani, who had accompanied him to Berlin in the aftermath of their failed pro-German coup in Iraq and often joined him on German radio in issuing public calls for jihad against the British and their Western allies. On May 10, 1942, in one of their shared radio broadcasts commemorating the first anniversary of the outbreak of their pro-Nazi Iraqi coup, al-Gaylani ended his speech with the appeal "I call on you, O Arabs, to unite as one, to organize and fight for your independence and your rights. Unite, O Arabs, and rise against our common enemy, treacherous England."[56]

For the mufti, as for al-Gaylani, however, the common enemy was not just Great Britain, but the entire Allied cause. The mufti often called upon the Muslims of the world to help Germany in the holy war it was waging against the British and their Western allies, especially the United States. Some of his radio broadcasts were devoted specifically to condemning American policy in the Middle East. In a radio broadcast from Berlin in March 1944, he denounced American policy with regard to the establishment of a Jewish homeland in Palestine: "No one [would have] ever thought," he thundered, "that 140 million Americans would become tools in Jewish hands. . . . How could the Americans dare to Judaize Palestine?"[57]

Many of his most passionate radio broadcasts were classically anti-Semitic, designed to incite hatred and violence against radical Islam's greatest enemy, the Jews. On November 2, 1943, at the public rally to protest the Balfour Declaration, al-Husseini used German radio to broadcast one of his most virulently anti-Semitic messages: "The overwhelming egoism which lies in the character of Jews, their unworthy belief that they are God's chosen nation and their assertion that all was created for them and that other people are animals," al-Husseini declared, "makes them incapable of being trusted." In this radio broadcast, which included an inflammatory tirade against both the Jews and the British, interspersed with citations of Koranic texts against the Jews,[58] the mufti said of the Jews: "They cannot mix with any other nation but live as parasites among the nations, suck out their blood, embezzle their property, corrupt their morals. . . . The divine anger and curse that the Holy Koran mentions with reference to the Jews is because of this unique character of the Jews."[59]

In another Berlin radio broadcast, on March 1, 1944, the mufti urged his fellow Arabs to murder their Jewish neighbors: "Kill the Jews wherever you find them. This pleases God, history and religion."[60]

The mufti made it abundantly clear that he fully supported Hitler's goal—the extermination of the Jews. "If, God forbid, England should be victorious, the Jews would dominate the world," he said in a November 11, 1942, broadcast. "But if, on the contrary, England loses and its allies are defeated, the Jewish question, which for us constitutes the greatest danger, would be finally resolved. . . ."[61] One year later, in his broadcast on Berlin radio, he praised Hitler for his results. "The Germans have never harmed any Muslim, and they are fighting our common enemy," he explained. "But most of all they have definitely solved the Jewish problem."[62]

On March 19, 1943, in a radio broadcast celebrating the birthday of the Prophet Muhammad, the mufti invoked Muhammad as a pretext for inciting Muslim anger and violence against the Prophet's enemy, the Jews. "Arabs and Moslems, on this occasion of the birthday of the Prophet, who crushed Jewish ambitions in the past and completely eliminated them from Moslem countries, thereby setting us an example, on such a day Moslems and Arabs should vow before God utterly to crush Jewish ambitions and prove that faith in God is greater than imperialism and far more powerful than the devilry which surrounds international Judaism."[63]

His broadcasts provide irrefutable evidence that he knew about the extermination of the Jews. In a radio broadcast from Berlin on September 21, 1944, al-Husseini spoke of "the eleven million Jews of the world." The mufti knew that in 1939 there were seventeen million Jews in the world.[64] The Israeli historian Moshe Pearlman, a contemporary of the mufti living in Jerusalem, concluded that the numbers used in this broadcast revealed the full extent of the mufti's knowledge. "Why 'eleven million'? No one outside Germany knew at the time the scale of Jewish extermination. It was known that before the war the Jewish population numbered nearly seventeen million. The ex-Mufti's figure was written off at the time as a slip of the tongue, or an error in the script. But now the facts are known. It was no arithmetic error. Haj Amin knew then what only Hitler, Himmler and Eichmann knew: that more than five million Jews had been liquidated."[65]

Haj Amin al-Husseini, Heinrich Himmler, and the Muslim Waffen-SS

In 1943, Heinrich Himmler placed Haj Amin al-Husseini in charge of recruiting Muslims into elite units to serve in the Nazi-occupied Balkans, North Africa, and the Middle East. It is an astonishing but often forgotten fact of history that as many as one hundred thousand Muslims in Europe were recruited by the mufti and fought for Germany during the course of World War II,[66] in divisions of the Waffen-SS. Under al-Husseini's leadership and direction, two of the best-known and most infamous Waffen-SS Nazi-Muslim divisions were established in Nazi-occupied Bosnia and in Croatia, which had been given the status of a separate state after the German conquest of Yugoslavia.[67] In April 1943, at the request of Himmler, al-Husseini traveled to the Balkans to help in the recruitment of Muslims for the Waffen-SS.[68] It was to be composed entirely of Bosnian Muslim volunteers.[69]

Al-Husseini was more than eager to help Himmler and his deputies in the SS organize the Bosnian Waffen-SS Handschar Division, which would both contribute significantly to the German war effort and play an instrumental role in the planned extermination of Bosnia's Jews. In a speech that the mufti delivered in March 1943, just a few weeks prior to leaving for Sarajevo, he said that "the hearts of all Muslims must today go out to our Islamic brothers in Bosnia, who are forced to endure a tragic fate. They are being persecuted by the Serbian and Communist bandits, who receive support from England and the Soviet Union. . . . They are being murdered, their possessions are robbed, and their villages are burned. England and its allies bear a great accountability before history for mishandling and murdering Europe's Muslims, just as they have done in Arabic lands and in India."[70]

Upon his arrival in Sarajevo, the mufti was greeted by cheering crowds and met with Bosnian Muslim leaders, who aided him in exhorting their Muslim followers to join the Waffen-SS. Bosnian Muslim religious leaders pressured their congregants, urging Muslims who came to pray at the city's mosques to volunteer to join the proposed Muslim Waffen-SS Division.[71] Al-Husseini himself visited all of the city's mosques and reviewed the Muslim Waffen-SS troops that he helped recruit in Bosnia in 1943 and 1944. Photographs of the mufti reviewing the troops appeared in the *Berliner Illustrierte Zeitung*, German newsreels, and other publications. One of several photographs of him reviewing these Bosnian Waffen-SS troops appeared on the cover of the popular Nazi magazine *Wiener Illustrierte* (*Vienna Illustrated*) January 12, 1944,[72] and was subsequently reprinted on several occasions as evidence of his collaboration with the Axis.[73] Kermit Roosevelt, grandson of President Theodore Roosevelt, interviewed the mufti in Cairo in June 1948 and wrote about al-Husseini's wartime radio broadcasts from Berlin: "This picture and the recordings of radio broadcasts do indeed prove collaboration."[74]

Charismatic and passionate as always, the mufti was demonstrably successful in his recruitment efforts. In his sermon at Sarajevo's largest mosque, he brought his audience to tears. To further recruitment, he wrote a book titled *Islam and the Jews,* which was distributed to Bosnian Muslim SS units during the war,[75] as part of his efforts to incite the murder of Bosnian Jews. To Himmler's delight, al-Husseini was eminently successful in these efforts: With his encouragement and incitement, the Bosnian Muslim Waffen-SS company that he recruited, the notorious "Handschar troopers," slaughtered 90 percent—12,600—of Bosnia's 14,000 Jews.[76] The mufti later recruited and sent other Bosnian Muslim military units to Hungary, where they aided in the killing of Jews.[77] The mufti's work in Bosnia was praised and supported by his friend Himmler, who established a special mullah military school in Dresden to train the Bosnian Muslim recruits.[78]

In January 1944, during a three-day visit with the Muslim Waffen-SS Handschar Division, al-Husseini gave a speech in which he made clear the basis of the Muslim alliance with Nazi Germany that he had done so much to forge and shape:

This division of Bosnian Muslims established with the help of Greater Germany is an example to Muslims in all countries. There is no other deliverance for them from imperialistic oppression than hard fighting to preserve their homes and faith. Many common interests exist between the Islamic world and Greater Germany, and those make cooperation a matter of course. The Reich is fighting against the same enemies who robbed the Muslims of their countries and suppressed their faith in Asia, Africa, and Europe. . . .

Friendship and collaboration between two peoples must be built on a firm foundation. The necessary ingredients here are common spiritual and material interests as well as the same ideal. The relationship between the Muslims and the Germans is built on this foundation. Never in its history has Germany attacked a Muslim nation. Germany battles world Jewry, Islam's principal enemy. Germany also battles England and its allies, who have persecuted millions of Muslims, as well as Bolshevism, which subjugates forty million Muslims and threatens the Islamic faith in other lands. Any one of these arguments would be enough of a foundation for a friendly relationship between two peoples. . . . My enemy's enemy is my friend. . . .[79]

In recruiting the Bosnian Waffen-SS, al-Husseini played an important role in Hitler's extermination of Europe's Jews. It was not, however, his only direct contribution to Hitler's Final Solution. In other ways, the mufti contributed actively to the Holocaust.

One of the ways in which he did so was to obstruct ransom negotiations that could have facilitated further European Jewish immigration to Palestine. In early 1946, the American journalist Edgar Ansel Mowrer, writing in the *New York Post,* documented a proposal made by the British government, in the spring of 1943, to permit four thousand Jewish refugee children from Hungary, Romania, Bulgaria, and Slovakia, accompanied by five hundred adults, to enter Palestine in exchange for the release of twenty thousand German prisoners of war. Himmler, Eichmann, and other German leaders were at first interested in the proposal and entered into negotiations with the British for the exchange of German POWs for the more than four thousand Jewish refugee children who might have fled to Palestine, but they subsequently withdrew from the negotiations when al-Husseini protested.[80] As a result, the Jewish children were sent to death camps in Poland. In his postwar affidavit at Nuremberg, Dieter Wisliceny, Eichmann's deputy, testified that the mufti's opposition had been responsible for the failure of these exchange negotiations.[81] After reviewing official

German correspondence about the negotiations, the distinguished Holocaust scholar Raul Hilberg also concluded that there was a definite connection, proof positive, between the mufti's protests and the end of the negotiations.[82]

On several other occasions, al-Husseini intervened actively with authorities of the Third Reich to prevent Jews from leaving Europe for Palestine. At one point he lobbied Hitler personally to block a plan to allow Jews to leave Hungary, again claiming that they would settle in Palestine and reinforce a new center of world Jewish power. In May and June 1943, the mufti sent letters to the Axis governments of Hungary, Romania, Bulgaria, and Italy in which he demanded that they withdraw their authorization for Jewish emigration and urged them instead to send their Jews to Poland,[83] where they would end up in Auschwitz and other Nazi death camps. In his May 6, 1943, letter to the Bulgarian foreign minister, he wrote "that it would be very beneficial to prevent the Jews from leaving their country. . . . With this in mind one avoids the danger they would bring. And this would be a thankful deed toward the Arab people."[84] The mufti's letter to the Italians, asking them to use their influence on Hungary, Romania, and Bulgaria to prevent Jewish immigration to Palestine, interfered with talks then under way for the ransoming of Jews from Italian-occupied Croatia.[85] Finally, at the urging of the mufti, Heinrich Himmler issued a prohibition against permitting any Jews to immigrate to Palestine from territories occupied by Germany.[86]

Exterminating the Jews of Palestine

Al-Husseini also participated in high-level Nazi discussions about the German war effort in the Middle East and in planning for the eventual extermination of the Jews of Palestine. Nazi Germany had made plans to expand the extermination of the Jews beyond the borders of Europe and into British-controlled Palestine. These plans, formulated in 1942 as the German conquest of the Middle East seemed quite plausible, would have implemented the mass slaughter of the Jews of Palestine.[87] In consultation with the mufti, the Nazi leadership had created a special Einsatzgruppe Egypt, a mobile SS squad, under the supervision of Adolf Eichmann, which was to carry out the mass murder of Palestinian Jewry. By the summer of 1942, anticipating a German military victory in the Middle East, the Einsatzgruppe Egypt had been standing by in Athens and was ready to disembark for Palestine, attached to German general Erwin Rommel's Afrika Korps, where it would have begun killing the close to half a million Jews then living in Palestine. This Middle Eastern death squad was led by SS Obersturmbannführer Walther Rauff, one of Eichmann's most trusted deputies and a confidant of al-Husseini's.

According to documents found by the Allied armies in Germany when they entered the country at the end of World War II, the mufti persistently urged Himmler and other Nazi leaders to consider bombing Jerusalem and Tel Aviv, where the vast majority of Palestine's Jewish community was concentrated. One of these documents, a secret report of the German air force command dated October 29, 1943, revealed that for the previous six months, al-Husseini had been proposing an air attack on Jerusalem as well as an attack on the more heavily Jewish-populated city of Tel Aviv. The air attack on Jerusalem was to have targeted the headquarters of the Jewish Agency, the provisional Jewish government of Palestine. According to this secret report, the mufti proposed that November 2, the anniversary of the British government's Balfour Declaration, should be celebrated by such an attack.[88]

At the same time, and again under pressure from al-Husseini, the German air command was considering an attack on military objectives along the Palestine coast.[89]

The same secret report described the mufti's efforts to secure an attack on Tel Aviv, which would have required the mobilization of an increased number of German army troops in the Middle East.[90] Hermann Göring, head of the German air force, eventually rejected the mufti's request on the pragmatic grounds that sufficient additional military forces were not available to be transferred from Europe to Palestine to successfully carry out such an attack.[91] Apparently, the mufti did not give up hopes for a German air offensive against Palestine, for on March 30, 1944, he again urged the German air force to bomb Jewish buildings in Jerusalem and Tel Aviv.[92] Again, the German air force command, under Göring, declined to carry out the mufti's request.

Unable to persuade the German air force to act on its own initiative, in late 1944 al-Husseini organized the dispatch of five parachuters to Palestine with ten containers of a toxin to poison Tel Aviv's water system. Fortunately, they were caught near Jericho before they could carry out their mission. A police report said that these ten containers held enough poison to kill 250,000 people.[93]

Escaping Indictment at Nuremberg

Had he been captured and imprisoned by the Allies at the end of World War II, Haj Amin al-Husseini would certainly have been indicted and convicted as a war criminal at Nuremberg, as were so many other leaders of Hitler's Nazi regime.

There is abundant evidence to document the charge that al-Husseini was guilty of war crimes, having actively advised and assisted the Nazi regime in its determination to carry out the systematic destruction of European Jewry. In June 1944, Adolf Eichmann's deputy Dieter Wisliceny told Dr. Rudolf Kastner, the Hungarian Jewish leader, that he was convinced the mufti had "played a role in the decision to exterminate the European Jews."[94] The importance of the mufti's role, insisted Wisliceny, "must not be disregarded. . . . The Mufti had repeatedly suggested to the various authorities with whom he was maintaining contact, above all to Hitler, Ribbentrop and Himmler, the extermination of European Jewry."[95]

In his testimony at the Nuremberg trials, Wisliceny, who was subsequently executed as a war criminal, was even more explicit: "The

Mufti was one of the initiators of the systematic extermination of European Jewry and had been a collaborator and adviser of Eichmann and Himmler in the execution of the plan."[96] Wisliceny's testimony gave proof positive of the mufti's guilt.

The mufti never attempted to disguise his Nazi beliefs or his wartime role as a mouthpiece for Hitler's genocide in the Arab world. His role in the extermination of the Jews of Bosnia, and his oft proclaimed desire to exterminate all the Jews of Europe and Palestine, cannot be excused simply as anti-Zionism.[97] It may be a coincidence that the decision to carry out the physical extermination of the Jews of Europe followed soon after his arrival in Germany.[98] From the mufti's perspective, it was providential. In fact, only two months after his initial meeting with Hitler on November 28, 1941, the infamous Wannsee Conference took place, in which the Nazi leadership produced their plan to systematically exterminate European Jewry.[99]

Bartley Crum, a member of the Anglo-American Committee on Palestine who visited Nuremberg to observe the war crimes trials, noted in his memoirs that he "spent some time talking to the American investigators who were reconstructing the Nazi conspiracy, for the prosecution from the massive archives which the Allies had unearthed."[100] Crum went on to report that "an Army intelligence officer, at three o'clock one afternoon, made it possible for me to enter a room and sit down at a table upon which was a thick file of documents. I opened the file and began to read. The record of the ex-Mufti's intrigues was fantastic. The file showed clearly that he climaxed a record of Facism, anti-British intrigues, and anti-Semitism by helping spearhead the extermination of European Jewry."[101]

The evidence against al-Husseini as a war criminal was so clear and convincing that Great Britain, France, and Yugoslavia considered moving for his indictment as part of the Nuremberg process. Each country (for its own reasons) ultimately declined to seek al-Husseini's indictment. The new British government of Clement Attlee was afraid that putting al-Husseini on trial would stir up even greater Arab hostility to Great Britain in the aftermath of World War II. The last thing

Britain needed was another uprising among the Arabs in Palestine, who continued to revere the mufti, or elsewhere in the Islamic Middle East where the British government continued to maintain a colonial presence. The British had no desire to risk Muslim ire in India, then on the verge of independence, and thus did nothing to extradite the mufti and get him on the road to Nuremberg. To be sure, many members of the British Parliament, outraged by the evidence of al-Husseini's role in instigating and encouraging the Nazi plan of exterminating European Jewry, demanded that the government take steps to extradite al-Husseini and try him as a war criminal.[102] The British government, however, took the position that the mufti "was not a war criminal in the technical sense of the term," since he had not served in enemy armed forces himself, nor was he an enemy national at the time he served in Germany.[103] It was decided that the mufti had not committed extraditable offenses under the Anglo-French treaty on extradition, and it would thus be a waste of time for the British government to seek his extradition.[104]

France, where anti-Semitism and sympathy for Nazi ideology remained strong even after the collapse of its pro-Nazi Vichy government, was more concerned about maintaining its presence in Muslim North Africa and the Islamic Middle East than in bringing al-Husseini to justice. Nor did the new postwar French government want to aggravate unrest among the Muslim populace of Algeria, Tunisia, or Morocco, for whom the mufti remained a hero. If they indicted him, it would likely make the mufti a martyr throughout the remaining French colonies within North Africa and the Middle East. Thus, like England, France concluded that the mufti had not committed extraditable offenses under the Anglo-French treaty on extradition.

So, too, Marshal Tito's government in postwar Yugoslavia did not demand al-Husseini's extradition and indictment as a war criminal at Nuremberg, despite overwhelming evidence of the mufti's collaboration with the Nazis, his role in the murder of thousands of Bosnian Croatians and Serbs, and his recruitment and formation of the Muslim Bosnian Waffen-SS Division that had been instrumental in the extermination of 90 percent of Bosnia's Jews. Tito understood that if he was to forge a united Yugoslav nation, the Muslims in Bosnia—many of whom had fought under the mufti during the war as members of the Handschar Division of his Bosnian Waffen-SS, and who constituted a not insignificant portion of Marshal Tito's constituency—must not have any excuse to resist his plans. The Muslim community of Bosnia, Tito recognized, remained unswervingly loyal to the mufti, even after the defeat of Nazi Germany. Thus, although there was a consensus that Haj Amin al-Husseini was guilty of war crimes, a convergence of political realities in the postwar world prevented him from being brought to justice.

The mufti satisfied and fulfilled all four criteria for indictment and conviction—conspiracy to wage aggressive war; crimes against peace; war crimes; and crimes against humanity—upon which war crimes guilt was judged at Nuremberg. In each of these areas, it was clear that al-Husseini was subject to indictment and conviction. One can only lament the fact that Haj Amin al-Husseini escaped judgment at Nuremberg. As we have documented, there is compelling and irrefutable historical evidence to support the conclusion of *The Nation*, a major American journal of opinion of the era, which editorialized in 1947 that the mufti was "by every criterion laid down at Nuremberg, a war criminal."[105] Having reviewed all of the available evidence, this is our conclusion as well.

The Mufti's Escape from Germany After World War II

As 1945 dawned, the handwriting on the wall seemed ominously imminent to the mufti: The eventual defeat of Hitler's Germany by the Allies, he realized, was only a matter of time. This time, the mufti was determined to abandon the sinking ship rather than be caught by the advancing Allied armies. Haj Amin al-Husseini was one of the great escape artists of the twentieth century. Time and again, he had kept one step ahead of whatever authorities were in hot pursuit of him. As Nazi

Germany collapsed, he played the role of Hitler's Houdini, preparing for his most daring escape.[106] With the help of friends in the SS, a German commercial airliner, reserved in advance, was ordered to stand by for takeoff. There was widespread speculation that the mufti would seek to gain sanctuary in the Muslim holy city of Mecca, where he would be safe from extradition and indictment at Nuremberg, even though Saudi Arabia was officially at war with the Axis powers. Under the law of the Koran, once in Mecca, the mufti could not be refused sanctuary. Haj Amin al-Husseini, however, chose to seek refuge elsewhere.

When he boarded the plane in Berlin on May 8, 1945, the day after Germany surrendered to the Allies, the destination given to the pilot was neighboring neutral Switzerland. Upon landing on Swiss soil, in Bern, the mufti was not welcomed with open arms, as he had expected. Denied political asylum by the Swiss, who anticipated he would be indicted as a war criminal, al-Husseini soon proceeded to France, where he would spend the next year living comfortably in a spacious villa in Rambouillet, a suburb of Paris. The government of the new French premier, Georges Bidault, many of whose members were still devoted to the rabidly pro-Nazi Vichy government, was in no rush to seek his extradition. Even General Charles de Gaulle, who had led the Free French Forces against Germany, was not calling for the mufti's imprisonment or extradition.[107] Instead of prison, the mufti and his entourage were allowed to stay in the villa under discreet police surveillance, living in luxury. Only in the late spring of 1946, when the wartime activities of the mufti would attract renewed attention owing to the revelations at the Nuremberg trials and a series of in-depth articles about him by journalist Edgar A. Mowrer in the *New York Post*,[108] was al-Husseini advised by the French government that it was time to leave France. He then made his escape, flying from Paris to Cairo, where he would receive political asylum and a hero's welcome from his friend and ally King Farouk of Egypt.

Chapter 4

The Mufti's Reflection:
What If Germany Had Conquered
Palestine and Britain?

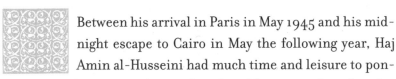 Between his arrival in Paris in May 1945 and his mid-night escape to Cairo in May the following year, Haj Amin al-Husseini had much time and leisure to pon-der his fate and his future: Over lavishly prepared meals at his villa, and during his numerous walks in the park and frequent visits to Paris, he could not help but imagine what might have been. What if the German military had been victorious at the decisive Battle of El Alamein in Egypt and had gone on to con-quer Palestine and the rest of the Middle East? What if Ger-many had won the Battle of Britain and conquered the British Isles? What if Churchill's government had then collapsed, to be replaced by a pro-Nazi puppet regime in London? What if Hitler had won the war? As he prepared to leave Europe to re-turn home to the Arab Middle East, the mufti imagined a coun-terfactual scenario, one that very well might have happened.[1]

In the spring of 1941, as Hitler was making his plans to invade the Soviet Union, Nazi Germany seem poised to dominate the world. Poland, France, Belgium, Holland, Norway, Denmark, Austria, Czechoslovakia, Yugoslavia, Greece, and Luxembourg had been conquered by Germany. Hitler's armies had gone "from one astonishing triumph to another."[2] Denmark had been defeated in three hours, Luxembourg in a day, Norway in two months, and the Netherlands, Belgium, and France within six weeks.[3] All of Europe, except for Sweden and Switzerland, which were neutral, was in the hands of Hitler's friends and allies: dictators or monarchs who ruled Fascist Italy, Vichy France, Franco's Spain, Portugal, the Balkan countries, Finland, and the Soviet Union.[4] By the end of June 1940, "Hitler was the master of the entire continent of Europe except for Russia."[5] Yet military historians have agreed that the invasion and destruction of the Soviet Union had become, against all odds, a "strategic obsession" to Hitler, "the strategic and ideological project closest to Hitler's heart."[6]

What if, al-Husseini imagined, in the late spring and summer of 1941, Hitler had postponed his invasion of the Soviet Union for a year and instead sent the bulk of his armies and air force to serve under General Erwin Rommel, who would then have been able to launch a victorious campaign of conquest throughout the Middle East? Hitler, like Napoleon Bonaparte, "seriously contemplated a military campaign throughout the Near East, following the route of another conqueror, Alexander the Great."[7] Hitler should have sent most of his army to fight with Rommel, who might very well have done what Alexander did and Bonaparte failed to do: He would have conquered the Middle East and led his armies victoriously to India.[8] There he would have linked up with the Japanese. Europe, Asia, Africa, and the Middle East might well have belonged to the victorious Axis powers. Future historians, the mufti mused, would probably agree that only Hitler's astonishing blunder in betraying his Soviet ally and invading Soviet Russia kept this scenario from happening.[9]

Had Hitler postponed Operation Barbarossa and instead sent his troops to Egypt rather than to Russia, the war might have taken an entirely different direction. What if . . . ? Reclining in his easy chair on the porch of his suburban Parisian villa, with his eyes closed, the mufti whimsically imagined what might have been.

From the beginning of World War II, Hitler had plans to conquer North Africa and the Middle East. When Germany's Italian allies declared war on Great Britain on June 10, 1940, the Italians' first objective had been to push the British out of Egypt. However, despite their superior numbers, the Italians were quickly defeated by the British and forced to retreat across Italian-ruled Libya. Hitler, fearing a total Italian collapse, sent an armored corps commanded by Rommel to regain the initiative in North Africa. Rommel, the celebrated desert commander who had already gained fame for his tactical genius in the German battles for Poland and France, arrived in North Africa in February 1941. Within a month, his Afrika Korps had the British on the run. By the beginning of 1942, Rommel's desert army had crossed into Egypt and come within striking distance of Cairo and the Suez Canal.[10]

Throughout the summer of 1942, Germany's Afrika Korps and Great Britain's Eighth Army attacked and counterattacked each other on several Egyptian battle fronts. On June 21, Rommel's army captured the key British-held port of Tobruk, taking thirty-five thousand prisoners. The British defeat "was second only to the capture of Singapore by the Japanese as the greatest British disaster of the war." Hitler was so impressed that he promoted Rommel to field marshal.[11] In September, British prime minister Winston Churchill, in the hope of gaining the initiative, placed one of Great Britain's top generals, Bernard L. Montgomery, in command of the Eighth Army. Churchill's hope soon proved futile. Despite the fact that Montgomery was able to motivate his soldiers and rebuild the weakened and demoralized army,[12] he and his troops were no match for the superior German army under the command of Rommel, the brilliant Desert Fox. Hitler's fortuitous decision to postpone his invasion of Soviet Russia and transfer the bulk of his armed forces to support Rommel in Egypt proved crucial to the German victories at El Alamein and, subsequently, elsewhere throughout the Middle East. By October 1942, Rommel's massively reinforced

Afrika Korps now numbered more than four hundred thousand men and two thousand armed tanks—double the number of Montgomery's men and machines.

At 9:30 p.m. on October 23, 1942, the British Eighth Army began its attack against the German defenses south of El Alamein.[13] Two days later, the Germans launched a major counteroffensive against Montgomery's Eighth Army, in an assault on the enemy lines at El Alamein itself. Within two weeks, the German victory at El Alamein was complete: British losses totaled more than twenty thousand casualties and thirty thousand prisoners; nearly all of their tanks and artillery were destroyed or captured.[14]

By winning the Battle of El Alamein, one of the decisive military engagements of World War II, Germany's famed desert commander Erwin Rommel had decisively turned the tide of the war in North Africa, paving the way for German military hegemony throughout North Africa and the Middle East. With El Alamein won, the road to Cairo was open. Germany was in occupation of Egypt, controlling the Suez Canal and within striking distance of the Middle Eastern oil fields. As one German officer remarked after the Nazi triumph: "Imagine, if we had not had that petrol, we would have lost the Middle East and with it, the war!" The news was delivered to an exultant Hitler, who immediately shared the report of Rommel's victory to Luftwaffe chief Hermann Göring and Foreign Minister von Ribbentrop. Together, they toasted Rommel's success and the Nazi future. Not since the surrender of France in June 1940 had the führer and his Reichministers known such a triumph. As Winston Churchill would later lament: "Before El Alamein we never had a defeat. After Alamein we never had a victory."[15]

The British retreat from Egypt was swift. When the German forces occupied the Suez Canal, the lifeline of the British Empire was in Hitler's hands. During the next few weeks, Rommel's Afrika Korps crossed the Sinai desert and entered Palestine, where they won victory after victory over the British in quick succession. Despite help from Palestine's Jewish defense brigades, the recently armed Haganah, the retreating British army could not regain the initiative against Rommel's onslaught. On November 18, 1942, Rommel's army marched up the coast of Palestine to capture the twin cities of Tel Aviv and Jaffa.[16] Inspired by the mufti's radio broadcasts from Berlin, the Arabs of Jaffa received the Germans joyously, dancing in the streets. With the capture of Jaffa and Tel Aviv assured, Rommel marched toward Jerusalem, entering the Holy City on November 20.[17]

During these momentous events, the mufti traveled from Berlin to Jerusalem, arriving in his native city on the same day as Rommel's army. In city after city—Jaffa, Hebron, Haifa, Tel Aviv, and Jerusalem—the mufti called for jihad, inspiring and mobilizing his Arab countrymen to rise up against the Jews and help the invading German army defeat the British and liberate Palestine. Quoting from *The Protocols of the Elders of Zion* as well as from the Koran, the mufti reminded his people that killing the Jews and liberating Jerusalem from the Zionists would be doing the work of Allah. Speaking from the Al-Aqsa Mosque, the mufti called for the extermination of Palestinian Jewry. "Kill the Jews of Palestine wherever you find them," he beseeched his impassioned audience, "this pleases God, history and religion."[18] Rioting everywhere, the Arabs of Jerusalem followed the mufti's ardent advice, killing thousands of Jews and destroying most of Jewish Jerusalem's homes and businesses. As al-Husseini would later confide to Rommel, "With your help and the help of Allah, Palestine like Germany will soon be *Judenrein*" (free of Jews).

The British retreat from Palestine made front-page news. The photographs of British troops boarding ships in Haifa's harbor were reminiscent of the pictures and newsreels from Dunkirk, where Germany also had won a resounding victory. But this time there was no next battle. Within a matter of weeks, the Arab Middle East had fallen to Axis hands, as Rommel's forces advanced from Cairo to Damascus, Baghdad, and Jerusalem, establishing Nazi hegemony wherever they went. After their victory at El Alamein, Rommel's Afrika Korps, aided by units of the German Twentieth Army, defeated the remnants of the retreating British Eighth Army in several battles before invading Palestine. After quickly vanquishing the British at Aleppo in northern

Syria, they easily captured Damascus. One by one, the major cities of Free French Syria fell to the invading German armies. Rommel's forces, having conquered Syria, crossed into Iraq, pursuing the British first to Mosul and then toward Baghdad.[19] By the time Rommel's Afrika Korps arrived in Palestine, Egypt, Syria, and Iraq were firmly under German control.

Shortly after Rommel's victory at El Alamein, the British high commissioner of Palestine, realizing that the German advance into Palestine was unstoppable and that the German army would soon occupy Jerusalem, made plans to evacuate the city before Rommel's forces arrived. On October 26, the high commissioner managed to flee Jerusalem for Haifa, feeling fortunate to have escaped with his life. After boarding a small plane piloted by a Royal Air Force officer under his command, he was flown to Haifa harbor. There, at midnight, he embarked by warship on the dangerous voyage to Great Britain. During the next few days, the remaining British officials of the British mandatory government in Palestine and of British army headquarters left their rooms and offices in the King David Hotel and drove out of the city. As they left, the British Union Jack was lowered from the hotel parapet.[20]

On November 2, 1942, the last of the British government officials and soldiers boarded several ships in Haifa harbor. Twenty-five years to the day after the Balfour Declaration, the British Mandate, with its promise of a Jewish homeland in Palestine, was no more.

As German troops entered Jerusalem in late November 1942, and the swastika flag flew over the city's German colony, the fate of the Jews of Palestine was sealed. Although there was some resistance by the Haganah, the military arm of the Jewish Agency, it was over within a few weeks. A remnant of Jewish freedom fighters resolved to retreat to the mountaintop of Masada, determined to reenact the heroic Jewish resistance against the Roman Empire in 70 CE. In the ultimate ironic twist of history, the Palestinian Jewish standoff against Nazi German forces at Masada in December 1942 ended with German soldiers advancing up the ramp of the very road the Romans had used to destroy the Jewish fortress at Masada nineteen centuries earlier. With that, all Jewish resistance to the German occupation of Palestine ended.

Nazi Germany had long planned to expand the extermination of the Jews beyond the borders of Europe and into British-controlled Palestine. In 1942, the Nazi leadership had created a special Einsatzgruppe Egypt, a mobile SS death squad, under the supervision of Adolf Eichmann, which was to carry out the mass murder of Jews in Palestine similar to the way the Final Solution had been carried out at Auschwitz and at the other Nazi death camps in Eastern Europe. By the following year, the Einsatzgruppe had been ready to go to Palestine and begin killing the close to half million Jews of Palestine, more than fifty thousand of whom had fled Europe to escape Nazi death camps like Auschwitz and Birkenau.[21] Even before the Battle of El Alamein, in the summer of 1942, the Einsatzgruppe Egypt had been standing by in Athens and was ready to disembark for Palestine, attached to General Rommel's Afrika Korps. This Middle Eastern death squad, similar to those operating throughout Eastern Europe during World War II, was led by SS Obersturmbannführer Walther Rauff,[22] one of Eichmann's most trusted deputies.

The November 16 order to round up the Jews and place them in a sealed city within Tel Aviv, first announced by SS Obersturmbannführer Rauff, was completed swiftly. (The order for the roundup of Palestinian Jewry, historians would later recount, took place exactly eleven months before the roundup of the Jews of Rome, 1,007 of whom were subsequently sent to their deaths at Auschwitz.) The mufti's close friend Adolf Eichmann was assigned the task of implementing the roundup order, a task for which he was well prepared and which he executed with deadly efficiency. The first death camps in Tel Aviv, modeled after the camps at Auschwitz and Birkenau, began operating shortly after Eichmann's arrival. Under Rauff and Eichmann's direction, and with the invaluable help of the mufti, the members of the SS Einsatzgruppe death squad enlisted hundreds of Palestinian Arab collaborators so that the "mass murder would continue under German leadership without interruption."[23] As Eichmann would later attest, his friend the mufti was instrumental in personally recruiting these Palestinian Arab collaborators, who were eager to facilitate the work of the Nazi death squad and thus enable the mufti to carry out his long promised jihad against Palestinian Jewry.

Within three months, all 450,000 Jews in Palestine had been exterminated. In Palestine, as in much of Europe, the Final Solution had been carried out with great efficiency and success. In early March 1944, speaking from his pulpit at the Al-Aqsa Mosque, the mufti joyously proclaimed that Palestine was "now and forever, *Judenrein*." Several days later over dinner at the King David Hotel, a former Jewish-owned establishment left standing in Jerusalem, Adolf Eichmann and Haj Amin al-Husseini rejoiced that together they had succeeded in bringing about the Final Solution of the Jewish problem, both in Europe and now in Palestine. "This is only the beginning," Eichmann promised his friend al-Husseini. "In our thousand-year Reich, there will soon be no Jews anywhere."

The following month, Hitler personally flew to Jerusalem, where he welcomed the mufti, his friend, ally, and collaborator in the Final Solution, and appointed him president of the newly established German protectorate of Palestine. "As I promised you at our historic meeting in November 1941," Hitler told the mufti, "Jerusalem and all of Palestine is now yours." The mufti was triumphant: He was now Hitler's designated führer of Palestine and of the entire Arab Middle East.

The Arab Higher Committee for Palestine was immediately disbanded and replaced by the new government of All-Palestine. The mufti was inaugurated as president of a free, independent Palestine, accountable only to the führer himself. In an inaugural ceremony in Jerusalem attended by the mufti's close friends Heinrich Himmler and Adolf Eichmann, al-Husseini publicly expressed his deep appreciation and loyalty to the Third Reich and pledged his full support to Adolf Hitler until complete victory was achieved.

With Rommel's military victories and Hitler's triumph in the Middle East complete, the age-old Islamic caliphate, which had been abolished two decades earlier by Turkey, was reestablished, with Haj Amin al-Husseini as its head. On the first Friday after the mufti's inauguration as the first president of the new All-Palestine state, al-Husseini attended a prayer service at the Al-Aqsa Mosque, at which the restoration of the Islamic caliphate was formally announced. At a celebratory dinner that evening, which Eichmann and Himmler also attended, al-Husseini was publicly designated and acclaimed as the caliph of the Islamic Middle East, the undisputed and absolute ruler of a new pan-Islamic empire, encompassing all the major cities of the Muslim world, including Cairo, Tehran, Beirut, Damascus, Baghdad, and Jerusalem. More than symbolically, perhaps, the dinner celebrating the new caliph was held at the King David Hotel, until recently the headquarters of the British high commissioner and the hated British mandatory government in Palestine. The British Mandate was no more. As Eichmann and Himmler noted proudly in their remarks that evening, their staunch friend and ally, and Hitler's loyal deputy, Haj Amin al-Husseini, who did so much to make Palestine *Judenrein* and to extend the Final Solution beyond Europe's borders, was now the true führer of the Arab world.

Within months of his inauguration as caliph and the final British exit from Palestine, al-Husseini had other good news to celebrate. Over the years, Haj Amin al-Husseini's hatred of the British had known no bounds. While Rommel's humiliating defeat of the British throughout the Middle East and the end of the detested British Mandate in Palestine had been music to the mufti's ears, he eagerly awaited the final defeat of Britain by Germany and its Axis allies and the demise of Churchill's government. In mid-April 1944, al-Husseini was exhilarated to hear that the German military defeat of Great Britain was finally complete. The Battle of Britain had been won. King George VI had been forced off the throne and replaced by his older brother, the pro-Nazi Duke of Windsor—the former king Edward VIII—whom Hitler had often entertained at Berchtesgaden. Sir Oswald Mosley, the charismatic leader of the anti-Semitic Union of British Fascists and a long-time friend and admirer of the Hitler regime, was released from prison, where Churchill had sent him in May 1940, and replaced Churchill as prime minister. Throughout the 1930s, Mosley—a former Conservative who had become a Labour Party member of Parliament, was a member of one of Great Britain's most aristocratic families, and whom many had assumed would be a future prime minister—had achieved special notoriety as the "Führer of British Fascism."[24] Mosley's Blackshirt followers had marched through London's Jewish East End in the 1930s, targeting Jewish homes and synagogues for attack and calling for the extermination of the Jews. Equally exhilarating was the news that Sir Oswald's choice for deputy prime minister was Lord Charles Stewart Henry Vane-Tempest-Stewart, the seventh Marquess of Londonderry and close friend and confidant of the Duke of Windsor, both before and after the duke's abdication as King Edward VIII. Lord Londonderry, a cousin of Winston Churchill, scion of one of Great Britain's wealthiest families, and a pillar of the British aristocracy, also had achieved well-deserved notoriety as the only British cabinet member to openly support the Nazis and as "Hitler's leading apologist in Great Britain."[25]

With the Duke of Windsor restored to his throne and Sir Oswald Mosley and Lord Londonderry governing the nation from 10 Downing Street, the Nazi defeat and takeover of Churchill's Britain was now complete. Hitler had long had secret plans for his invasion of Great Britain. Among them was the Gestapo "Arrest List for Great Britain," with Churchill's name on it,[26] which immediately had been put into effect. Winston Churchill and the members of his government had been taken into custody by the Gestapo the day after German troops entered London.[27] Churchill and several of his senior cabinet ministers were immediately placed under house arrest in London, awaiting deportation to Auschwitz, where they would soon be executed as war criminals. More than two thousand other prominent British leaders—members of Parliament, professors, scientists, bankers, captains of industry, and churchmen, including the archbishop of Canterbury—were rounded up over the next few days. Like Churchill, they were soon shipped to Auschwitz. Within the first week of the Nazi occupation, Gestapo

troops were everywhere in Great Britain, from Windsor Castle to Westminster Abbey, and had established bases of operation in cities
throughout England. Churchill's birthplace, Blenheim Palace, just
outside of Oxford, which had been built by Churchill's ancestor the
first Duke of Marlborough in the early 1700s, had been taken over by
the Nazis to serve as Gestapo headquarters.

Under Hitler's specific orders, moreover, Nazi-occupied Britain
had been made *Judenrein*. Although the exact numbers of British Jews
who perished in the gas chambers of the death camps set up in Manchester, Leeds, and London have never been published, Eichmann,
who had presided over their executions with his usual deadly efficiency, boasted later that they amounted to more than a hundred thousand. Many of the most eminent leaders of British Jewry, however,
were sent immediately to Auschwitz. One of the first to be executed
there was the seventy-four-year-old Sir Herbert Samuel, the British
politician and statesman who, as the first high commissioner of Palestine, had appointed al-Husseini grand mufti in 1921. Samuel's personal appeal for clemency to the mufti had been in vain. His son Edwin
perished with his father at Auschwitz. The initial Nazi roundup of London Jews also included three prominent members of the Rothschild
banking family: James de Rothschild, the well-known Jewish philan-
thropist and Zionist, who since 1929 had been serving as a Liberal
Party member of Parliament, and his cousins Anthony Gustav de Rothschild, presiding head of the family's London banking firm, and Baron
Nathaniel Mayer Victor Rothschild, the eminent Cambridge University
biologist. No fewer than one hundred other members of the extended
Rothschild family were arrested in the initial Nazi roundup, all destined for deportation to Auschwitz or to the new Nazi death camp facil-
ity in Leeds. So, too, was Joseph Hertz, the distinguished chief rabbi of
the British Commonwealth, and Chaim Weizmann, the brilliant Manchester University chemist and Zionist leader who had been influential
in convincing British foreign minister Arthur James Balfour to issue
the Balfour Declaration in 1917. Had there ever been a state of Israel, as
promised in the Balfour Declaration, it was always assumed that Chaim

Weizmann would have been its first president. On the Saturday after the beginning of the Nazi roundup of London Jewry, moreover, the entire congregation of London's historic Bevis Marks Synagogue was arrested during Sabbath worship services and taken away by the Gestapo, in preparation for deportation to the gas chambers of Leeds or Auschwitz.

Two prominent American Jews—Bernard Baruch, the influential Wall Street financier and FDR's trusted presidential adviser, whom Hitler had listed as the "No.1 Jew" in America,[28] and U.S. Supreme Court justice Felix Frankfurter—were in London at the time, having been dispatched by Franklin Roosevelt at the behest of his wife, Eleanor, on a mission of mercy to try to save the leadership of British Jewry before the advent of the expected German occupation. The Nazi invasion and occupation, however, occurred so swiftly that, as misfortune would have it, Baruch and Frankfurter, caught up in the chaos of the unexpectedly quick Nazi invasion and thus still in London on the first day of the Nazi occupation of the city, were unable to escape. Both, having dined together the previous evening with James de Rothschild, to whom they had brought an urgent message from Franklin and Eleanor Roosevelt urging him to leave London immediately, were arrested by Gestapo agents as they tried to hail a taxi near the British Foreign Office at Whitehall. Both had planned to meet with their old friend Winston Churchill at 10 Downing Street later that afternoon. Their scheduled meeting, of course, never took place. Tragically, all three would briefly meet, one last time, the following week, while awaiting their shared fate outside one of the gas chambers at Auschwitz.

Haj Amin al-Husseini was exhilarated by news of the Nazi defeat and occupation of England. Adolf Eichmann wrote al-Husseini what he had been overheard telling friends in Berlin: that "the Führer, in his next New Year's proclamation, will proudly announce" that all Europe, including Great Britain, has been made *Judenrein*—"free of Jews." This was the news that he had been eagerly anticipating for many months. "I was delighted to hear," al-Husseini happily wrote his friend Eichmann, "that Britain like Palestine, and the rest of Europe, will now be completely *Judenrein*. Allah be praised!" In Mosley's England, the mufti prophesied, radical Islam will grow and prosper: "Mosques will dwarf St. Paul's Cathedral and Westminster Abbey." Arabs would soon replace Jews in London and in Oxford, Leeds, Cambridge, and Manchester. Mosques would soon outnumber churches on the streets of the British capital, which journalists and pundits alike would later rename Londonistan.[29] "By the twenty-first century," al-Husseini predicted, "London will boast a thousand mosques and will be the unofficial Muslim capital of Europe."[30] British liberal democracy would be no more. "Hitler's Reich and radical Islam," al-Husseini wrote Eichmann, "would now reign supreme in the British Isles."

Of course, the mufti knew that this would never be. . . .

Chapter 5

The Mufti's Return to the Middle East

Introduction: The Mufti's Escape

Shortly before midnight on May 28, 1946, Haj Amin al-Husseini, in disguise and using the false name and passport of Ma'ruf al-Dawalibi, a member of the Syrian embassy staff in Paris,[1] boarded an American TWA flight leaving Orly airport for Cairo. The following day, after an uneventful flight via Rome and Athens, the mufti arrived in Cairo.

As his plane approached the Cairo airport, al-Husseini could not help but reflect upon his good fortune; he had certainly lived a charmed life. Neither the Churchill nor the Attlee government in Great Britain, nor Marshal Tito's government in Yugoslavia, had succeeded in its efforts to extradite him from France so that he could be put on trial for war crimes. As al-Husseini would later note in his memoirs, from the moment of his arrival in Paris on May 19, 1945, the French government had gone out of its way to protect him, rejecting the repeated demands of the British and Allied commands for his extradition.[2] Having miraculously escaped indictment, he was now returning home to his beloved Middle East, where he would be free to assume his rightful place among the leadership of Islam and resume his life's mission of jihad against his hated enemies, the British and the Jews.

His good fortune was even more remarkable, al-Husseini reflected, given the fate of so many of his former friends and comrades in Nazi Germany. Most of them—Himmler, Goebbels, and Göring, among others—were already dead or awaiting execution by the Allies. Albert Speer, Hitler's gifted architect and munitions minister, was languishing in Spandau Prison, where he would remain for twenty years. Only his friend Adolf Eichmann, alone among the Nazi leadership with whom he had worked so closely during the war years, had escaped. Eichmann, al-Husseini had been told, had found temporary refuge and was living incognito in Argentina, which would soon become a haven for other Nazis fleeing postwar Germany. One day, the mufti mused, he and his old friend Eichmann would meet again, in Cairo or perhaps in Bueno Aires.

Al-Husseini's well-planned escape from Paris had been a complete success. In London, Winston Churchill demanded in Parliament that al-Husseini be captured in Egypt. Prime Minister Clement Attlee responded by stating that he would take the matter under advisement and would consult with the British ambassador to Egypt to facilitate the mufti's extradition. The mufti's midnight escape from Paris had surprised everyone.[3] King Farouk of Egypt had promised him a safe refuge and made good on his promise. Al-Husseini was safe and secure in Cairo, where he received political asylum, enjoying the patronage and hospitality of King Farouk's rabidly anti-British Egyptian government. While Adolf Hitler had died by his own hand in a bunker in Berlin, al-Husseini would live on to further his and the führer's dreams. His arrival in Cairo, he fervently hoped, would usher in a new chapter in his life and a new chapter in the history of Islam. During the next twenty-eight years, his hopes would be realized beyond his wildest expectations.

In Cairo, al-Husseini received a hero's welcome. He was fifty-one years old. He had aged noticeably since the days of his active leadership of the Palestine National Movement during the 1920s and 1930s. His beard, originally reddish brown, was graying softly and was now white at the tip.[4] His face, however, remained unlined and youthful. Still handsome, serene and elegant in appearance, he seemed younger than his years. Like the good wine he was fond of drinking, he felt that he had improved with age. He was at peace with himself, back home at last. After years of exile, self-imposed and otherwise, he had returned, as he always knew he would, to his beloved Arab Middle East.

Al-Husseini was greeted with great warmth by his wartime friend and ally King Farouk. Farouk, reciprocating perhaps for al-Husseini's earlier offer to him of a safe political refuge in Hitler's Berlin, immediately made good on his promise to the mufti. The mufti stayed briefly at the Metropolitan Hotel in the center of the city. He then left for Heliopolis, where he met with old friends and members of the royal family. On June 19, after being received warmly at Abdeen Palace by the head of King Farouk's palace court, al-Husseini was granted a personal audience with Farouk, who was delighted to meet with his old friend. At the end of their conversation, the king invited al-Husseini to take up residence in Inshas Palace.[5] After spending almost three weeks as the king's guest, al-Husseini was transferred to the royal family's al-Ma'amurah summer palace, where he was visited by King Farouk the following week. At this second meeting between the Egyptian monarch and the mufti, they discussed the future of Palestine and the need to protect the Al-Aqsa Mosque and the Dome of the Rock from the Jews. Arab and Muslim unity was essential, they concluded.[6] Farouk ended the conversation by telling al-Husseini, "I am pleased that you are here and hope to benefit from your experience."[7] Throughout the next six years of his reign, prior to the military coup that would depose him in 1952, King Farouk remained the mufti's friend and patron and frequently invited al-Husseini to be his guest at his al-Ma'amurah summer palace or at his even more luxurious Koubbeh Palace in Cairo, where the king and the mufti would spend many leisurely hours walking and talking in the splendid palace gardens.

The Mufti and His Protégés

Within weeks of his arrival in Egypt, al-Husseini met with several old friends and political allies, including Hassan al-Banna, founder of the Muslim Brotherhood, and the Muslim Brotherhood's increasingly influential theoretician Sayyid Qutb. Al-Husseini also made new acquaintances and political allies, in both Heliopolis and Cairo. One of them was Yasser Arafat, a precociously ambitious seventeen-year-old student and political agitator who had been born and raised in Cairo. Arafat and al-Husseini were, in fact, distantly related: Arafat's mother was the daughter of the mufti's first cousin. Two years before Arafat's birth on August 24, 1929, his parents had arrived in Cairo and settled in the middle-class Sakakini neighborhood of the city,[8] where the young Arafat spent his youth and where al-Husseini first met him, at a family gathering, during the summer of 1946. The mufti quickly took upon himself the role of Arafat's mentor. He instilled in Arafat a burning desire to wage terrorist war against the Jews. In their many long walks together in downtown Cairo, and in innumerable political discussions that would frequently continue for hours into the night, al-Husseini would regale the young Arafat with stories of Nazi Germany and the führer and share with his impressionable cousin his plans for the defeat of the Zionists and the Islamization of Jerusalem, his vision of a *Judenrein* Palestine, and his hopes for preventing the creation of a new state of Israel.

As he sat with his young cousin, the mufti saw a future filled with promise. Here was a young man, he mused with satisfaction, who was learning well the lessons that the mufti sought to teach the next generation. Realizing that his credibility had been compromised by years of political intrigue, and facing the grim reality of his advancing age, he recognized that in his young cousin he could see his dreams fulfilled. In giving his blessing to Arafat, the mufti realized, he was ensuring the future of his vision.

Al-Husseini would also share with Arafat his plans for resuming his position as president of the Arab Higher Committee for Palestine, and thus as the unchallenged leader of the Palestinian Arabs, as well as his dreams of becoming the recognized leader of radical Islam throughout the Middle East. Founded in 1936, the Arab Higher Committee had been disbanded by the British mandatory government, which had held the mufti and his associates in the committee responsible for the 1936 Arab riots that had taken hundreds of British and Jewish lives in Palestine.[9] The mufti's plans to resume his leadership were facilitated by his cousin and close associate Jamel al-Husseini, who shortly after the war had been permitted by the British mandatory government to return to Palestine.[10] Within weeks of Haj Amin al-Husseini's arrival in Cairo, his cousin Jamel had announced the reactivation of the Arab Higher Committee as the official representative of the Arabs of Palestine and, together with Hassan al-Banna, publicly urged the reinstatement of Haj Amin as its president. There was no question as to who was to be the leader of the committee. Testifying before the Anglo-American Committee on Palestine (a blue-ribbon commission established jointly by the British and American governments to make policy recommendations concerning the future governance and political leadership of Palestine), Jamel al-Husseini stated emphatically that the Arabs of Palestine "find themselves deprived of their chief leader, the Grand Mufti, for whom they cannot accept any substitute."[11] The mufti alone, reiterated Jamel al-Husseini, could speak on behalf of the Arabs of Palestine. The issue of Haj Amin al-Husseini's involvement with Nazi Germany did come up during the committee hearings; but despite the overwhelming evidence against him, realpolitik prevailed, and his reinstatement as president of the Arab Higher Committee was approved by the Anglo-American Committee.

The Mufti's All-Palestinian Government for Palestine

In the aftermath of the creation of the state of Israel in May 1948, much of the mufti's time and energies were devoted to his goal of establishing a new All-Palestine Arab government in Palestine. On May 15, 1948, the day after Israel declared its independence, the Arab Higher Committee announced its intention to set up such a provisional government, under the presidency of al-Husseini, with its capital in Jerusalem (or, if that was not possible, in Nablus).[12] After twelve years in exile, al-Husseini longed to return to the city of which he was nominally the mufti and to assume the presidency of a Palestinian state.

In Cairo, on January 5, 1948, his Arab Higher Committee had first publicly announced its intention of establishing a new Palestinian Arab government as soon as the British mandatory government departed Palestine and the anticipated declaration of Jewish statehood took place. Recognizing that events were moving quickly—the end of the British Mandate was scheduled to take effect on May 15—al-Husseini acted decisively. On March 30, 1948, he had presented to the United Nations a formal Arab charter for Palestine. Although not binding in any way, it declared the claim of the Arabs, represented by al-Husseini's Arab Higher Committee, to sovereignty over all of Palestine.

On September 27, 1948, the Arab Higher Committee for Palestine convened in Gaza and announced the formation of the All-Palestine government. On September 28, al-Husseini arrived in Gaza. It was a momentous moment, as it was the first time since his departure in 1937 that he stood on Palestinian soil. It was a joyous day. The decision to create Hukumat 'umum Falastina, the All-Palestine government, was the first step in what he believed would lead to the liberation of all of Palestine. On September 30, amid much fanfare, al-Husseini was unanimously elected by the delegates as president. Assembled around him were many of his comrades in arms from the 1936 intifada.

A formal photo session followed, at which the mufti and his supporters joyously proclaimed the establishment of a free, democratic Arab state in the whole of Palestine. With that announcement came the formal Declaration of Independence by the new government: "Inasmuch as the Arab Palestine People have the sacred natural rights for freedom and independence so far subdued by British colonialism and Zionism, we, members of the National Assembly, meeting in Gaza, declare on October 1, 1948, the independence of all Palestine, full independence, and the establishment in all Palestine of a free democratic state in which freedom and equal rights are guaranteed to all citizens; and in line with its Arab sister states to carry on in the building of Arab culture and glory."[13] As president of the new government, al-Husseini chose as his prime minister his close friend and associate Ahmed Hilmi Abd al-Baqi.

On October 12, Egypt, Syria, and Lebanon recognized the All-Palestine government. Jordan, however, did not agree to recognition. King Abdullah, who had a pathological distrust (indeed, hatred) of al-Husseini, immediately made it clear to other nations in the Arab League that he would strongly oppose the creation of an independent Palestinian government headed by the mufti,[14] which would have thwarted Jordanian hegemony in Palestine. Moving quickly, Abdullah convened the Palestine Arab Congress in Amman, denounced the mufti's new Palestinian government, and called for Jordan to play an active role in the future of the area.

Meanwhile, the United States made its position clear. On October 14, Acting Secretary of State Robert A. Lovett announced that the United States would not grant recognition. Lovett stated four reasons for the U.S. decision. First, the United States had granted de facto recognition to Israel on May 14 and would not recognize a government that claimed land already under the authority of an established, recognized government. Second, in the judgment of the United States, the All-Palestine government had not conformed to the normal attributes of government, as it could not perform even the most minimal administrative or governmental functions. Third, it had not held elections; and fourth, it did not control the area over which it claimed sovereignty. The United States pointed out that Egypt controlled Gaza, Jordan controlled what was soon to be known as the West Bank of the Hashemite Kingdom of Jordan, and Israel had sovereignty over the balance of what had been British mandatory Palestine.

On December 1, the Second Palestine Arab Congress convened in Jericho, then controlled by Jordan. To no one's surprise, the congress invited King Abdullah to unite the existing Kingdom of Jordan with the area of Palestine under Jordanian control. On December 13, the Parliament of Jordan approved the request. Despite vigorous protest by al-Husseini and his All-Palestine government, de facto annexation took place on May 17, 1949, when the Jordanian military government over the area was replaced by a civilian administration. On April 11, 1950, elections for a new Jordanian Parliament were held on what was then called the East Bank as well as in the newly annexed West Bank of the Kingdom of Jordan. On April 24, the newly elected Parliament ratified the annexation.

The fury of Haj Amin al-Husseini knew no bounds. He had been betrayed. His government was a fiction. It controlled no land. To add insult to injury, the Egyptian government of King Farouk, which had so warmly welcomed the mufti to Cairo only two years earlier, ordered the All-Palestine government out of Gaza. The Egyptian government had come to view the All-Palestine government as a political and diplomatic liability and as an embarrassment. Against his will, al-Husseini was relocated to Egypt, where he lived with his freedom of movement severely restricted.[15]

Al-Husseini's reappointment to the presidency of the Arab Higher Committee was public confirmation, both symbolic and real, that the mufti had returned to political leadership and power in his native Palestine. His presidency of the Arab Higher Committee provided Yasser Arafat with an avenue for political advancement and influence as well. Over the next few years, many of the Arab Higher Committee's meetings, over which the mufti presided and which Arafat regularly attended, were held for the mufti's convenience in Cairo. In the years to

*Portrait of Haj Amin al-Husseini, at the
height of his power, in Jerusalem, 1937:
grand mufti of Jerusalem, president of
the Supreme Muslim Council, president of
the Arab Higher Committee for Palestine.*

Al-Husseini awaits
his first meeting with
Adolf Hitler in the Reich
Chancellery, Berlin,
November 28, 1941.

Hitler and al-Husseini, November 28, 1941.

Al-Husseini shakes hands with an unidentified Nazi official during a reception in Berlin, circa 1941–1943. © USHMM, COURTESY OF CENTRAL ZIONIST ARCHIVES

Al-Husseini poses with Nazi officials at a reception in Berlin, circa 1941–1943. © USHMM, COURTESY OF GEORGE BIRMAN

*Grand Mufti Haj Amin al-Husseini (left) with Indian freedom fighter
Chandra Bose (center) and Iraqi former prime minister Rashid Ali al-Gaylani
(right) during an official visit to Berlin to discuss the political situation with
Nazi leaders, January 23, 1943.* © USHMM, COURTESY OF YIVO INSTITUTE

*Al-Husseini meets with Heinrich Himmler on an official visit to Germany,
July 4, 1943. The photograph is signed by Himmler and translates,
"His Eminence, the Grand Mufti. In remembrance."*

© USHMM, COURTESY OF YAD VASHEM PHOTO ARCHIVES

Al-Husseini with Himmler.

© USHMM, COURTESY OF YAD VASHEM PHOTO ARCHIVES

Al-Husseini inspects the rifle of a Bosnian Muslim recruit to the Waffen-SS, Bosnia-Hercegovina, July 1943.

© BUNDESARCHIV

The mufti reviewing Bosnian troops of the Waffen-SS. This is a reproduction of the front page of the Wiener Illustrierte *(Vienna Illustrated) of January 12, 1944.*

Al-Husseini poses with a unit of Bosnian Muslim recruits to the Waffen-SS, Bosnia-Hercegovina, July 1943. © BUNDESARCHIV

Al-Husseini in the company of German SS and Bosnian members
of the Waffen-SS during an official visit to Bosnia, 1943.

© USHMM, COURTESY OF ROBERT KEMPNER

Al-Husseini inspects Bosnian Muslim recruits to the Waffen-SS,
Bosnia-Hercegovina, July 1943. © BUNDESARCHIV

*Al-Husseini greets
a Bosnian member
of the Waffen-SS
during his visit to
Bosnia, 1943.*
© USHMM, COURTESY OF
ROBERT KEMPNER

*Al-Husseini reviews Bosnian Muslim recruits to the Waffen-SS,
Bosnia-Hercegovina, 1943.* © USHMM, COURTESY OF ROBERT KEMPNER

come, Arafat would play an increasingly important role within the Arab Higher Committee as al-Husseini's trusted confidant and lieutenant.

Another protégé of the mufti, and for many years one of his most trusted allies and loyal political supporters, was future Egyptian president Anwar Al Sadat. Sadat, like his close friend and associate Gamal Abdel Nasser, whom he succeeded as president of Egypt, had begun his political career in the mid-1930s as a teenage activist with the Muslim Brotherhood. It was through his early political activity with the brotherhood that Sadat (like Nasser) had first met al-Husseini. Both Sadat and Nasser boasted a long history of pro-Nazi sympathies and anti-Semitic speeches.[16] In his autobiography, *In Search of Identity,* Sadat candidly admitted that he was inspired by Hitler's Germany.[17] Like his friend Nasser, Sadat was recruited by the mufti to engage in espionage activity on behalf of the Third Reich. During World War II, Sadat had worked for the mufti as a spy for Nazi Germany in British-occupied Egypt.[18] He later served a term in prison for his role in these pro-German activities. Sadat's attitude did not change after World War II. In 1953, while serving as a close associate and political confidant of al-Husseini, Sadat published a letter in the Egyptian weekly *Al-Mussawar,* addressed posthumously to Hitler, in which he expressed sorrow over the defeat of the Third Reich and hailed Hitler as the "immortal leader of Germany."[19] In a speech celebrating the birthday of the Prophet Muhammad on April 25, 1972, Sadat declared: "Nobody can ever decide the fate of Jerusalem. We shall re-take it with the help of God out of the hands of those of whom the Koran said 'It was written of them that they [the Jews] shall be demeaned and made wretched . . . condemned to humiliation and misery. . . . They [the Jews] are a nation of liars and traitors, contrivers of plots, a people born for deeds of treachery.' "[20] In the years before he concluded a peace treaty with Israel, Sadat often quoted anti-Semitic verses from the Koran to illustrate what kind of treatment Muslims would impose on Jews when Egypt defeated Israel. In an address before the National Press Club in Washington, D.C., in 1975, in the course of an official state visit during the Gerald Ford administration, Sadat justified the November 10, 1975, UN General Assembly resolution equating Zionism with racism, stating that the Egyptian economy had once been controlled by the Jews.[21]

By 1970, several protégés of the mufti, or associates or relatives of the mufti's circle, had risen to positions of political prominence and leadership within radical Islam. Yasser Arafat had become head of the Palestine Liberation Organization (PLO). That same year, Anwar Al Sadat succeeded to the presidency of Egypt. By 1970, Saddam Hussein, the nephew and adopted son of another of al-Husseini's longtime protégés and supporters, Khairallah Talfah, had risen to prominence in Iraqi politics as one of the leaders of Iraq's Ba'ath Party, which had first seized power in Iraq in 1963. Throughout the 1970s, Saddam Hussein would consolidate his power over Iraq's Ba'ath Party and its radical Islamic government and, in 1979 following a military coup, would formally assume the presidency of Iraq.

The Uncle and the Mufti

The story of the close relationship of Khairallah Talfah (Saddam Hussein's uncle) with the mufti is a significant, albeit forgotten, chapter in the extraordinary public career and legacy of Haj Amin al-Husseini and in the political history of radical Islam in the second half of the twentieth century. Khairallah Talfah was an Iraqi army officer and passionate Arab nationalist who had been one of al-Husseini's most trusted lieutenants in their short-lived pro-Nazi coup that had briefly returned Rashid Ali al-Gaylani to power in Iraq in April 1941. Talfah deeply opposed British control of the political and military structure of Iraq. A fervent admirer of Hitler, he was known to actively favor the victory of Nazi Germany. With the failure of their coup due to British military intervention, al-Husseini, al-Gaylani, and several of their supporters subsequently fled the country. They soon found a political haven in Berlin, where they spent the rest of the war as honored guests of the Nazi regime. Talfah and several of his fellow officers who had participated in the pro-Nazi uprising, however, were not so lucky. Many were imprisoned, and some were executed. Khairallah Talfah himself was dismissed from the military and jailed for five years.[22]

The events of the al-Gaylani coup and its aftermath had, as the mufti would later learn, a profound effect on the life of Talfah's impressionable young nephew Saddam Hussein, who was only nine years old when al-Husseini returned to the Middle East. In the following years, the young Saddam would often inquire about his uncle, only to be told that he was in jail.[23] As Saddam would later recall, his close relationship with his uncle was vital to his political development.[24] It also fueled his anti-British and deep-seated anti-Jewish ideology and his belief that the Zionist entity, the state of Israel, must be eradicated. Khairallah Talfah, like the mufti, was a virulent anti-Semite whose Hitlerian hatred of the Jews led him to suggest, for decades after the Holocaust, that Jews were insects and thus, like all insects and other vermin infecting the body politic, should be exterminated. In 1981, Talfah published a scurrilously anti-Semitic pamphlet, widely distributed by the Iraqi Ba'ath Party, entitled *Three God Should Not Have Made: Persians, Jews and Flies.*[25] Jews, Talfah wrote, were a "mixture of the dirt and leftovers of diverse peoples,"[26] who, like flies, were a trifling creation "whom we do not understand God's purpose in creating." Talfah had a solution to the Jewish problem: "There is a certain insecticide for every type of insect," he declared.[27]

To Saddam Hussein, as to his uncle and to his mentor the mufti, it was especially evident that Israel, the hated Zionist entity, must be eradicated. For Saddam Hussein and his Ba'athist supporters, Israel was always an artificial implant in the Middle East, "a multi-tentacled octopus," a "deadly cancer," or an "AIDS virus" to be burned up, as Saddam threatened to do shortly before the first Gulf War.[28] As late as 2002, Saddam Hussein declared on Iraqi television: "Palestine is Arab and must be liberated from the river to the sea and all the Zionists who immigrated to the land of Palestine must leave."[29] In Saddam's vision of the world, as in that of Khairallah Talfah and Haj Amin al-Husseini, Jews were by definition "outsiders," "aliens," and enemies of the Arab nation.

Beginning in 1947, shortly after his uncle's release from prison, Saddam Hussein lived at his uncle Khairallah's home in Tikrit, a small town 115 miles from Baghdad, where Saddam began attending school. Khairallah Talfah, like his friend al-Husseini, remained faithful to the idea of radical Islam, a political faith that he imbued in his nephew. The young Saddam Hussein, one can imagine, sat mesmerized as his beloved uncle regaled him with stories of the al-Gaylani coup and of the dreams that he, the mufti, and their old colleagues had of ridding both Iraq and Palestine of the infidel Zionists and of waging jihad against the British enemies of Islam, their Jewish allies, and indeed the entire corrupt, pro-Zionist West. Above all, he indoctrinated his nephew with a burning desire to liberate their native Iraq from British and Western control and to lead another military coup that would bring Iraqi Arab nationalists like themselves the freedom and power that the abortive al-Gaylani coup had not achieved. There can be little doubt that under the tutelage of Khairallah Talfah, the young Saddam Hussein came to share the mufti's virulently anti-Zionist and anti-Western ideology.

Saddam attended a nationalistic secondary school in Baghdad and studied for three years at Iraq's School of Law before dropping out. In 1957, at the age of twenty, he joined the newly formed Ba'ath Party, whose goal it was to win Iraqi independence from British control. In 1964, Saddam was put in charge of the party's military organization.[30] In 1968, he was appointed to the second most important post in the Ba'ath Party government, becoming the right-hand man to Iraqi president Ahmad Hassan al-Bakr.[31] It was a position of power that he would hold for the next decade, until assuming the Iraq presidency himself. Throughout his rise to prominence in Ba'ath Party politics, his uncle Khairallah remained his closest political confidant and adviser.

After his return to the Middle East in 1946, al-Husseini was a frequent visitor to Baghdad. In 1959, he moved his own residence and his

Arab Higher Committee office to Beirut, Lebanon, from where he often visited Baghdad.[32] In May 1962, he was in Baghdad for several weeks to participate in a World Islamic Congress that he had been instrumental in convening.[33] It is not implausible to speculate that on one or more of these visits to Baghdad, the mufti met and spoke with Saddam Hussein in the company of his uncle Khairallah, who had remained one of al-Husseini's most loyal friends and supporters in the Iraqi capital.

Haj Amin al-Husseini, the Creation of the State of Israel, and the Palestine National Movement

Throughout his lifelong dedication to radical Islam, al-Husseini was consumed by hatred of the Jews and especially of the Zionist infidels who had settled in his beloved Palestine, usurping his hometown, his beloved Jerusalem, whose holy sites were so sacred to the entire Islamic world. Much of his political and terrorist activity, as head of the Arab Higher Committee, was directed toward trying to prevent or abort the creation of a Jewish state in Palestine. On November 29, 1947, months before the actual creation of the state of Israel and the end of British rule in Palestine the following May, the United Nations General Assembly had voted to accept the principle of establishing two states in Palestine, one Arab and one Jewish. Throughout most of the Arab world, opposition to the UN partition vote soon erupted into violence. Al-Husseini's Arab Higher Committee immediately condemned the UN decision, declaring a three-day general strike in protest,[34] and Arab mobs began rioting in Jerusalem and elsewhere throughout Palestine. Radical Arab politicians and intellectuals in Egypt, led by al-Husseini, Nasser, Qutb, Arafat, and Sadat, had vocally and violently opposed the partition of Palestine as they would the actual establishment of a Jewish state in Palestine six months later. When on May 14, 1948, David Ben-Gurion declared the independence of a sovereign Jewish state to be called Israel, their response was immediate and emphatic. As the Arab armies rolled to what they thought would be a swift and decisive victory over the Jews, al-Husseini eagerly awaited the destruction of the Jewish state.

Their demands that Egypt and its Arab allies immediately launch a war of aggression against the new Jewish state were also answered immediately: Within hours of Israel's declaration of independence, the Arab League, which had been founded in March 1945 by all the sovereign Arab states of the Middle East—Egypt, Iraq, Syria, Lebanon, Saudi Arabia, Yemen, Libya, and Transjordan (later renamed the Hashemite Kingdom of Jordan)—declared war on the newly declared state. By the next day, an Egyptian army estimated at two hundred thousand men had been mobilized for war. The first attack on Israel came from the air, as Egyptian aircraft bombed Israel's largest city, Tel Aviv,[35] shelling and destroying numerous civilian homes. As the Egyptian air attacks persisted, many Israeli civilians were killed. With malicious intent, the central bus station in Tel Aviv was targeted for attack from the air.

Later on the first day of Arab hostilities, May 15, 1948, the Egyptian Foreign Ministry officially informed the United Nations Security Council that with the termination of the British Mandate and Israel's declaration of statehood, "Egyptian armed forces have started to enter Palestine."[36] On the morning of May 15, the Arab war for Palestine gained momentum as the Arab Liberation Army, under the command of the mufti's old comrade Fawzi al-Kawukji, attacked Neve Yaakov, a Jewish suburb just north of Jerusalem, and Jerusalem itself. Al-Kawukji, like the mufti, had been an accomplice of Rashid Ali al-Gaylani in their pro-Nazi Iraqi coup against the British in April 1941.[37] Like the mufti, when the revolt collapsed, he had escaped to Nazi Germany, where he had married a German woman,[38] a member of the Nazi Party, and actively assisted al-Husseini in his efforts on behalf of the Third Reich. Also, like the mufti, the escape of Fawzi al-Kawukji, who arrived in Cairo via France, had been widely reported and applauded in the Arab press. With the Israeli declaration of independence, al-Kawukji's Arab Liberation Army, on direct orders from the mufti, took the offensive in igniting what the mufti hoped would be a true jihad, a quick and complete war of extermination against the Jews and their new Jewish state.

Rashid Ali al-Gaylani, who together with the mufti and al-Kawukji had spent the war years in Berlin working for the Third Reich after the collapse of his abortive pro-Nazi Iraqi coup, had also managed to escape Europe. He was given sanctuary by King Ibn Saud in Saudi Arabia, from where he actively supported their new Arab war of extermination against Israel and its Jews. The initial means selected was the targeting of civilians. The Arab air force dropped bombs on civilian population centers that had no military or strategic value.[39] The goal, for al-Husseini, al-Kawukji, and their terrorist followers, was to finish the job Hitler had started. "This will be a total war of extermination,"[40] they vowed.

Al-Husseini immediately cabled his friend and benefactor King Farouk his congratulations on Egypt's declaration of war against Israel.[41] Their delight was shared by the vast majority of Muslim Egypt and the Islamic Middle East, who were united in their calls for Israel's destruction. Everywhere in the Egyptian capital of Cairo, on May 15, calls for jihad against the new Jewish state were being proclaimed. The mufti himself was one of the first to call for a holy war, ordering his "Muslim brothers to murder the Jews. Murder them all."[42] This same call was made by his friend the sheikh of Al-Azhar. "The hour of the Holy War has struck," proclaimed the sheikh. "All Arab fighters must look upon the struggle for Palestine as a religious duty."[43] As the Arab League's secretary general, Abdul Rahman Hassan Azzam Pasha, candidly put it: "This will be a war of extermination and a momentous massacre, which will be spoken of like the Mongolian massacres and the Crusades."[44] Al-Husseini's spokesman Ahmad Shuqairy, later to become the first chairman of the PLO, announced that the goal of the new Arab war against Israel was "the elimination of the Jewish state."[45] Jerusalem, the mufti told his supporters and friends, would soon become *Judenrein*.

During the late spring and summer of 1948, much of the mufti's rage was directed at the United States and the pro-Zionist government of President Harry Truman, which had become the first nation to officially grant de facto recognition to the new Jewish state after its independence had been declared. For the mufti, the United States had come to replace Great Britain as the symbol of Western decadence, secularism, and Zionism that the new leaders of Islam were obligated to oppose and destroy. Increasingly, in the aftermath of 1948, calls for jihad against the West by al-Husseini, Qutb, and Arafat, and later by their new colleagues and disciples among the leadership of radical Islam, would be directed at the United States rather than Great Britain.

Al-Husseini's hopes for the defeat and destruction of Israel were also enhanced by the coup that overthrew King Farouk of Egypt. While the affable Farouk had happily granted al-Husseini political asylum and hospitality after the mufti's arrival in Egypt in 1946, the corrupt and inefficient Farouk government had become far too pro-Western and insufficiently militant in its anti-Zionism for the mufti's tastes. Much to al-Husseini's delight, on July 23, 1952, Farouk was deposed in a military coup by a group of army officers, among whom was the mufti's friend and protégé Colonel Gamal Abdel Nasser. Nasser, who often referred to *The Protocols of the Elders of Zion* as one of his favorite books, shared al-Husseini's all-consuming hatred of the Jewish people. Another Egyptian officer who took part in the coup was Lieutenant Colonel Anwar Al Sadat,[46] another protégé and ideological soul-mate of the mufti. Hostilities against Israel orchestrated by the new Nasser regime would lead inevitably to the Suez crisis and Sinai campaign of 1956. It was Nasser and his deputy Sadat, moreover, who would later orchestrate and launch the 1967 Six-Day War against Israel, in which the Nasser-led Arab armies hoped to finally defeat and destroy the Jewish state. Nasser would remain, perhaps, the preeminent leader of the Islamic Middle East until his death in 1970, when he would be succeeded by Sadat as president of Egypt, who together with Yasser Arafat would assume Nasser's mantle of leadership within the Islamic Middle East.

Al-Husseini and the Assassination of King Abdullah

The anger of al-Husseini was directed in particular at King Abdullah of Jordan. Abdullah, the mufti believed, had usurped what was to have been a sovereign part of Arab Palestine and in so doing had betrayed the Arab people. His annexation of that land had doomed the mufti's dream of achieving an independent Palestinian Arab state.

A growing enmity between Abdullah and the mufti had been brewing since their first meeting in Jerusalem in 1921. "My father," Abdullah continually reminded his followers, "always told me to beware of preachers."[47] Their enmity only deepened after the mufti's return to the Middle East in 1946, when each came to view the other as a treacherous political enemy and rival. Alone among the Arab leaders of his generation, Abdullah was a moderate with a generally pro-Western outlook, who was ready to accept the existence of the new state of Israel and to consider signing a separate peace agreement with the new Jewish state. "I was astonished at what I saw of the Jewish settlements," King Abdullah had written in his memoirs, published in 1946. "They have colonized the sand dunes, drawn water from them, and transformed them into a paradise."[48] He had further angered al-Husseini and his followers in stating that "the Jews had their rights to their Holy Places in the Old City" of Jerusalem.[49]

Such behavior by an Arab ruler was inexcusable, the mufti raged. He, like other moderate leaders, had become tools of the Zionist infidels, traitors to the radical Islamic cause, who were betraying both Allah and their fellow Muslims. Such betrayal, preached al-Husseini, could not and must never be tolerated. They were deserving of violent retribution by the Islamic people they had betrayed. Abdullah's opposition to the mufti's dream of an Arab state in Palestine, with his Arab Higher Committee as its government and al-Husseini as its president, was the final straw. It was Abdullah's final act of betrayal, one that the mufti and his followers could not and would not ever forgive or forget.

On July 15, 1951, the moderate prime minister of Lebanon, Riad

Bey al-Solh—who had also earned the condemnation of al-Husseini and his radical Islamic colleagues for his apparent willingness to support a cease-fire in the Arab war against Israel—was assassinated in Amman. Al-Solh had journeyed to Amman to encourage Abdullah to proceed with a peace treaty with Israel. Supporters of al-Husseini immediately denounced both men as traitors. While attending a memorial service for al-Solh at the Al-Aqsa Mosque in Jerusalem on July 20, King Abdullah of Jordan was himself assassinated, gunned down by a twenty-three-year-old Palestinian, Mustafa Shukri Ashu.[50] As Abdullah fell to the ground, his fifteen-year-old grandson Hussein, who would succeed him on the Jordanian throne, witnessed with horror the murder of his beloved grandfather. More than forty years later, King Hussein would refer to that moment in moving terms, when he returned to Jerusalem to speak at the funeral of assassinated Israeli leader Yitzhak Rabin.[51]

Al-Husseini always denied having any connection with the assassination, but his denials are far from persuasive. Several of the mufti's family and supporters were in fact arrested in the investigation following Abdullah's slaying. Indeed, one of the six assassins convicted and sentenced to death, in the ensuing trial, was Dr. Musa Abdullah al-Husseini,[52] a cousin of the mufti. As scholars agree, there is no doubt that the mufti instigated the assassination of King Abdullah.

These assassinations were part of a wave of mufti-inspired political killings of moderate Arab leaders that swept the Middle East in the aftermath of the establishment of the state of Israel. Much to the anger and outrage of al-Husseini and his allies in the militantly anti-Israel Muslim Brotherhood, Egypt's moderate prime minister Mahmoud an-Nukrashi Pasha made it known that he did not want to send Egypt's army into combat against Israel. For al-Husseini and the leaders of the Muslim Brotherhood, this was an unforgivable sin. For this crime, Pasha fell to an assassin's bullet as he left his office in Cairo on December 28, 1948. A member of the Muslim Brotherhood fired the shot. Al-Husseini and the Muslim Brotherhood had conspired secretly in his assassination, as they would conspire together in the assassination of King Abdullah.

The Violent Ideology of Sayyid Qutb

Haj Amin al-Husseini was not alone in his condemnation and indictment of moderate Arab leaders like Abdullah. Sayyid Qutb, the eminent Muslim Brotherhood writer and theoretician, shared his sentiments. In 1981, not long after signing a peace treaty with Israel, Egyptian president Anwar Al Sadat was assassinated by members of the Egyptian terrorist group Islamic Jihad, an offshoot of the Muslim Brotherhood, who were all admirers and disciples of Qutb and al-Husseini. A moderate Arab leader, al-Husseini, Qutb, and their disciples fervently believed, was a traitor to radical Islam and could not be permitted to survive and govern within the Islamic world.

The virulently anti-Western ideology of Qutb's thought had its genesis in his visit to the United States, where, as an official of the Egyptian Ministry of Education, he was sent on a special study mission in November 1948. Qutb later recounted his horror at what he witnessed in America. Everywhere in America, he wrote, even religion is measured in material terms. Churches in America, he said, "operate like businesses, competing for clients and for publicity, and using the same methods as stores and theaters to attract customers and audiences. . . . To attract clientele, churches advertise shamelessly and offer what Americans most seek—'a good time' or 'fun.' The result is that church recreation halls, with the blessing of the priesthood, hold dances where people of both sexes meet, mix, and touch."[53] He noted with evident disgust that "the dance is inflamed by the notes of the gramophone; the dance-hall becomes a whirl of heels and thighs, arms enfold hips, lips and breasts meet, and the air is full of lust."[54] He also quoted the Kinsey reports on sexual behavior to document his disgust with American immorality. This perception of the West and its ways, popularized by Qutb in his writings, has shaped two generations of radical Islamic thought and attitudes about America and the West.

Sayyid Qutb's ideology shares much in common with the worldview of the terrorist Islamic Jihad organization, which was inspired by the radical Islamic revolution that swept Iran in 1979 under the leadership of Ayatollah Khomeini. For Qutb, as for Khomeini, the evil of Western influence is personified by the United States—or "the Great Satan," as termed by Khomeini. Consequently, Israel, as the agent of the United States in the Middle East, is termed "the Little Satan."[55] Qutb's denunciations generated some controversy in his native Egypt, where some moderate leaders in the Farouk and later Nasser governments still hoped to maintain ties with, and receive financial aid from, the United States. Indeed, so vehement were Qutb's denunciations of America and its way of life that in 1952 he left his post at the Ministry of Education to devote his time and energies exclusively to the Muslim Brotherhood. He soon became the brotherhood's leading ideologue and theoretician and was appointed editor of its official journal, *Al-Ikhwan al-Muslimun.*[56] Qutb, like his friend al-Husseini, had at first enjoyed close relations with Nasser and his new regime, which had overthrown King Farouk. Unlike al-Husseini, however, Qutb quickly parted company with Nasser and his new government, whose secular policies he actively opposed. As a result, beginning in 1954 Qutb would spend several years in prison in Nasser's Egypt. He died in 1966—executed upon orders of the Nasser regime for his treasonous activities. But his legacy would be an enduring one. Qutb's anti-Western Muslim polemic *Signposts,* which the mufti and other radical Islamic leaders often quoted, would become vital reading for all in the jihadist movement.

The impact of the jihadist ideologue Sayyid Qutb on the perpetrators of the September 11, 2001, terrorist attacks on the World Trade Center and Pentagon has been well documented. Qutb had a particularly important influence on terrorist leader Osama bin Laden. As a student at King Abdulaziz University in Jeddah in the late 1970s, bin Laden first became associated with the Muslim Brotherhood while studying religion with Sayyid Qutb's brother Mohammad,[57] one of the university's most prominent teachers of Islamic studies and the chief interpreter of Sayyid Qutb's written works.[58]

The anti-Jewish invective inspired by Qutb's widely quoted writings has also been central to the ideological development of two generations of radical Islamic terrorist leaders, from the mullahs of Hamas and Khomeini and Mahmoud Ahmadinejad's Iran, to the leaders of Hezbollah and al-Qaeda. Thus, for example, Ayatollah Khomeini said in his 1970 "Programme for the Establishment of an Islamic Government":

> We must protest and make the people aware that the Jews and their foreign backers are opposed to the very foundations of Islam and wish to establish Jewish domination throughout the world. Since they are a cunning and resourceful people, I fear that—God forbid!— they may one day achieve this goal and that the apathy shown by some of us may allow a Jew to rule over us one day. May God never let us see such a day.[59]

The Mufti's Later Years:
The 1950s and 1960s in Cairo and Beirut

In hindsight, 1951 was a watershed year for Haj Amin al-Husseini. The assassination of King Abdullah of Jordan had removed a major voice for political moderation from the scene. Although his blatant role in the Jordanian king's assassination had generated some controversy and criticism, even among several of his friends, it had been applauded by his allies in the Muslim Brotherhood, who had conspired with him in the assassination, and had enhanced his stature within the radical Islamic world. In the immediate aftermath of Abdullah's assassination, al-Husseini presided over a meeting of the World Islamic Congress held in Karachi; and in his role as president of the Arab Higher Committee and its new All-Palestine government, he continued his travels and meetings with world leaders, where he was treated as an official Arab head of state. He maintained bases of operation in Syria and Egypt.

In 1955, he joined Nasser of Egypt, Nehru of India, Tito of Yugoslavia, Nkrumah of Ghana, and Chou En-lai of China at the Afro-

Asian non-aligned conference held in Bandung, Indonesia. Haj Amin al-Husseini was determined to maintain a Palestinian Arab presence in all international forums where he knew they would be welcome. The Palestinian Arab delegation to the United Nations was led by his close friend and associate Issa Nakhleh, who also served as the permanent representative of the Arab Higher Committee for Palestine at the UN. On a regular basis, memorandums were submitted to the appropriate UN committees, and the words of al-Husseini still rang in the halls of international power. In August 1959, he decided to move the head-quarters of the Arab Higher Committee from Cairo to Beirut,[60] where he took up permanent residence. Beirut would remain his home and political base for the rest of his life.

On May 11, 1960, in a surprise action, Israeli agents abducted the fugitive Nazi war criminal Adolf Eichmann from the streets of Buenos Aires. At his trial, Israeli prosecutors tried to persuade Eichmann to elaborate on his relations with the mufti. Eichmann always claimed that he could recall meeting the mufti only once, at a Berlin cocktail party. This claim was, of course, an immense distortion of the truth, for there is irrefutable historical evidence to document the close work-ing relationship between Eichmann and the mufti during the Third Reich. In the aftermath of the Eichmann trial, however, the mufti's fol-lowers, writing in newspapers in Damascus, Beirut, Cairo, and Amman, wrote glowingly of Eichmann. In his memoirs, the mufti later thanked Eichmann for his discretion and praised him as "gallant and noble" for having denied, while in Israeli custody, "that there had been any connection between the two men."[61]

The later 1960s were a time of decline for al-Husseini. In 1963, Iraq's prime minister Abd al-Karim Qasim, a supporter of al-Husseini, was overthrown. The new government withdrew its support for the mufti and the All-Palestine government. Following the death on June 29, 1963, of Ahmed Hilmi Abd al-Baqi, prime minister of the All-Palestine government, the Arab League withdrew its support for al-Husseini by declaring the seat of the Palestinian representative at the league to be vacant. In September, over the mufti's objections,

Ahmed Shuqairy was appointed by Nasser to be the Palestinian representative at the Arab League. In 1964, a new organization was created
to replace the Arab Higher Committee and the All-Palestine government. In May of that year, 422 delegates gathered in Jerusalem to create the Palestine Liberation Organization, which al-Husseini assumed
he would be elected to head. Once again, Ahmed Shuqairy, who had
emerged as the mufti's main rival, was victorious and was formally
elected as chairman of the PLO. Al-Husseini was furious. "The opposition to Mr. Shukeiri," reported *The New York Times,* "centers around
Hajj Amin al-Husseini, the Grand Mufti of Jerusalem, who claims to be
the proper and legal representative of the Palestinian people."[62] Outraged, al-Husseini's Arab Higher Committee put out a statement calling the new organization "a colonialist, Zionist conspiracy aiming at
the liquidation of the Palestinian cause."[63] Further marginalized by the
Arab League, which recognized the PLO as the representative of the
Palestinian Arab people, al-Husseini suffered yet another blow when,
in 1966, Syria withdrew its support for his All-Palestine government.
Haj Amin al-Husseini seemed to be finished as an important political
player.

The 1967 crisis in the Middle East offered al-Husseini a brief return to center stage. King Hussein of Jordan and President Nasser of
Egypt were in the midst of a war of words and nerves as the year
opened. Nasser backed Shuqairy and the PLO, and Shuqairy adopted
the position that Jordan was a part of Palestine rather than an independent Arab state. While Shuqairy was correct historically, the British
having severed Jordan from the original Palestine Mandate in the
1920s, King Hussein was not prepared to surrender his kingdom or his
life. Moreover, despite his power struggle with the new leadership of
the PLO, Haj Amin al-Husseini was still viewed by many Palestinian
Arabs as their leader. On March 1, 1967, King Hussein, in a calculated
political move designed to neutralize the threat posed by Nasser and
Shuqairy, invited al-Husseini to return to Jerusalem. Despite what he
knew to have been al-Husseini's direct responsibility for the death of
his beloved grandfather King Abdullah, Hussein remembered the old

adage "The enemy of my enemy is my friend" and temporarily embraced the mufti as a welcomed ally in his struggle against Nasser and the PLO.

Al-Husseini's brief return to Jerusalem was a great personal triumph and gave him immense satisfaction. Despite all the pitfalls, missteps, failed plans, misplaced alliances, and tragic betrayals, for the first time in thirty years he was back in his beloved Jerusalem and felt the warm adulation of the Arabs of Palestine wash over his aging person. While visiting the Holy City, he stayed in the personal residence of King Hussein at Beit Hanina. All of the leaders of Arab Jerusalem, religious, secular, and nationalist, greeted him with deference, reverence, and enthusiasm. Al-Husseini was to speak of that time in Jerusalem with these affecting words: "While the plane flew around Jerusalem's airport, I saw the Dome of the Rock smiling at me. I left a part of myself in every corner of the city and on every one of its hills."[64] As he prayed in the Al-Aqsa Mosque, he felt a new surge of hope and renewal. He was home at last. That night, when he dined with King Hussein at his palace in Amman, they raised their glasses to toast what al-Husseini hoped would be a long and enduring alliance. It was their common enemies that had brought them together. Within a few months, however, all of this would be forgotten as Nasser and Hussein put aside their enmity and realigned themselves against Israel in preparation for what was to become known as the Six-Day War.

At dawn on June 11, 1967, Israel's military triumph was complete. The dream of Arab victory had turned into a nightmare of defeat. All of the mufti's hopes that Palestine would be liberated were destroyed. He knew now that he would never live to see the liberation of Palestine.

If only the Arabs had struck Israel first. If only they had succeeded in destroying Israel's air force on the ground. If only Egypt, Jordan, and Syria had better coordinated their war plans. All of the what-ifs replayed in al-Husseini's mind as he realized that his lifelong hopes for the liberation of Palestine would not become a reality.

In the aftermath of Israel's stunning victory in the Six-Day War, al-Husseini briefly visited Saudi Arabia. The Saudi royal family was angry with Nasser, who constantly attacked them and their rule. Once again, the principle "The enemy of my enemy is my friend" worked its magic for the mufti and his new patrons. The Saudis welcomed Haj Amin al-Husseini with open arms. King Faisal, a virulent anti-Semite who, like al-Husseini, revered *The Protocols of the Elders of Zion,* embraced the mufti and came to value his advice and counsel. In public and in private, the mufti's role was welcomed and acknowledged. As one Saudi newspaper noted, "The journalists smilingly nod polite assent and make vigorous motions with their head. The King quotes from chapter 3 of *The Protocols of the Elders of Zion* to reinforce his argument. It is said that his thoughts are influenced by those of Hajj Amin al-Husseini, former Mufti of Jerusalem. King Faisal even uses Hajj Amin al-Husseini's own words."[65] In September 1967, the ideological influence of al-Husseini was felt again when the Arab summit held in Khartoum adopted his long-standing "three no's" as official policy: "There will be no peace nor negotiation with the Zionist state and no relinquishment of any part of the occupied Arab territories."

When his rival Ahmed Shuqairy was forced to resign as chairman of the PLO on December 24, 1967, following the debacle of the 1967 Arab-Israeli war, Haj Amin al-Husseini felt a sense of triumph and vindication. On February 4, 1969, al-Husseini's cousin and most devoted protégé Yasser Arafat was elected as the new chairman of the PLO. With Arafat's election, al-Husseini accepted the reality of the PLO as the representative organization of the Palestinian Arab people and willingly handed over the mantle of radical Palestinian Arab leadership to his younger cousin. As Muheideen al-Husseini, the mufti's son-in-law, would later recall: "Hajj Amin felt that Arafat would be the right leader for the Palestinian nation after him. He thought he could carry the responsibility"[66] of leadership and continue his mentor's legacy of uncompromising opposition to the state of Israel.

Yes, thought Haj Amin al-Husseini, there was hope. His young cousin Yasser Arafat was determined to continue the battle. He was prepared to organize a war of national liberation, and the mufti understood that although it was only the start of a long struggle, with faith and fortitude the battle might still be won. It was Arafat who coined the slogan "Revolution Until Victory." These words carried resonance with al-Husseini. As each of his expected triumphs turned to defeat and despair, he simply turned the page and hurtled forward to confront the next challenge. Now, as he approached the sunset of his life, the old warrior could look with satisfaction on the fact that the torch would be carried by a younger, equally determined member of his own family. Yes, he mused, Arafat would suffer setbacks, but he had learned the lessons of the mufti's own life and legend.

No matter what would follow, he knew the Palestinian Arab cause would be in good hands.

With Arafat's election as PLO chairman, al-Husseini retired to his home in Beirut, from where he continued to play an informal yet influential role in the Palestine National Movement, advising Arafat on his unfolding war of terror against the state of Israel and the Jewish people.

Haj Amin al-Husseini spent the last years of his life in Beirut, Lebanon, and died there on July 4, 1974. Most notable among the mourners at al-Husseini's funeral was Yasser Arafat. According to newspaper reports, Arafat arrived with "tears in his eyes."[67] Lebanese president Suleiman Franjieh and King Hussein of Jordan sent representatives, as did other Arab heads of state. It is not impossible to imagine that among the mourners would have been Saddam Hussein's uncle Khairallah Talfah, the mufti's devoted friend for more than forty years. A large crowd, thousands of mourners,[68] attended the funeral as well.

When Haj Amin al-Husseini died, the Supreme Muslim Council, of which he had been the founding president, asked the Israeli government for permission to bring his body back to Jerusalem for burial at Haram al-Sharif. Permission was denied, and three days later al-Husseini was buried, amid much pomp and circumstance, in the cemetery of the Fallen of the Palestinian Revolution, in Beirut. It was clear to all the mourners who gathered to pay their last respects to the mufti that when the lifelong goals of al-Husseini were eventually realized—when the liberation of Jerusalem from the Zionists and the destruction of their illegitimate Jewish state in Palestine were finally achieved—the mortal remains of Haj Amin al-Husseini would be brought back to Jerusalem for burial. Then, and only then, would their beloved mufti rest in peace for eternity in a truly *Judenrein* Islamic holy city, the capital of a new and enduring Palestinian Arab state that, like the Third Reich envisioned by Hitler and al-Husseini, would last for a thousand years.

Today, sixty years after the Holocaust, the wartime career and historical significance of Hitler's mufti should be better remembered and understood. In the Arab world, the effects of the mufti's historic November 28, 1941, meeting with the führer, and of radical Islam's subsequent wartime alliance with Hitler, have been long-lasting. The Muslim-Nazi alliance that the mufti forged with Hitler has in real ways continued to this day.

The death of the mufti did not end the debate about his life and legacy. To his supporters, Haj Amin al-Husseini was a hero of epic proportions. He was the George Washington of the radical Islamic world. Much like Atatürk in Turkey and Nehru in India, the mufti had won great acclaim in his early years as a charismatic national leader who many foreign leaders believed would lead his people into statehood. His close friend and supporter Issa Nakhleh, who for more than three decades served as the Arab Higher Committee's representative at the United Nations, described him as a great Palestinian patriot, the century's "greatest Palestinian leader, who spent his entire life defending Palestinian rights" and working for Palestinian Arab independence.[69] Yasser Arafat, who would succeed the mufti as head of the Palestine Liberation Organization in 1969, always spoke with great pride on being the mufti's student and protégé, referring to him as "our hero al-Husseini," as a heroic "symbol of withstanding world pressure, having remained an Arab leader in spite of demands to have him replaced because of his Nazi ties."[70] To the leaders of radical Islam in the latter half of the twentieth century, the mufti was viewed as both hero and mentor.

A very different, and more accurate, view of al-Husseini was offered by Edgar Ansel Mowrer, the Pulitzer Prize–winning foreign correspondent and nationally syndicated columnist. "As a murderer," wrote Mowrer, "this man ranks with the great killers of history. As an enemy of the United Nations, he was surpassed only by Hitler. In the evil of his intentions, Haj Amin equaled Hitler."[71] For his critics, then and now, Haj Amin al-Husseini had become a true icon of evil—a murderer and terrorist who justified the use of terror to achieve his political ends. His legacy is still with us today.

Chapter 6

Mandate for Hate:
Haj Amin al-Husseini and
the Islamization of Anti-Semitism

"I am a Jew." These were the last words that Daniel Pearl, the *Wall Street Journal* reporter, uttered before his decapitation by Islamic terrorists in Pakistan in 2004. His killing was the culmination and fulfillment of the viciously anti-Jewish ideology of Haj Amin al-Husseini, an ideology that has inspired decades of Jew hatred throughout the Islamic world. The horrifying murder cruelly exemplified the existential threat that this ideology now represents. To be born a Jew has become, for many radical Islamists today as it was for Hitler and for Haj Amin al-Husseini, a mandate for hate.

Radical Islam is the preeminent source of anti-Semitism in the modern world. In recent decades, Jew hatred and the widespread circulation and distribution of anti-Semitic literature, such as *The Protocols of the Elders of Zion,* have increased dramatically and exponentially throughout the Islamic Middle East. "Kill the Jews. . . . This pleases God, history and religion": The fatwa proclaimed by the mufti on German radio in 1943 has become a slogan that has inspired generations of radical Islamic terrorists, from Yasser Arafat and Osama bin Laden to Ahmed Omar Saeed Sheikh, the Muslim terrorist who masterminded the brutal kidnapping and barbaric murder of Daniel Pearl in Pakistan. As the founding father of radical Islamic anti-Semitism in the twentieth century, al-Husseini remains the inextricable and enduring link between the old anti-Semitism of pre-Holocaust Europe and the Jew hatred and Holocaust denial that now permeates the Muslim world.

Today more than ever, anti-Semitism is publicly endorsed by Arab governments, disseminated by the Arab media, taught in Muslim schools and universities, and preached in mosques. Indeed, it can be said without fear of exaggeration that classical anti-Semitism is now a major and inextricable component of the Arab intellectual life of our time, as it was in the intellectual and cultural life of Nazi Germany during the 1930s and 1940s.[1]

The roots of Islamic anti-Semitism run deep. They were invigorated by the radical Islamic and Nazi collaboration, inspired and fostered by the mufti, during World War II. The enduring anti-Jewish legacy of Nazism, which the mufti did much to shape and further during the 1950s and 1960s, has found an appreciative audience in the contemporary Islamic world, where an especially virulent strain of Jew hatred, the likes of which has not been seen since the Holocaust, finds widespread expression in books, magazines, newspapers, radio and television, and the Internet.

Contemporary Muslim anti-Semitism is also deeply rooted in Islamic religious teachings and political tradition. Since the founding of Islam, Jews have had to live with the enduring legacy of Muhammad's historic antipathy toward the Jews of Medina. His anger toward the Jews who opposed him in Medina, recorded in the Koran, was followed by his merciless subjugation of them, in Medina and many other cities, as Muhammad and his followers embarked on their wars of conquest.

This hostility set the tone for Islam's subsequent attitude toward the Jews, and toward Judaism, over the centuries, a hostility that has become more virulent since the end of World War II. As descendants of those who opposed the founder of Islam and refused to accept the new faith he promulgated, Jews would forever be condemned by many Muslims as infidels.[2]

Contemporary Islamic anti-Semitic speakers and publications invoke Muhammad's teaching in the Koran that the Jews are the greatest enemies of mankind. This verse, as well as other Koranic verses singling out Jews for special condemnation by the Islamic faith, have become increasingly popular in recent years with Muslim clerics the world over.[3] Maliciously anti-Jewish pronouncements, many more vitriolic than others, are found throughout the Koran. Jews are accused of cowardice, greed, and chicanery, vilified as monkeys and pigs,[4] and condemned as "corruptors of Scripture."[5]

These accusations, first articulated by Muhammad in angry response to his rejection by the Jews, have ever since been regarded by many Muslims as God's word. In recent decades, the leaders of radical Islam have continued to invoke Muhammad's divinely based antipathy to the Jews, citing his teachings in the Koran to justify their call for a jihad, which every devout Muslim is obligated to carry out against the Jews. For radical Islamists today, as for the grand mufti before them, Muhammad's divinely inspired hatred of the Jews has been the all-important pretext for the continuing Islamic war of terrorism against the Jewish people and the Jewish state.

Since the time of Muhammad, Jews have been denigrated as *dhimmis*—second-class citizens—in Muslim societies, where they have traditionally been treated as tolerated minorities, inferior and subservient to Muslims.[6] During his reign, the caliph of Baghad, Harun al-Rashid (786–809), enacted legislation requiring Jews to wear a yellow belt and a tall conical cap. This landmark Muslim legal decree was the inspiration for the humiliating yellow badge that Jews were forced to wear in medieval Europe and, more recently, in Nazi-occupied European countries.[7] Even in the relatively more tolerant Islamic Ottoman Empire, where many Jews sought refuge in the aftermath of their expulsion from Spain in 1492, laws were enacted restricting the number and location of synagogues and prohibiting their construction in proximity to mosques.[8]

The centuries that followed the caliph's decree witnessed a rising tide of hostility and violence toward Jews throughout the Muslim world. During the nineteenth century especially, Jews were massacred by Muslims on numerous occasions and in numerous cities throughout the Middle East. Muslim rioters attacked and murdered Jews in Aleppo in 1853, in Damascus in 1848 and 1890, in Cairo in 1844 and 1901–1902, in Alexandria in 1870 and 1881,[9] and on the Tunisian island of Djerba in 1864.[10] In Tunis itself, in 1869, eighteen Jews were murdered in the space of a few months by Muslims. Between 1864 and 1880, more than five hundred Jews were murdered by Muslims in Morocco, often in broad daylight.[11] At the beginning of the twentieth century, rampages against Jews by Muslims also occurred in the Moroccan cities of Casablanca and Fez.[12] Indeed, in Fez, on April 18, 1912, Muslim riots resulted in the killing of sixty Jews and the sacking of the Jewish Quarter.[13] The tragic tradition of Muslim anti-Semitism is venerable indeed.

The Protocols of the Elders of Zion, Mein Kampf, and Islamic Anti-Semitic Literature

In the decades since World War II, hatred of the Jews has been fanned throughout the Islamic world by the mass circulation of notoriously anti-Semitic publications, including *The Protocols of the Elders of Zion* and Hitler's viciously anti-Semitic autobiography, *Mein Kampf,* a development encouraged and promoted by Haj Amin al-Husseini.

The Protocols of the Elders of Zion is an infamous forgery dating from czarist Russia that purported to document the existence of a secret Jewish conspiracy to rule the world. Despite the fact that the *Protocols* had been discredited before the 1920s, they continued to be accepted as authoritative scholarship throughout much of the Islamic world. From his earliest years, the mufti had viewed the *Protocols* as such. In fact, Haj Amin al-Husseini grew up in a family that accepted the authenticity of the *Protocols*. In 1918, Haj Amin's cousin Musa Kasim Pasha al-Husseini, the mayor of Jerusalem, told the Zionist leader Chaim Weizmann that he had received a copy of *The Protocols of the Elders of Zion* from a British officer of the military administration of Palestine and asked Weizmann whether the Zionist leaders were also "the elders of Zion" and whether they shared the same conspiratorial program.[14] Just three years later, in 1921, shortly after Haj Amin al-Husseini was appointed mufti of Jerusalem, the first of many Arabic-language translations of the *Protocols* was published,[15] with al-Husseini's enthusiastic support and endorsement. During the 1920s, allegations of a Jewish international cabal to control the world through treachery and secret violence, as depicted in the *Protocols*, found an appreciative audience among the Arabs of Palestine. Only two months after al-Husseini's appointment, a new anti-Jewish riot broke out in Jerusalem, instigated by the mufti's propaganda, including the new translation in the Arab press of the *Protocols*. In 1929, in his testimony before the Shaw commission of inquiry appointed by the British Colonial Office to investigate the massacre of the Jews of Hebron and Jerusalem, al-Husseini admitted that he had distributed Arabic translations of the *Protocols* in Palestine and firmly asserted his belief in their authenticity. It was the Jewish-Zionist cabal described in the *Protocols*, al-Husseini told the Shaw commission, that was responsible for the increased Jewish immigration to Palestine of the 1920s, and the illegitimate efforts of the Jewish immigrants to take Palestine away from the Arabs and take possession of Islamic holy sites in Hebron and Jerusalem.

Haj Amin al-Husseini and Adolf Hitler shared a deep and abiding admiration for the *Protocols*. Hitler's defeat and suicide in 1945 did not deter the mufti from carrying on the führer's mission of republishing and disseminating the *Protocols* throughout the Middle East. In subsequent decades, as a result of the mufti's unceasing efforts, *The Protocols of the Elders of Zion* would be published in Arabic many times as well as in a number of different translations[16] and would enjoy best-selling status in Islamic capitals from Cairo to Tehran and Damascus. There have now been at least nine different Arabic translations of the *Protocols* and innumerable editions, more than in any other language, and it remains required reading in a number of Arab universities.[17] One Arabic edition of the text, published in 1968, was translated by Shawqi Abd al-Nasser, brother of the Egyptian president[18] and a devoted protégé and supporter of the mufti.

The *Protocols* have been publicly praised and recommended by various monarchs, presidents, prime ministers, and other political and intellectual leaders of radical Islam. On numerous occasions, for example, Egyptian president Gamal Abdel Nasser praised the book and recommended that it be widely read. Nasser told an interviewer from an Indian newspaper, "I will give you an English copy. It proves clearly, to quote from the *Protocols,* that 'three hundred Zionists, each of whom knows all the others, govern the fate of European continents and they elect their successors from their entourage.' "[19] King Faisal of Saudi Arabia ordered that all Saudi hotels have copies of the *Protocols* as bedside reading[20] and often gave copies of the czarist forgery to the guests of his regime. Then U.S. secretary of state Henry Kissinger was among the many visiting diplomats to receive a copy of the *Protocols* from the Saudi monarch.[21] When King Faisal presented the *Protocols,* along with an anthology of anti-Semitic writings, to French journalists who accompanied French foreign minister Michel Jobert on his visit to Saudi Arabia in January 1974, officials noted that it was among the king's favorite books.[22]

Hamas, which evolved from the Muslim Brotherhood and which the mufti had promoted enthusiastically from its inception, invokes the *Protocols* in Article 32 of its charter, stating that the ongoing conspiratorial conduct of world Zionism, Israel, and the Jewish people "is the best proof of what is said [in the *Protocols*]."[23] Spokesmen for the government of Iran, from the era of Ayatollah Khomeini to the present, have embraced the *Protocols* and often serialized the book in daily newspapers.[24] Most recently, it was made available in English at the Iranian exhibition booth at the 2005 Frankfurt International Book Fair.[25] Hundreds of Arab periodicals regularly quote or summarize the *Protocols,* referring to them as the definitive word on the international Jewish Zionist conspiracy. The Lebanese newspaper *Al-Anwar* reported that a recent edition of the book hit the top of its nonfiction best-seller list.[26] On November 6, 2000, the first day of the Muslim holy month of Ramadan, twenty-two television stations in the Arab world broadcast the first segment of a forty-part Egyptian television series, *Knights Without a Horse,* which depicted the Jewish plot to rule the world as presented in the *Protocols.* For the mufti, as for two generations of later radical Islamists, much of the evil, hatred, treachery, and violence in the world was attributable to Jewish plots and conspiracies hatched by the "Elders of Zion," as described in the *Protocols.*

Hitler's *Mein Kampf,* a favorite anti-Semitic publication of the grand mufti and his protégés, has similarly enjoyed a wide and appreciative radical Islamic audience in recent decades. Indeed, if the *Protocols* is the most popular anti-Semitic tract in the Arab world, *Mein Kampf* could be considered a close second.[27] Hitler's hate-filled and virulently anti-Jewish autobiography has been available in Arabic since 1963 and remains a perennial best seller in several Islamic countries.[28] After the Six-Day War in 1967, Israeli soldiers discovered that many Egyptian prisoners carried small paperback editions of *Mein Kampf,* translated into Arabic by an official of the Arab Information Center in Cairo. The translator, who was known as el-Hadj, had been a leading official in the Nazi Propaganda Ministry; his real name was Luis Heiden.[29] He took this new name after he fled to Egypt following the war and converted to Islam. When *Mein Kampf* was republished by Yasser Arafat's Palestinian National Authority in 2001, shortly after the September 11 terrorist attacks on the World Trade Center and the Pentagon, it achieved best-seller status throughout the Arab world.

New Arabic editions of *Mein Kampf* have recently appeared in Turkey, Lebanon, and Saudi Arabia, and it is always available in Arabic translation in London bookstores.[30] While *Mein Kampf* continues to enjoy a wide and appreciative Islamic audience, *Schindler's List,* a film portraying the suffering of Jews under Nazi rule, is banned in most Arab countries.[31]

The Blood Libel Accusation in the Islamic Middle East

Since the early 1960s, the Arab media, at the urging of Haj Amin al-Husseini and his cohorts, have resurrected the notorious blood libel accusation, routinely charging Jews with committing the ritual murder of Muslim and Christian children during the Passover holiday. The Jews were accused of using the children's blood in the unleavened bread eaten at the Passover meal. Accusations of ritual murder had been directed by Muslim leaders against Jews throughout the nineteenth century in Syria, Palestine, and Egypt.[32] For al-Husseini, the blood libel was not malicious rumor or libel, but historical fact. From his youth, al-Husseini had believed in the credibility of these accusations of Jewish ritual murder. Such accusations gained new momentum and popularity after al-Husseini's arrival in Egypt in the late 1940s. During the 1950s and 1960s, the regime of Egyptian president Gamal Abdel Nasser published and disseminated many works accusing Jews of ritual murder, which subsequently gained a wide audience through the Arab press, radio broadcasts, and school textbooks.[33] In 1962, at the suggestion of al-Husseini, the Egyptian Ministry of Education reissued *Talmudic Sacrifices* by Habib Faris, first published in 1890 in Cairo. In the introduction, the editor notes that the book constitutes "an explicit documentation of indictment, based upon clear-cut evidence that the Jewish people permitted the shedding of blood as religious duty enjoined in the Talmud."[34] In his 1964 book, *The Danger of World Jewry to Islam and Christianity,* the Egyptian writer Abdallah al-Tall argued that "the God of the Jews is not content with animal sacrifices" but "must be appeased with human sacrifices." Thus, wrote al-Tall, "the Jewish custom of slaughtering children and exacting their blood to mix it with their *matzot* on Passover."[35] In his book *Illumina-*

tions on Zionism, published in Cairo in 1969, Mustafa al-Sa'dani, one of the mufti's favorite authors, devotes more than thirty pages to the blood libel,[36] accepting allegations of Jewish ritual murder as historical fact. So, too, the Egyptian author Aisha Abd al-Rahman treats the draining of children's blood at Passover as "a recognized Jewish ritual" in her book *The Enemies of Mankind.* In this book, published in Cairo in 1968, she also refers to Jews by such epithets as "sickness," "plague," and "noxious germ."[37]

In more recent decades, similar blood libel accusations have continued to appear in the Arab media. Newspapers in Qatar, Egypt, Saudi Arabia, Kuwait, Bahrain, and Jordan have reprinted similar claims about Jews and Israelis.[38] *Al-Ahram,* one of the major government-sponsored daily newspapers in Egypt, devoted a special series of articles to discussing in great detail how Jews used the blood of non-Jews to bake their Passover matzo. In a similar vein, an Egyptian intellectual, writing in *Al-Akhbar* in March 2001, explained that the Talmud (which he described as being the Jews' second holiest book) required the blood of non-Jews to be used in the preparation of the traditional matzo eaten by Jews during their Passover holiday.[39] On January 1, 2000, an Arab weekly paper in Damascus invoked the blood libel, claiming that the matzo of Israel "is soaked with the blood of the Iraqis, descendants of the Babylonians, the Lebanese, the descendants of the Sidonese, and the Palestinians, the descendants of the Canaanites. This Matzah is kneaded by American weaponry and the missiles of hatred pointed at both Muslim and Christian Arabs. . . ."[40] In March 2002, Dr. Umayma Ahmed al-Jalahma stated in the Saudi government daily *Al-Riyadh:* "The Jews spilling human blood to prepare pastry for their holidays is a well-established fact, historically and legally, all throughout history. This was one of the main reasons for the persecution and exile that were their lot in Europe and Asia."[41]

Yasser Arafat and other Arab political leaders close to the mufti have also thrown their weight behind the blood libel and charges of Jewish ritual murder. On April 24, 1970, Yasser Arafat's Fatah radio broadcast that "reports from the captured homeland tell that the Zionist enemy has begun to kidnap small children from the streets. Afterwards the occupying forces take the blood of the children and throw away their empty bodies. The inhabitants of Gaza have seen this with their own eyes."[42] In August 1972, King Faisal of Saudi Arabia reported in the Egyptian magazine *Al-Mussawar* that while he was in Paris, "the police discovered five murdered children. Their blood had been drained and it turned out that some Jews had murdered them in order to take their blood and mix it with the bread that they eat on that [Passover] day."[43] The following year, in November 1973, Faisal stated that "it was necessary to understand the Jewish religious obligation to obtain non-Jewish blood in order to comprehend the crimes of Zionism."[44]

In 1984, Syrian defense minister Mustafa Tlass published a book called *The Matzah of Zion,* in which he discussed the infamous Damascus affair of 1840, in which the Jews of Damascus, Syria, were falsely accused of ritual murder after a Capuchin friar and his Muslim servant had mysteriously disappeared.[45] In *The Matzah of Zion,* Tlass claimed that the Jews of Damascus had indeed murdered the friar and his servant to use their blood to make the holiday matzo for Passover. In the book's preface, Tlass ominously warned: "The Jew can . . . kill you and take your blood in order to make his Zionist bread. . . . I hope that I will have done my duty in presenting the practices of the enemy of our historic nation. Allah aid this project."[46] In 2001, an Egyptian producer announced that he was adapting Tlass's book into a movie. "It will be," he said, "the Arab answer to *Schindler's List.*"[47]

The blood libel myth was predicated, in part, on the demonization of the Jews and on the belief that the Jews were inherently evil, depraved, and treacherous. This belief was given widespread coverage and credence throughout the Islamic world in 1968 by a conference that was held at Al-Azhar University in Cairo, the leading Islamic university in the Middle East,[48] attended by delegates from twenty-four Islamic countries. In the papers presented at the conference, which were subsequently published in a book entitled *Arab Theologians on Jews and Israel,*[49] the conference participants vilified Jews as the "Enemies of God," the "Enemies of Humanity," and "the Dogs of Humanity," while portraying the evil of the Jews "as immutable and permanent."[50] The state of Israel was described as a culmination "of historical and cultural depravity."[51] The Bible of Israel was referred to in pejorative terms as a "counterfeit work,"[52] while Jews were accused of "treachery" at all times and wherever they might reside. "Treachery was the business of Jews throughout the ages and times," alleged one of the Arab theologians speaking at the conference, al-Husseini's friend Hassan Khaled, the mufti of Lebanon, "as it was their instinct to break their covenant with others and resort to treachery as soon as they had any chance to betray others."[53]

Mahmoud Abbas, the Palestinian National Authority, and Holocaust Denial in the Middle East

As other forms of anti-Semitism, such as the blood libel and ritual murder allegations, have become increasingly widespread in the Islamic world in recent years, so has Holocaust denial become a new weapon in the radical Islamic campaign to demonize and vilify the Jews.[54]

From its inception, Holocaust denial has attracted widespread support in the Islamic Middle East. The government of Saudi Arabia paid for the publication of a number of books accusing Jews of creating a myth of the Holocaust in order to win support for Israel.[55] The Cyprus-based PLO publication *El-Istiqlal,* founded by PLO chief Yasser Arafat, trumpeted the Holocaust denial thesis under the headline BURNING OF THE JEWS IN THE NAZI DEATH CHAMBERS IS THE LIE OF THE TWEN-TIETH CENTURY.[56] The July 1990 issue of *Balsam*—published by the Palestinian Red Crescent Society, the Red Cross affiliate of the PLO, whose director was Dr. Fathi Arafat, a medical doctor and brother of Yasser Arafat—featured an article alleging that "the lie concerning the gas chambers enabled the Jews to establish the State of Israel."[57] The Nazi gas chambers "were a Jewish hoax to bilk funds for Israel from

Germany," claimed the article's author. "Without German money," he alleged, "Israel would be unable to survive."[58]

Saudi Arabia has also surreptitiously helped to finance anti-Semitic Holocaust denial literature in the West, such as *Anti-Zion* (originally entitled *The Jews on Trial*) and *The Six Million Reconsidered*, written by an American neo-Nazi, William Grimstad, registered as a Saudi agent with the U.S. Department of Justice in 1977. These publications were mailed to all members of the United States Senate and the British Parliament in 1981 and 1982 by the World Islamic Congress.[59] This organization, as noted earlier, had been founded in 1931 by Haj Amin al-Husseini, who had served as its president until his death in 1974. With its headquarters in Pakistan, and with close ties to the PLO, the World Islamic Congress has from its creation served as a base for radical Islamic anti-Semitism and terrorist activity against Israel and the West.

Arab attempts to minimize or deny the Holocaust date back more than forty years. The first of many Arab heads of state to advance such a view was Egyptian president Gamal Abdel Nasser, who told a German newspaper that "no person, not even the most simple one, takes seriously the lie of the six million Jews who were murdered."[60] Since the early 1980s, however, Holocaust denial has found increasingly frequent expression, throughout the Islamic Middle East, in the writings and pronouncements of Arab politicians and heads of state, in articles and columns by journalists, and in the publications and resolutions of Islamic terrorist organizations such as the PLO and Hamas. One of the preeminent Holocaust deniers among the political leadership of radical Islam has been Mahmoud Abbas, one of the cofounders with Yasser Arafat of the Palestinian Arab terrorist group Fatah and Arafat's successor as president of the Palestinian National Authority and as chairman of the PLO. Mahmoud Abbas (also known as Abu Mazen) is the author of a 1983 book titled *The Other Side: The Secret Relationship Between Nazism and the Zionist Movement*, which was originally his doctoral dissertation, completed in 1975 at Moscow Oriental College in the Soviet Union.[61] In *The Other Side*, Abbas claims that the Nazis killed only a few hundred thousand Jews, not six million, and that the Zionist movement "was a partner in the slaughter of the Jews" during the Third Reich.[62] Abbas denies that the Nazi gas chambers were used to murder Jews, quoting an allegedly authoritative study to that effect by the notorious French Holocaust denier Robert Faurisson.[63] A central argument of Abbas's book is his allegation that postwar Zionists greatly exaggerated the number of Jewish victims of the Holocaust for their own political purposes.[64] As Abbas argued: "During World War II, forty million people of different nations of the world were killed. The German people sacrificed ten million; the Soviet people twenty million; and the rest [of those killed] were from Yugoslavia, Poland, and other peoples. But after the war it was announced that six million Jews were among the victims, and that the war of annihilation had been aimed first of all against the Jews, and only then against the rest of the peoples of Europe. The truth of the matter is that no one can verify this number, or completely deny it."[65]

Less than two years after it was completed in Russia, Abbas's PhD dissertation was translated into Arabic and published in Jordan, with a new introduction by its author. It is now accepted as a standard work of Holocaust denial widely cited by Arab academics, politicians, and propagandists alike.[66] Abbas has repeatedly refused to retract or repudiate the outrageous claims and assertions that he made in his now classic work. Indeed, shortly after his appointment as Arafat's prime minister, Abbas, who is widely considered to be a Palestinian moderate, reasserted his views about the Holocaust in a May 28, 2003, interview with journalists from the Israeli daily *Yediot Aharonot*.[67]

Other Palestinian leaders, politicians, and diplomats have followed suit, espousing Abbas's line. In 1978, for example, in the midst of the political activity surrounding the historic diplomatic summit at Camp David attended by Jimmy Carter, Menachem Begin, and Anwar Al Sadat, Holocaust denial found public expression in a memorandum submitted to presidents Carter and Sadat by the Palestinian Arab diplomat Issa Nakhleh. Nakhleh, one of the mufti's closest political confidants and collaborators and a noted Holocaust denier,[68] had served for several decades as the permanent representative of the Arab Higher Committee for Palestine at the United Nations. "The hoax of the six million Jews who supposedly perished in Europe," Nakhleh stated emphatically, "has been used by the Zionists to win sympathy for the Jewish occupation of the Palestine homeland."[69] Holocaust denial has now become a widely shared view, endorsed and promoted by many Arab politicians, diplomats, and pundits throughout the Islamic Middle East. It has now become another standard radical Islamic calumny against the Jews.[70]

Since the 1990s, Holocaust denial has become ever more popular throughout the Arab media. This is true even in Egypt and Jordan, the two Arab countries that have diplomatic relations with the state of Israel. Among the newspapers that have consistently featured Holocaust denial are the Jordanian daily *Al-Arab al-Yom,* the Syrian daily *Teshreen,* the English-language Iranian *Tehran Times,* and the Palestinian National Authority's *Al-Hayat al-Jadida.*[71] A January 31, 2000, article in *Teshreen,* the official newspaper of the ruling Ba'ath Party in Syria, claimed that Israel used "the legend of the Holocaust as a sword hanging over the necks of all those who oppose Zionism" and was seeking "to strangle any voice that reveals the truth."[72] In a similar vein, the English-language *Tehran Times* has maintained that its own researchers have proved that Jewish claims about the Holocaust have been fraudulent and unverifiable, fabrications of a Zionist plot.[73]

In July 1998, an especially virulent essay entitled "Jewish Control of the World Media" appeared in *Al-Hayat al-Jadida* that tried to explain how the Jews got away with falsifying the history of World War II. The essay's author, Seif Ali al-Jarwan, argued that international public opinion, controlled and manipulated by the Zionists, grossly exaggerated the German persecutions and fabricated horrendous stories about the mass murder of European Jewry and the use of gas chambers to exterminate millions of Jews. Al-Jarwan, writing for a newspaper officially published under the auspices and direction of Yasser Arafat, went on to assert that the Holocaust was a fabrication of the world Jewish conspiracy:

The truth is that such persecution was a malicious fabrication by the Jews. It is a myth which they named 'The Holocaust' in order to rouse empathy. Credible historians challenge this Jewish [myth], calling for [more] persuasive evidence to be presented. The Los Angeles Historical Society declared that it would grant U.S. $50,000 to anyone who could prove Jews had been gassed to death. Jews exerted intense pressure and cast accusations of anti-Semitism everywhere in order to silence this challenge. Even if Hitler's onslaught facilitated the persecution of Jews to some degree, Jews certainly benefited from its aftermath. . . .[74]

The Palestinian National Authority's television station, also operating under the authorization and direction of Yasser Arafat, has frequently denied basic facts of the Holocaust in its reporting. In an August 25, 1997, cultural affairs program on Palestinian National Authority television that evoked Israel's annual commemoration of the Holocaust, the moderator informed his audience: "It is well-known that every year the Jews exaggerate what the Nazis did to them. They claim there were six million killed, but precise scientific research demonstrates that there were no more than four hundred thousand."[75] In another Palestinian National Authority cultural affairs television program that aired in 1997, Hassan al-Agha, professor at the Islamic University in Gaza and a political confidant of Yasser Arafat, declared that "the Jews view it [the Holocaust] as a profitable activity so they inflate the number of victims all the time. In ten years, I do not know what number they will reach. . . . As you know, when it comes to economics and investments, the Jews have been very experienced even since the days of *The Merchant of Venice.*"[76]

Several prominent Muslim religious leaders in the Islamic Middle East have also rejected the facts of the Holocaust. One of the most vocal and notorious Holocaust deniers in the Palestinian National Authority, Sheikh Ikrima Sabri, who had been appointed by Arafat as grand mufti of Jerusalem, told *The New York Times* in March 2000: "We believe the number of six million is exaggerated. The Jews are using this issue, in many ways, also to blackmail the Germans financially. . . . The Holocaust is protecting Israel."[77] In this interview, held at the time of Pope John Paul II's historic visit to Israel, during which the mufti publicly rejected an invitation to meet with the pope,[78] Sheikh Ikrima Sabri added: "It's certainly not our fault that Hitler hated the Jews. Weren't they hated pretty much everywhere?"[79] These are sentiments that the sheikh's predecessor as mufti, Haj Amin al-Husseini, would certainly have shared. In other interviews with journalists and reporters, Sheikh Ikrima Sabri, the highest appointed cleric in the Palestinian National Authority, repeated his claim that the number of six million dead is exaggerated. "There are a lot of stories and we don't know which are true and which are false," he told one American writer in his Jerusalem office. "It happened. There is no doubt about that. But a lot of people are suspicious about the number. Now [former Israeli prime minister Ariel] Sharon is trying to make a new Holocaust of the Palestinian people!"[80] Sabri couldn't point to Israeli death camps and, when pressed, said that taking land was akin to murder. "Besides, Hitler didn't kill the Jews," he said. "That's why we still have Jews today!"[81]

In most Western countries, blatant Holocaust deniers such as Mahmoud Abbas and Sheikh Ikrima Sabri have been publicly ostracized or regarded as pariahs. In New Zealand, Canterbury University issued an apology for having accepted a master's thesis denying the Holocaust, while the French minister of education actually revoked a PhD that had been awarded to a Holocaust denier at the University of Nantes. So, too, a Polish university professor who denied the Holocaust was dismissed from his faculty position.[82] In Canada and many European countries, including Austria, France, and Switzerland, Holocaust denial is now a criminal offense.

Not so in the Islamic Middle East, where several notorious Holocaust deniers have found a safe haven following indictment for the crime of Holocaust denial in their European home countries. Several have turned to the radical Islamic world, and in recent years especially to Iran, for help when facing prosecution at home for illegal activities. For instance, Wolfgang Fröhlich, an Austrian neo-Nazi engineer and author of the Holocaust denial book *The Gas Chamber Fraud,* sought and found refuge in Iran in May 2000 rather than face trial and a prison term for promulgating Holocaust denial in Austria.[83] He reportedly still resides in Iran, now as a welcomed guest of the Ahmadinejad regime.

The popularity that Holocaust denial was enjoying throughout the Islamic Middle East generally, and in Iran especially, was reflected in the response to the trial of Roger Garaudy in France in 1998. Garaudy, one of Europe's most notorious Holocaust deniers, had been charged with violating a 1990 French law that made it illegal to deny historical events that have been designated as crimes against humanity, and with inciting racial hatred. These charges, for which he was convicted in 1998, stemmed from his 1995 book, *The Founding Myths of Modern Israel,* in which he states that "there was no Nazi pogrom or genocide during World War II and that Jews essentially fabricated the Holocaust for their financial and political gain."[84]

As the trial unfolded, Garaudy was hailed as a hero throughout the Islamic Middle East. Although Garaudy had converted from Catholicism to Islam in 1982 and had married a Jerusalem-born Palestinian woman, it was primarily his outspoken and audacious denial of the Holocaust that evoked the public acclaim and celebrity he received throughout the Muslim world.[85] The Holocaust revisionist message of his book, whose Arabic translation became a best seller in many countries of the Middle East, clearly resonated among his appreciative Muslim readers, who made the book a runaway best seller. The former president of Iran, Ali Akbar Hashemi Rafsanjani, announced in a sermon on Radio Tehran that Garaudy's personal scholarship on the subject had convinced him that "Hitler had only killed twenty thousand Jews and not six million," and he added that Garaudy's only crime was that he had cast doubt on the historical falsehoods and fabrications of Zionist propaganda.[86]

Ali Akbar Hashemi Rafsanjani's Radio Tehran sermon was notably illustrative of the widespread support that Holocaust denial and its advocates and promoters have enjoyed in contemporary Iran. Since the beginning of the Ayatollah Khomeini regime in the early 1980s, Holocaust denial had coexisted alongside other virulent forms of Jew hatred and anti-Semitism, including the obsessive state promotion of *The Protocols of the Elders of Zion.* In 2000, the leading Iranian newspaper, the *Tehran Times,* insisted in an editorial that the Holocaust was "one of the greatest frauds of the twentieth century."[87] The following year, in April 2001, then president of Iran Ayatollah Khomeini would publicly proclaim that "there is evidence which shows that Zionists had close relations with German Nazis and exaggerated statistics on Jewish killings. There is even evidence on hand that a large number of non-Jewish hooligans and thugs of Eastern Europe were forced to emigrate to Palestine as Jews . . . to install in the heart of the Islamic world an anti-Islamic state under the guise of supporting the victims of racism."[88]

Islamic Holocaust Denial Comes of Age

Perhaps the best-known and most widely publicized event relating to Holocaust denial in the Islamic Middle East took place in 2006, when Iranian president Mahmoud Ahmadinejad, amid great fanfare, convened an international conference on the Holocaust to which most of the world's most celebrated and notorious Holocaust deniers were invited. This was not the first symposium devoted to Holocaust denial convened in the Middle East. In August 2002, for example, the Zayed Center for Coordination and Follow-Up, an Arab League think tank whose chairman, Zayed bin Sultan al-Nahayan, served as deputy prime minister of the United Arab Emirates, promoted a Holocaust denial symposium in Abu Dhabi.[89] But the conference convened by Mahmoud Ahmadinejad was the most notoriously celebrated and publicized gathering of its kind. In recent years, Iran has become the center of Holocaust denial in the Islamic Middle East, and Mahmoud Ahmadinejad is its most virulent and vocal champion. In December 2005, the new Iranian president, while declaring his intention to "wipe Israel off the map," announced that "we do not accept" the claim that "Hitler killed millions of innocent Jews in furnaces."[90] The Holocaust was a "fairy tale" to protect Israel, alleged Ahmadinejad. "They [the Jews] have fabricated a legend under the name of 'Massacre of the Jews,' and they hold it higher than God himself, religion itself and the prophets themselves,"[91] he claimed. Ahmadinejad's remarks struck a responsive chord throughout much of the Islamic Middle East, where they were widely applauded and praised. Khaled Mashaal, the political leader of the terrorist group Hamas, described Ahmadinejad's comments as "courageous" and stated that the "Muslim people will defend Iran because it voices what they have in their hearts."[92] Ahmadinejad's statements denying the extent of the Holocaust were followed by a cartoon contest, sponsored by Ahmadinejad's Iranian regime, which organized an international exhibition of anti-Holocaust cartoons in Tehran and distributed cash prizes to cartoonists who best mocked Israel and the Holocaust. When asked about the future, the exhibition organizer stated "that the project will continue as long as the Jewish state has not been destroyed."[93]

On December 5, 2006, Ahmadinejad announced that Iran would sponsor an international conference to examine the historiography of the Holocaust, specifically addressing the questions of whether the Holocaust had been exaggerated or whether it actually took place, as well as whether the gas chambers had actually been used by the Nazis. In so doing, he announced, Iran would be encouraging scholarly debate and honest research on the subject of the Holocaust, which Ahmadinejad claimed could not be done in several European countries in which it was a crime to deny the Holocaust.[94]

Amid much fanfare and press coverage the following week, more than sixty invitees from thirty countries gathered in Tehran to participate in the two-day conference hosted by the Ahmadinejad regime. The conference brought together a rogues' gallery of Holocaust deniers and anti-Semites from around the world, including white supremacists and neo-Nazis, radical anti-Israel and pro-Palestinian activists, and radical Islamic clerics with close ties to Hamas, Hezbollah, and other Islamic terrorist groups. Attendees included the American racist

David Duke, former Imperial Wizard of the Ku Klux Klan, and Bradley R. Smith, one of the leading American propagandists for the Holocaust denial movement. Also participating were Wolfgang Fröhlich, the Austrian neo-Nazi author of *The Gas Chamber Fraud*, and Mohammed Hegazi, an Australian-based champion of Palestinian terrorist activity who has described suicide bombings against Israel as "the noblest form of self-sacrifice" and who claims that Australia is controlled by "Jewish supremacists in New York." Another notable conference participant was Robert Faurisson, the notorious Holocaust denier from France who had been suspended from his academic post at Lyon University and fined by a court in Paris for the crime of Holocaust denial, and who argued in his conference speech "that the Holocaust was a myth created to justify the occupation of Palestine, meaning the creation of Israel."[95] In his prepared remarks, distributed by the Iranian Foreign Ministry, David Duke claimed that the gas chambers in which millions perished "actually did not exist." Rather, argued Duke, the "inventions about what happened to Europe's Jews were part of a plot. Depicting Jews as the overwhelming victims of the Holocaust gave the moral high ground to the Allies as victors of the war and allowed Jews to establish a state on the occupied land of Palestine." Another American Holocaust denier, Veronica Lake, stated unequivocally that "the Jews made money in Auschwitz,"[96] a claim ludicrous even by the outrageous standards of contemporary Holocaust denial.

The Tehran conference was unprecedented in a number of horrific ways. Never before had an assemblage of Holocaust deniers been given the respectability of state sponsorship. The conference in Tehran was convened under the official sponsorship of the Ahmadinejad government. Invitations to participants were sent out by the Iranian Foreign Ministry. The conference itself was held on government property. The lavish hospitality of the Iranian government, which generously funded the travel and accommodations of those in attendance, was noticeable everywhere. Receiving a standing ovation, Ahmadinejad himself opened the conference with welcoming remarks in which he reiterated his claim that the Holocaust was a fairy tale fabricated by the Jews and in which he called for the destruction of Israel in a new, twenty-first-century Holocaust in the Middle East. His call for this new Holocaust, at a gathering dedicated to denying the first one, was met with deafening applause.

Not a single scholar of the mainstream field of Holocaust studies was present at the conference. No Israeli scholars were permitted to attend.[97] Iran also denied a visa to Khaled Kasab Mahameed, a Muslim lawyer from the Israeli city of Nazareth who had opened the world's first Holocaust museum for Arabs, the Arab Institute for the Holocaust Research & Education,[98] and who had hoped to speak at the conference.

The Iranian government's state sponsorship of its Holocaust denial conference was an event unprecedented in the annals of modern anti-Semitism. It was an event that Haj Amin al-Husseini, had he lived to attend the conference, would have been the first to applaud and approve. Ahmadinejad's impassioned call for Israel's destruction and for a new Holocaust to complete the extermination of the Jews that Hitler and the mufti had begun was a historic vindication of the mufti's life's work. For Ahmadinejad and his cohorts, the mufti's infamous call to genocide—"Kill the Jews. . . . This pleases God, history and religion"— remained an inescapably relevant and enduring message that they were dedicated to transmitting to a new generation.

Chapter 7

The Mufti's Legacy:
Jew Hatred, Jihad, and Terror

Islamic Anti-Semitism in a New Age of Terror:
Blaming the Jews for September 11

The radical Islamic terrorist attacks on the World Trade Center and the Pentagon on September 11, 2001, shocked America and the world. For America, and for the West, it was a day of infamy comparable to, if not greater than, Pearl Harbor. This murderous slaughter of innocent civilians ushered in a new and unprecedented era in the history of radical Islamic terrorism.

The perpetrators of September 11 shared much in common with the Nazi perpetrators of the Holocaust. Anti-Semitic conspiracy theories, which have their genesis in *The Protocols of the Elders of Zion*, lie at the heart of the radical Islamic ideology and worldview that served as the pretext for September 11. In the aftermath of September 11, radical Islam would blame the attacks on the World Trade Center on "the Elders of Zion" and on the Jews.[1] Barely two weeks after September 11, a columnist in the Egyptian newspaper *Al-Wafd* wrote that the Zionists must have known in advance that the September 11 attacks were impending but refused to share the information with the United States "in order to sow disputes and troubles" throughout the world. "Proof is found," the columnist added, "in the Protocols of the Wise Men of Zion."[2]

The September 11 terrorist attacks against the United States were welcomed by many in the Muslim world. The grand mufti of Jerusalem, Sheikh Ikrima Sabri, preaching his Friday sermon at the Al-Aqsa Mosque, called openly for the destruction of Israel, Great Britain, and the United States: "Oh Allah, destroy America, for she is ruled by Zionist Jews. . . . Allah will paint the White House black!"[3] For the sheikh, such prayerful calls for global jihad were nothing new. Well before September 11, Sabri, who served as the supreme religious leader of the Palestinian National Authority, had prayed in public for the destruction of America. "Oh, Allah, destroy America as it is controlled by Zionist Jews," he implored during his weekly sermon at the Al-Aqsa Mosque on July 11, 1997. Two months later he repeated his appeal, adding: "Cast [the Americans] into their own traps and cover the White House with black!" It was a prayer he would repeat again just two weeks before the September 11 terrorist attacks.[4]

The Egyptian-based journal of the Muslim Brotherhood, to which Haj Amin al-Husseini had once contributed anti-Semitic and anti-Western diatribes, hailed Osama bin Laden "as a hero in the full sense of the word" and prayed that his followers would eventually "eradicate America."[5] For the Muslim Brotherhood, to whose malicious ideology al-Husseini had been so fervently devoted, the September 11 terror attacks were nothing less than "divine retribution," not least because the Americans "preferred the apes [that is, the Jews] to human beings, treating human beings from outside the U.S. cheaply, supporting homosexuals and usury."[6] Perhaps the most dramatic—and explicit—response came from the Hamas weekly *Al-Risala* in Gaza, in its issue of September 13, 2001: "Allah has answered our prayers."[7]

Almost immediately in the aftermath of September 11, throughout the Islamic world, blame for the terrorist attacks was placed on the Zionists, Israel, and the Jews. The Syrian ambassador to Tehran was quoted as saying that "the Israelis have been involved in these incidents and no Jewish employee was present in the World Trade Organization building on that day." In the Jordanian newspaper *Al-Dustour* on September 13, 2001, an article appeared that argued, in the conspiratorial tradition of *The Protocols of the Elders of Zion,* that the Twin Towers massacre was in fact "the act of the great Jewish Zionist mastermind that controls the world economy, media and politics . . . ," and the diabolical Zionist plot "was rapidly leading the world to global disaster."[8] The Egyptian sheikh Muhammad al-Gameia, former imam of the Islamic Cultural Center and Mosque of New York, who had paid homage to Haj Amin al-Husseini as a hero and spiritual mentor, also had little doubt that the Jews were behind the September 11 terrorist attacks. "The Jewish element is as Allah described," asserted al-Gameia. "We know they have always broken agreements, unjustly murdered the prophets, and betrayed the faith."[9] Explaining that "only the Jews" were capable of destroying the World Trade Center, the sheikh added that "if it became known to the American people, they would have done to the Jews what Hitler did."[10] In Kuwait, there were reports that New York rabbis "told their followers to take their money out of the stock market before September 11."[11] In Egypt and other Muslim countries, the Mossad was blamed for the attack.

The conspiratorial theory that the Mossad, Israel's intelligence service, was behind the Twin Tower attacks gained widespread credence throughout the radical Islamic world in the aftermath of September 11 and enjoyed great credence in Pakistan. In support of this anti-Zionist conspiracy theory, the *Jihad Times* and other media in Pakistan stated as fact that four thousand Israelis and Jews working in the World Trade Center had been ordered by the Mossad not to show up for work on September 11. The terrorist attacks, it was alleged, had been ordered by "the Elders of Zion" in response to criticism of Israel and Zionism at the Third UN World Conference Against Racism held in Durban, South Africa, in the weeks before the attacks.[12]

Fatwas and Holy War:
Al-Husseini's Legacy as a Pioneer of Modern Jihad

During the 1920s and 1930s, Haj Amin al-Husseini was one of the first radical Islamic leaders to issue fatwas, or religious rulings, calling for jihad, or holy war, against Great Britain, the United States, the Jews, and the West. Since World War I, during which al-Husseini served as an officer in the Ottoman Turkish army, the fatwa has served as a major instrument by which Islamic religious leaders have impelled their followers to engage in acts of jihad, which invariably involved acts of violence and terrorism.

The first twentieth-century use of the fatwa to declare an Islamic holy war against the British and its Western allies was invoked during World War I by the Ottoman Turkish sultan Sheikh ul-Islam, in support of the German-Turkish war effort led by Kaiser Wilhelm II. It is likely that the Turkish sultan's idea of World War I as a holy war against the British was one that al-Husseini passionately shared, envisioning it also as a jihad against the Jewish supporters of Lord Balfour and his pro-Zionist British government. Swiftly translated into Arabic, Persian, Urdu, and Tartar, the Turkish sultan's fatwa was a truly global call to jihad, addressed to the approximately 120 million Muslims then living under British, French, and Russian rule.[13] It was the first of many such twentieth- and twenty-first-century proclamations of holy war in the emerging struggle between radical Islam and the West.

Shortly after being appointed grand mufti in 1921, al-Husseini declared a fatwa of jihad against Great Britain and the Jews in response to the British decision to affirm its support for the creation of a Jewish homeland in Palestine. After the outbreak of the Arab Revolt in Palestine in April 1936, and the declaration of a state of emergency by the British mandatory government, the newly established Arab Higher Committee for Palestine, of which al-Husseini had been elected president, called for a general strike against the British, urging other Arab leaders to join in a jihad *watani,* or "patriotic struggle," to "work for

rescuing the country from [British] imperialism and Jewish coloniza-
tion. . . ."[14] After the British expelled al-Husseini from Palestine in
September 1937, the mufti helped establish the Central Committee of
the Jihad, also known as the General Command of the Arab Revolt,
which under his direction issued the following fatwa against the
British: "The fighters . . . have sold themselves to Allah and they have
set out in [obedience] to Him, only in order to strive for His goal, for
the jihad in His way. . . . They try to get ahead of one another [in hur-
rying] to the battlefield of jihad and martyrdom, in order to support
what is right, to establish justice and to defend the noble community
and their holy country. . . . We call upon any Muslim [or] Arab to set
out for jihad in the way of Allah and to help the fighters in defending
the holy land."[15]

In Iraq in May 1941, in the immediate aftermath of the failed pro-
German coup that he had been so instrumental in launching, the mufti
issued what was perhaps his best-known fatwa, a summons to a holy
war against Great Britain. In the mufti's fatwa against Britain, he invited "my Moslem brothers throughout the world to join in the Holy
War for God, for the defense of Islam and her lands against her enemy
[the British]. . . . In Palestine the English have committed unheard of
barbarisms. . . . I invite you, O Brothers, to join in the War for God to
preserve Islam, your independence and your lands from English aggression."[16]

During the next four years, as his radio broadcasts from Berlin
were transmitted throughout the Islamic world, the mufti issued several other calls to jihad against the British, its Western Allies, and the
Jews, calls for holy war that often cited the Koran.[17] In these radio
broadcasts to the Middle East, the mufti elaborated upon the claim that
Jews were vilified by the Koran, the now so familiar claim that subsequent generations of radical Islamic terrorist leaders have invoked.
"They cannot mix with any other nation but live as parasites among the
nations, suck out their blood, embezzle their property and corrupt
their morals," al-Husseini asserted in his radio broadcast of November 2,
1943, in which he also called upon his fellow Arabs "to rise and fight" a

holy war against the British and the Jews. "The divine anger and the curse that the Koran mentions with reference to the Jews," proclaimed the mufti, "is because of this unique character of the Jews."[18] In this, as in other areas, he made enduring contributions to both the rhetoric and the practice of the modern Islamic fatwa that laid the foundation for contemporary Islamic terrorism.

After his return to the Middle East in 1946, al-Husseini once again resorted to the fatwa, issuing religious rulings to mobilize Arab support for a new Islamic holy war to prevent the creation and future existence of a Jewish state in Palestine. In May 1948, at the beginning of Israel's War of Independence, the mufti called for Arabs throughout the Islamic Middle East to wage a holy war against the newly established Jewish state. The goal of this jihad, he emphasized, was the extermination of the Jews and the destruction of their state of Israel.

His calls for a holy war were directed not only at the British and the Jews, but increasingly at America as well. In a famous radio broadcast from Berlin in March 1944, he denounced American policy in support of the establishment of a Jewish homeland in Palestine: "No one ever thought," he thundered, that 140 million Americans "would become tools in Jewish hands. . . ." How could America "dare to Judaize Palestine?" American intentions were now "clear," he claimed, and reflected America's demonic effort to establish a "Jewish empire in the Arab world,"[19] an effort that he called upon his fellow Muslims to fight and oppose. It was, quite simply, their religious obligation to do so.

It may well have been Sheikh ul-Islam's use of the fatwa during World War I that first inspired al-Husseini to issue his subsequent fatwas. In so doing, al-Husseini was a true pioneer. For al-Husseini in the 1930s, as for his ideological heirs in the 1990s, these religious rulings "provided the legal and moral dispensation for acts of terrorism that are deemed to fulfill the duty of Jihad."[20] In his calls for global jihad, Haj Amin al-Husseini was setting a precedent for future fatwas: for the fatwa of the Ayatollah Khomeini, calling for the killing of Salman Rushdie, author of *The Satanic Verses,* in 1989; for the fatwas of the Egyptian sheikh Omar Abd al-Rahman, which provided the religious justification for the 1981 assassination of Anwar Al Sadat and for the first terrorist attack on the World Trade Center in 1993;[21] and for Osama bin Laden's infamous 1996 fatwa calling on all Muslims to wage jihad against the United States and Israel, which would provide the religious justification for the Islamic terrorist attacks of September 11. "Our Muslim brothers throughout the world . . . are asking you to participate with them against their enemies, who are also your enemies—the Israelis and the Americans—by causing them as much harm as can possibly be achieved,"[22] asserted bin Laden. In an even more explicit and notorious fatwa of February 22, 1998, bin Laden proclaimed that "in order to obey the Almighty . . . to kill and fight Americans and their allies, whether civilian or military, it is an obligation for every Muslim who is able to do so in any country. . . . In the name of Allah, we call upon every Muslim, who believes in Allah and asks for forgiveness, to abide by Allah's order by killing Americans and stealing their money anywhere, anytime, and whenever possible."

These fatwas were new warrants for genocide in the ongoing war of the mufti and his protégés who seek to complete, posthumously, Hitler's war against the Jews.

The Mufti and Arafat:
The Fathers of Modern Islamic Terrorism

During the 1950s, with al-Husseini's encouragement, Yasser Arafat began recruiting followers for Fatah, his Palestinian terrorist guerrilla group, which took its name from the Koranic word for "conquest."[23] In 1965, Arafat's Fatah terrorists began attacking Israelis, shortly after Egyptian president Gamal Abdel Nasser created the Palestine Liberation Organization.[24] In 1969, Arafat merged Fatah with the PLO, and in that same year he succeeded his mentor al-Husseini as leader of the Palestine National Movement.

Arafat continued the mufti's legacy by recruiting Nazis and neo-Nazis for Fatah and the PLO. In 1969, the PLO recruited two former

Nazi instructors, Erich Altern, a leader of the Gestapo's Jewish affairs section, and Willy Berner, who was an SS officer in the Mauthausen extermination camp.[25] Another former Nazi, Johann Schuller, was found supplying arms to Fatah. Belgian Jean Tireault, secretary of the neo-Nazi organization La Nation Européenne, also went on the Fatah payroll. Another Belgian, neo-Nazi Karl van der Put, recruited volunteers for the PLO.[26] During the 1970s, German neo-Nazi Otto Albrecht was arrested in West Germany with PLO identity papers after the PLO had given him $1.2 million to buy weapons.[27]

Like al-Husseini, Arafat was a ruthless murderer whose career was built on terrorism and violence. In continuing this tradition, Arafat introduced his longtime PLO associate Hani al-Hassan to Romanian president Nicolae Ceaușescu in October 1972, saying: "This is my brother. . . . He is the one who, just a few months ago, prepared our answer to the Olympic Committee's decision not to allow a team of Palestinian athletes to participate in the Munich games. He is the brain who put our organization's name on the front page of every single newspaper."[28]

Arafat was referring to the September 5, 1972, massacre of eleven Israeli athletes by a team of PLO terrorists during the Olympic Games in Munich, a brutal deed that shocked the world. So did the murder the following year of Cleo A. Noel, U.S. ambassador to Sudan, and his chargé d'affaires, George Curtis Moore,[29] another crime executed by Arafat's PLO. Arafat was directly implicated in the October 1985 seizure by Palestinian terrorists of the Italian cruise ship *Achille Lauro*, in which a disabled Jewish passenger, Leon Klinghoffer, was singled out for killing, a terrorist act that Pope John Paul II publicly condemned as "a grave act of violence against innocent and defenseless persons."[30]

In his almost four-decade career as leader of the PLO, Arafat was involved in innumerable terrorist attacks against Israeli and other Jewish civilians, ranging from the hijacking of planes to the recruitment and training of terrorist bombers. Arafat, like al-Husseini, targeted Jews just because they were Jews: Jews at prayer in synagogues throughout Israel and Europe and even helpless children in nurseries and on school buses. His direction and sponsorship of terrorist attacks against Israeli civilians as well as Jewish students and tourists in Israel became an almost daily occurrence during the intifada that raged between 2000 and 2002. More than 640 Israeli civilians were killed in 2001 and 2002 alone. It was also during this intifada that Arafat and his Palestinian National Authority were implicated in the bombing of French synagogues and other acts of anti-Semitic violence and terrorism against Jewish communal leaders and institutions in France. During the last three months of 2000 alone, Arab-Muslim violence aimed at French Jews, inspired by Arafat's intifada, included forty-five fire bombings, forty-three attacks on synagogues, and thirty-nine assaults on Jews as they were leaving their places of worship.[31] This was in fact the fifth intifada in eighty years. In orchestrating the first intifada of the twenty-first century, Arafat was following in the footsteps of al-Husseini and continuing the tactics and legacy of terror that the mufti had introduced.

The Arab response to the Israeli War of Independence had been inspired and promoted by Islamist jihadists, led by al-Husseini, the young Yasser Arafat, and their allies in the Muslim Brotherhood, whose express purpose was genocidal: They had called for a holy war against the Jews of Palestine. Their objective had been, as the mufti candidly put it and reiterated throughout his political career, to "murder the Jews," to "murder them all." In the aftermath of Israel's War of Independence, the mufti and Arafat continued to mobilize Palestinian Arab terrorists, who throughout the 1950s and early 1960s targeted the Jewish civilian population of Israel for attack and extermination. Haj Amin al-Husseini had first established his credentials as a terrorist leader by organizing and carrying out terrorist attacks against the civilian Jews of Palestine during the 1920s and 1930s. The mufti's enduring influence and legacy as one of the founding fathers of modern Islamic terrorism was widely felt throughout the latter half of the twentieth century and the first decade of the twenty-first: The targeting of innocent Jewish civilians, which he pioneered, became a hallmark of all radical Islamic terrorist activity against Israel from the 1950s to the present. In his policy of targeting Jews just because they were Jews, al-Husseini provided the inspiration and precedent for a new generation of radical Islamic terrorist leaders, all of whom advocated suicide bombing attacks inside Israel as a religiously mandated and justified tactic in their ongoing holy war against Israel and its Jews.

Mahmoud Abbas, Arafat's successor as head of the Palestinian National Authority, also frequently justified and glorified suicide bomber attacks in the name of jihad against Israel and its allies in the West. In January 2005, Abbas publicly praised Palestinian suicide bombers, saying that "Allah loves the martyr,"[32] and in May 2006 he paid homage to the Palestinian terrorists who had carried out suicide bomber attacks against Israel as "our heroes."[33] On January 11, 2007, addressing a rally of 250,000 Palestinian Arabs in Ramallah in honor of the forty-second anniversary of the founding of Fatah and commemorating the first terrorist attack by Fatah against Israel on January 1, 1965, Abbas called for Palestinians to turn their guns and rifles on Israeli Jews, saying that "we have a legitimate right to direct our guns against Israeli occupation. . . . Our rifles, all our rifles, are aimed at the Occupation."[34]

As Islamist jihadists who had called for a holy war against the Jews of Palestine and their allies in the West, Haj Amin al-Husseini and Yasser Arafat shared a common goal both had failed to achieve: to destroy Israel and create a Palestinian Arab state in its place. In truth, Arafat's enduring legacy was merely a continuation of the failed legacy of al-Husseini. Both were determined to liberate Palestine from the Zionists. But in their rejection of political compromise and moderation, both failed to achieve their dreams of Palestinian Arab statehood. Both chose to align their Palestine Liberation Movement with a superpower. The mufti chose Nazi Germany. Arafat chose the Soviet Union. Both lived to witness the demise of their chosen patron.

Both seized on terror as a vehicle for achieving their political ends, justifying and glorifying acts of terror in the name of Palestinian Arab statehood and jihad. Both al-Husseini and Arafat internationalized terrorism, using it as an effective political strategy to gain widespread recognition and support for their Palestinian Arab cause.[35]

Only in his attire did Arafat differ profoundly from his beloved mentor as a terrorist leader. As if created by central casting, Arafat personified the public's image of the murderous Islamic terrorist. While al-Husseini always wore the long traditional robes and red tarboosh headdress of his clerical office, Arafat was invariably attired in his military fatigues, wearing a gun dramatically visible in his holster, his photogenic symbol of revolution until victory. Arafat, who was bald, always wore his trademark kaffiyeh headdress, draped down over his stomach and chest in such a fashion that it resembled the map of Palestine.

From his leadership of the first murderous intifada against the Jews of Palestine in 1920 until his death in 1974, Haj Amin al-Husseini remained an unrepentant terrorist leader. Until his death in 2004, Yasser Arafat, who often paid homage to the mufti as his hero and mentor, also remained a terrorist leader, equally unrepentant. Arafat—implicated in the murders of thousands of Christians, Jews, Israelis, Europeans, and Americans—well deserved the reputation that he shared with the mufti as one of the fathers of Islamic terrorism in our time.

Haj Amin al-Husseini and the Terrorists of Hamas

While Haj Amin al-Husseini may be best remembered as the revered mentor of Yasser Arafat, it must not be forgotten that he was also the inspiration for the leaders of Hamas, which continues its ongoing campaign of terror and violence against the state of Israel. Following in the footsteps of the PLO, Hamas ushered in a new era in radical Islamic terrorist violence by launching suicide bomber attacks inside Israel, a new and more violent tactic in anti-Jewish terror and violence that al-Husseini would undoubtedly have applauded. The ideology of Hamas, which reflects the legacy of al-Husseini with an unmistakable clarity, may be found in the words of its covenant, adopted on August 18, 1988:

> The enemies [the Jews] have been scheming for a long time . . . and have accumulated huge and influential wealth. With their money, they took control of the world media. . . . With their money they stirred revolutions in various parts of the globe. . . . They stood behind the French Revolution, the Communist Revolution and most of the revolutions we hear about. . . . With their money they formed secret organizations—such as the Freemasons, Rotary Clubs and the Lions—which are spreading around the world, in order to destroy societies and carry out Zionist interests. . . . They stood behind World War I . . . and formed the League of Nations through which they could rule the world. They were behind World War II, through which they made huge financial gains. . . . There is no war going on anywhere without them having their finger in it. . . . The Day of Judgement will not come about until Moslems fight Jews and kill them. Then, the Jews will hide behind rocks and trees, and the rocks and trees will cry out: "O Moslem, there is a Jew hiding behind me, come and kill him."[36]

Hamas leaflets, widely distributed in recent years, further promote this view. They vilify Jews as "the Brothers of the Apes, the killers of the Prophets, blood suckers and warmongers," the "enemy of God and mankind," the "descendants of treachery and deceit," "the Zionist culprits who poisoned the water in the past, killed infants, women and elders,"[37] and openly proclaim "the war is open until Israel ceases to exist and until the last Jew in the world is eliminated."[38]

In creating Hamas, the organization's founder and spiritual leader, Sheikh Ahmad Yassin, a devoted admirer of al-Husseini, formulated the concept that Palestine should "become the central battlefield" between the forces of radical Islam and Israel and its Western allies, in a radical Islamic jihad against Israel, America, and the pro-Israel West. Participation in the intifada, argued Yassin, the first stage of this holy war, would bring about Israel's eventual destruction and the establish-ment of a nationalist pan-Islamic state in Palestine. The creation of this state, the very type al-Husseini had envisioned, would in turn be the precursor of a global holy war, waged by Hamas and the leaders of radical Islam against Israel's allies in America and the West.[39] Thirty-two years after his death, the vision of al-Husseini was to be affirmed as Hamas assumed the leadership of the Palestinian people. Following the victory of Hamas in the Palestinian elections held on January 25, 2006, Khaled Mashaal, the leader of Hamas, gave a speech in Damas-cus in which he declared: "I bring good tidings to our beloved Prophet Muhammad: Allah's promise and the Prophet's prophecy of our victory in Palestine over the Jews and over the oppressive Zionists has begun to come true." The leaders of Hamas continue to seek to undermine and reverse the work of the more moderate Palestinian nationalist fac-tions, some of which have reluctantly accepted Israel's right to exist. The opposition to Israel's existence is much more intransigent in Hamas than it is today among some secular Palestinian nationalists. This is an intransigence that the mufti would have shared.

In the aftermath of these elections, a civil war erupted between Hamas and the Palestinian National Authority let by Mahmoud Abbas. In June 2007, Hamas was victorious, seizing power in Gaza. Just as the mufti had viewed his All-Palestine government as a mere prelude to the conquest of all of Palestine, the Hamas triumph in Gaza is viewed today by radical Islam as only the first step in the creation of an Islamic state in all of Palestine. Both the mufti and Hamas based their dreams and hopes on the belief in the inevitable triumph of radical Islam over the Jews and the West.

The mufti and Hamas were both willing to kill fellow Palestinians who stood in the way of their ultimate triumph. The brutal killings por-trayed graphically in the news media from Gaza in 2007 were entirely reminiscent of the mufti's elimination of his rivals in the 1920s and 1930s. The mufti and Hamas both cited *The Protocols of the Elders of Zion* in their war against the Jews. Their willingness to believe and promulgate the most vicious forms of anti-Jewish rhetoric became a hallmark of their pursuit of victory. The decisions to align their struggles with world powers whose views were antithetical to peace and international goodwill were clear and equally dangerous. The mufti's decision to align with Hitler's Germany found its contemporary analogue in Hamas's decision to align itself with Iran. Both claimed as their objective the goal to "wipe Israel off the map." From the mufti's All-Palestine government in Gaza to the Hamas government in Gaza of today, it is clear that the aims and goals of radical Islam have remained consistent through the years.

Hitler, al-Husseini, and the Terrorists of September 11

On November 18, 1947, Adolf Hitler's close confidant Albert Speer recorded the following in his Spandau Prison diary:

> I recall his ordering showings in the Chancellery of the films of burning London, of the sea of flames over Warsaw, of exploding convoys, and the rapture with which he watched those films. I never saw him so worked up as toward the end of the war, when in a kind of delirium he pictured for himself and for us the destruction of New York in a hurricane of fire. He described the skyscrapers being turned into gigantic burning torches, collapsing upon one another, the glow of the exploding city illuminating the dark sky.

On September 11, 2001, this horrific vision became a terrible reality.

This new reality affirmed the unbroken line of continuity from generation to generation, an unbroken chain of terror from Adolf Hitler, Haj Amin al-Husseini, Sayyid Qutb, and Yasser Arafat to Hamas's founder and spiritual leader, Sheikh Ahmad Yassin, Sheikh Omar Abd al-Rahman, and Ramzi Yousef, who planned the World

Trade Center bombing of 1993, to Osama bin Laden and Mohammed Atta, to Ahmed Omar Saeed Sheikh, the Pakistani Muslim terrorist who planned the kidnapping and murder of U.S. journalist Daniel Pearl, and to Iranian president Mahmoud Ahmadinejad. The radical Islamic jihadists, like the Nazis before them, are simultaneously anti-American, anti-Western, and anti-Jewish. The mufti's close ties to Hitler and his inner circle, his role as a trusted confidant of Himmler and Eichmann, and his enthusiastic embrace of Hitler's Final Solution provide the common thread linking past to present. Just as the mufti was and remains the link between the old fascism and the new, so has he been the inextricable link between the old anti-Semitism and the new radical Islamic anti-Semitism that has spread and metastasized throughout the Arab world in the decades since World War II.

The roots of present-day radical Islamic terrorism can, in many ways, be attributed to the mufti. Haj Amin al-Husseini has been, and remains, the inspiration for the leaders of the PLO, Hamas, Hezbollah, Islamic Jihad, al-Qaeda, and other radical Islamic groups to continue their campaigns of violence and terror against Israel, the United States, and their allies and friends. The terrorism, fanaticism, and ruthlessness of the Palestine National Movement reflect the mufti's enduring legacy and influence. Today, more than thirty years after his death, Haj Amin al-Husseini deserves recognition as the icon of evil that he was, as the father of radical Islamic anti-Semitism and political terrorism as we know it today. Al-Husseini's notorious fatwas, calling for the defeat and destruction of Israel, Great Britain, and the United States—like the religious rulings of Sheikh Omar Abd al-Rahman, Osama bin Laden, and other terrorists who would follow him—became new warrants for genocide in the clash of civilizations between radical Islam and the West and in the ongoing war of the mufti and his follow-ers who sought to carry out, posthumously, Hitler's war against the Jews. The radical Islam that the mufti and his followers promoted and espoused during the 1930s and 1940s has today become dominant in much of the Islamic world and has continued to be the ideological source and inspiration for global anti-Semitism, jihad, and terrorism throughout the latter half of the twentieth century and into the twenty-first.

The challenge of terror from radical Islam is the great issue of our time. As Adolf Hitler and Haj Amin al-Husseini were decisively defeated in their day, the new icons of evil must be unconditionally vanquished in ours.

Acknowledgments

In writing this book over the years, we have been helped along by the advice, encouragement, and cooperation of a number of people. We owe a special debt of gratitude to the late Eliahu Elath, the former Israeli ambassador to the United States and president of the Hebrew University in Jerusalem, who first encouraged us to write a book about the life and legacy of the mufti, his role in the Holocaust and in the rise of radical Islam. In 1937, Elath had been an official working in the political department of the Jewish Agency in Jerusalem. At that critical time in the history of the Middle East, Elath prepared a manuscript for internal consumption on the mufti and his role in the struggle for Palestine. In 1968, this manuscript was published in Hebrew by the Office of the Prime Minister. Many years later, Dr. Elath authorized us to have his work translated into English. In a letter dated August 8, 1988, Dr. Elath wrote, "I congratulate you on the very idea of publishing such a book, as the Mufti's role in the Shoah has never been fully done in a work of research and historic detail. Alas, there are still many of his followers around." In subsequent communications, Dr. Elath continued to urge us to write such a book that would document the mufti's unholy legacy as the founding father of Islamic anti-Semitism and terrorism, a legacy that tragically still endures. In this book, we have tried to tell the story of the mufti's enduring legacy of evil, a story that Eliahu Elath believed needed to be more widely known and better understood. We only wish that he had lived to read this book, the writing of which he helped to inspire.

We wish to extend our deep appreciation to Sir Martin Gilbert for his extraordinary support and advice in the process of completing this book. Sir Martin, the official biographer of Winston Churchill, made a number of constructive suggestions and provided sources from his private archives and files. While we have incorporated many of Sir Martin's suggestions, we realize that our conclusions and interpretations may not all be in complete accordance with Sir Martin's views. He should not be held accountable for any errors of historical fact or interpretation. All of the conclusions and interpretations in this book are solely those of the authors.

We would also like to express our appreciation to three cherished friends, Professor Jonathan D. Sarna, Dr. Joseph R. Goldyne, and David Apfelbaum, who took time out of their busy schedules to read and comment on portions of this book. We are especially indebted to them for their invaluable comments on the chapters of this book that they read. David Dalin would additionally like to thank his Hoover Institution colleague and friend Douglas J. Feith for his continuing advice and encouragement on this book project.

The publication of this book provides us with a welcome opportunity to acknowledge our thanks to several other colleagues and friends who have spoken with us about material relating to the subject of this book. We would like to express our deep appreciation to each of the following individuals, whose sharing of their thoughts and general encouragement have helped to make this a better book: Professor Robert P. George, Sarah and William Stern, Professor Bernard Lewis, William

Kristol, Dov Zakheim, Michael Novak, Tevi Troy, Andrew and Deborah Leeds, Brian and Rosalind Henning, Irvin Ungar, Joseph Bottum, William Doino Jr., David Wormser, Luis Fleischman, Reed Rubinstein, Dick Seeley, Charles Liebling, Leslie Kane, Michael Jankelowitz, Zvi Jankelowitz, Oded Yinon, and Rabbi Leonid Feldman.

Thirty years ago, Trish Bransten encouraged the authors to write this book. We are delighted to thank her and to acknowledge her inspiration. We would like to thank Professor David Engel, who many years ago translated for us Eliahu Elath's manuscript on the mufti, as well as a little-known and long out of print German book about the mufti, written by Kurt Fischer-Weth, that was published in Germany in 1943. Antonia Clark and Monika Hunt were extremely helpful with additional translation work. Technical assistance was provided by Robyn Lipsky, John Moses Lewandowski, Diane Spagnoli, and Richard Lerner. Frances Stark, producer of *The John Rothmann Program* on KGO-810 AM, provided ongoing, extraordinary help and encouragement throughout the process of preparing this manuscript for publication.

We would like to acknowledge our appreciation to Judith Cohen, director of the Photographic Reference Collection at the United States Holocaust Memorial Museum, and to Caroline Waddell, the photo reference coordinator at the museum, for their gracious assistance in helping us to locate and secure the photographs that we have included in this volume.

We would also like to express our thanks and appreciation to our agent, Alexander Hoyt, who has had faith in this book project since its inception and has been a continuous source of encouragement throughout the research and writing of the manuscript.

We owe a special debt of thanks to Will Murphy, our editor at Random House, for his careful reading and editing of our book manuscript and his many excellent suggestions for its improvement. His continuing good advice and encouragement has been invaluable throughout. We are deeply grateful to Lea Beresford, editorial assistant to Will Murphy at Random House, for her unfailing patience and good humor in answering our many questions throughout the editing process. Dennis Ambrose, associate copy chief at Random House, was always available and extremely helpful during the ,proofreading and editing process. Thanks also to our copyeditor, Sona Vogel; our publicist, London King; her assistant, Maria Braeckel; and Courtney Turco.

This book evolved, in part, from an article, "Hitler's Mufti," written by David Dalin, that was published in the journal *First Things.* Dalin would like to thank Joseph Bottum and Richard John Neuhaus, the editor and editor in chief of *First Things,* for publishing this earlier article and for their ongoing encouragement of his writing.

As both authors and parents, we owe an immeasurable debt of gratitude to our children. David Dalin would like to express his deep thanks and appreciation to his daughter, Simona Dalin, and son, Barry Dalin, whose love and support continue to be a source of encouragement and inspiration for all that he does. John Rothmann would like to offer a special thank-you to his son Joel, who allowed him to use, not borrow, his laptop computer. Samuel Rothmann was always willing to help his technologically challenged father at critical moments along the way. Our children's continuing love and support has been a blessing for both of us.

Chronology of the Mufti's Life

1895 Born in Jerusalem.

1912 Attended Al-Azhar University in Cairo, studying Islamic philosophy.

1913 Made a pilgrimage to Mecca, entitling him to the title Haj.

1914 Returned to Jerusalem and enlisted in the Turkish army.

1918 Spent five months as a clerk in the office of Gabriel Pasha Haddad, Arab adviser to the military governor of Jerusalem. Worked for five months for Reuters Press Service translating press messages into Arabic.

1920 Arrested for his direct responsibility for the anti-Jewish riots in Jerusalem April 4–5. Let out on bail, jumped bail, was tried and sentenced in absentia to ten years' imprisonment.

   July 1—Sir Herbert Samuel becomes high commissioner for Palestine.

July 7—Samuel issues full amnesty for all prisoners sentenced by military courts, but not al-Husseini. Seven weeks later, a special pardon for al-Husseini is issued by Samuel.

1921 May 8—Selected as mufti of Jerusalem, succeeding his half-brother Sheikh Kamal al-Husseini.

1922 May 1—Selected to be president of the Supreme Muslim Council.

1929 August—Anti-Jewish riots break out in Palestine. The mufti's involvement is directly established by the royal commission investigating the disturbances.

1931 December 7—The mufti establishes the World Islamic Congress at a meeting held in Jerusalem. Al-Husseini is elected president.

1934 Heads a delegation of the World Islamic Congress to Mecca to mediate between Saudi Arabia and Yemen during their border war.

1936 April 19—Two Jews killed in Jaffa.

April 21—General strike proclaimed in Nablus.

April 25—At a meeting in Nablus, the Arab Higher Committee is organized with al-Husseini as president.

1937 January 12—The mufti testifies before the royal commission. The commission establishes the direct responsibility of the mufti and the Arab Higher Committee for increasing violence. Mufti removed as head of the Supreme Muslim Council.

July 17—British attempt to arrest the mufti. The mufti hides in the Al-Aqsa Mosque area.

October 15—The mufti flees from Palestine to Beirut, to Damascus, and then to Iraq.

1939–1941 Mufti in Iraq. Attempts to organize a pro-German coup.

1941 May 29—Flees Iraq.

June 1—Arrives in Tehran.

September—Flees Iran, arrives in Turkey, spending a month in the Italian embassy.

October 11—Arrives in Italy.

October 27—In Rome, the mufti meets with Benito Mussolini.

November 6—Arrives in Berlin.

November 28—Meets with German foreign minister Joachim von Ribbentrop.

November 28—Meets with Adolf Hitler.

1941–1945 Remains in Germany. Participates in and leads anti-Jewish meetings, broadcasts over German radio, encourages German anti-Jewish activity, and organizes the Arab Legion to fight alongside the Germans.

1945 May 7—Leaves Berlin and arrives in Bern, Switzerland.

May 19—Arrives in France, is arrested, and housed in villa at Rambouillet near Paris.

July—Officially placed on the United Nations list of war criminals.

1946 May 29—Arrives in Cairo.

June 20—Egypt announces that the mufti has been given refuge by King Farouk.

1948 March 30—The mufti, as president of the Arab Higher Committee, has "Arab Charter for Palestine" presented to the United Nations.

May 14—State of Israel established.

September 28—The mufti arrives in Gaza, entering Palestine for the first time in eleven years.

September 30—The mufti is unanimously elected president of the All-Palestine government by the Palestine National Assembly.

December 20—King Abdullah appoints a new mufti in place of al-Husseini.

1951 July 20—King Abdullah killed on orders from the mufti.

The mufti presides over World Islamic Congress in Karachi, West Pakistan.

1955 The mufti attends the Afro-Asian conference in Bandung, Indonesia.

1959 Settles in Beirut.

1967 March 1—Visits Jerusalem for the first time in thirty years.

Visits Riyadh as the guest of King Faisal.

1974 July 4—The mufti dies in Beirut.

July 5—The Supreme Muslim Council of Jerusalem asks to bring the mufti's body back to Jerusalem for burial. Request denied by the Israeli government.

Appendix:
Correspondence and Documents

Mufti's Letter to Hitler, 20 January 1941

Baghdad, 20 January 1941

Excellency:

England, that relentless and crafty enemy of the true liberty of peoples, has never tired of forging chains to enslave and subjugate the Arab people, sometimes in the name of a perfidious League of Nations and sometimes by flaunting false and hypocritical sentiments of humanity for the others, but always, in truth, for the most imperialistic designs camouflaged by the principles of democracy and of a mendacious internationalism.

By a geographic coincidence, the Arab people find themselves at the center of the land and sea crossroads, which form, according to the English, the principal hub of "Imperial British communications." For this reason, no means were spared to create perpetual obstacles hampering the freedom and development of the Arab people. One might even say that the relative peace which has lasted for more than a century between France and England has been due in good measure to the tacit understanding between these two Powers to keep the Arab populations under their yoke, thus observing the law of an ignoble division, which in any case established an equilibrium of ambitions without touching the sensitive artery of "sacred" British communications! This division of influence between France and England, moreover, served to break the resistance and the reactions of the Arabs by leaving them to grapple with the various strong powers. But English policy could not for long defy the awakening of Arab nationalism; hence the incessant activity of England in creating new obstacles against the achievement of independence by the Arabs and against their liberty. And so it is the dismal history of the past decades, which offers to the eyes of the world the spectacle of a continuous and desperate struggle.

In Iraq, England, in her traditional policy of divide and rule, conceived the plan of settling several million Hindus brought over from British India side by side with the indigenous Arab population. The plan was foiled by a bloody revolution and so England has to submit to the fait accompli, and devote her attention to the immediate exploitation of Iraq petroleum. In a word, King Faisal I accepted a modus vivendi and, despite the opposition of the majority of the people, signed a treaty with England, thus purchasing the relative independence of the country at the price of petroleum concessions. The attitude of Turkey, favoring the annexation of Mosul to the territory, imposed on the late King the need for this policy.

As for Syria, she was handed over to France—this to break her national unity and impoverish her economically in order to be able the better to subdue her nationalist spirit. After 18 years of struggle, she was able to wrest from France the lame treaty of 1936, recognizing her independence, but at the price of concessions and unilateral reservations. And then England emerged to bar the road to liberty for Syria and came to an agreement with Turkey to neutralize the effect of the Franco-Syrian treaty; this was done in agreement with the Jews who feared an independent Syria next to her sister, Palestine, who was in a state of revolt. It was at this time that the Anglo-French-Turkish agreement against the Axis Powers came into being. Such was the prelude in 1938 to the question of Alexandretta and Antioch, which was to end in the cession by France of the said region to Turkey, on the one hand, and the abrogation, sine qua non of the Treaty of 1939 between France and Syria. Thus, it was another "very democratic" maneuver on the part of England at the expense of Syria—this despite the commissions and the reports of investigations of the League of Nations, all favorable to the Syrian thesis.

I pass in turn to Egypt. Now, since 1882, England has established herself there "temporarily!" because the people, in revolt, demanded of the Khedive a national constitution, which was to place a curb on the extravagance of the Prince and organize the budget according to the interests and the needs of the country. But so-called democratic England occupied the country in order to save the throne of the Khedive on the pretext of assuring order in Alexandria, while perfidious Albion with her own fingers spun intrigues and fomented troubles and disorders by means of her own agents-provocateurs. The truth is, what was involved was the Suez Canal and . . . imperial communications. Egypt waited until 1936 to obtain likewise her lame treaty with the familiar reservations. This fact was not due to British generosity—far from it—but quite simply to the breakdown of the balance of forces in the Mediterranean, since Italy was taking a stronger and more threatening stand against British "interests."

Now, after so many other countries of the Arabian peninsula, there comes Palestine. Her case, Your Excellency, is well known to you because she, too, has had to suffer from the perfidy of the English. It is a case of creating an obstacle to the unity and independence of the Arab countries by pitting them directly against the Jews of the entire world, dangerous enemies, whose secret arms are money, corruption, and intrigues, in addition, moreover, to the bayonets of the British. For 20 years now we have been face to face with these various forces. Armed with an invincible faith in their cause, the Arabs of Palestine have fought with the most rudimentary means. The question of Palestine, moreover, has united all the Arab countries in a common hatred for the English and the Jews. If a common enemy is the prelude to the formation of national unity, one may say that the Palestine problem has hastened this unity. From the international point of view, the Jews of the entire world have given their allegiance to England in the hope that, if she is victorious, she will be able to make their dreams come true in Palestine and even in the neighboring Arab countries. If the Arabs are aided in defeating the Zionist aims, the Jews, and especially those of the United States, will be so demoralized at seeing the object of their dreams fade into nothingness that they will lose their enthusiasm for aiding Great Britain and will retreat before the catastrophe.

I beg Your Excellency not to be vexed with me for having related in summary fashion the history of Arab antagonism toward England, because it seemed to me necessary to throw into relief the fundamental causes which arouse the Arab world against the English. I have been anxious especially to state clearly that these causes have their deep roots in primordial interests and vital problems and not in futile questions with superficial and transitory effects. The warmest sympathy of the Arab peoples for Germany and the Axis is now and henceforth an established fact. No propaganda can change this truth. Freed from certain material impediments, the Arab peoples are everywhere prepared to act, as is proper, against the common enemy and to take their stand with enthusiasm on the side of the Axis to do their part in the well-deserved defeat of the Anglo-Jewish coalition.

Arab nationalism owes to Your Excellency a debt of gratitude and of recognition for having again and again brought up in ringing speeches the question of Palestine. I am anxious here to reiterate my thanks to Your Excellency and to assure Your Excellency of the sentiments of friendship, of sympathy, and of admiration which the Arab people pledges to Your Excellency, great Fuhrer, and to the courageous German people.

I take this occasion to delegate to the German Government my private secretary in order to initiate in the name of the strongest and largest Arab organization and in my own name the negotiations necessary for sincere and loyal cooperation in all fields.

I may add resolutely that the Arabs are disposed to throw their weight into the scales and to offer their blood in the sacred struggle for their rights and their national aspirations, provided that certain interests of a moral and material order are assured. It is a matter of taking the necessary precautions against a perfidious and powerful enemy; it is necessary to take into account the means and the strength in order to enter the fight with the greatest chance of success. This foresight is indispensable, especially since England is obliged to act and react with all her might in view of the strategic nature of the Arab countries, which could then endanger imperial communications and paralyze all connections between India and the Mediterranean and Turkey via the Persian Gulf, at the same time bringing about an end to the exploitation and sale of petroleum for the benefit of England.

I conclude by wishing Your Excellency a long and happy life and brilliant victory and prosperity for the great German people and for the Axis in the very near future.

I beg Your Excellency to believe in my sentiments of great friendship, of gratitude, and of admiration.

Grand Mufti of Palestine
Mohammed Amin El Husseini

Hitler's Response to the Mufti, 8 April 1941, from Freiherr von Weizsacker

Berlin, 8 April 1941

To His Eminence
The Grand Mufti
M. Haj Amin al Husayni
Baghdad

Your Eminence:

The Führer has received the letter of January 20, which you sent him through your private secretary. He has noted with great interest and sympathy your statements about the national struggle of the Arabs and has been pleased with the friendly words that you addressed to him on behalf of Arab nationalism and on your own behalf. Through Foreign Minister von Ribbentrop he sends his regards and his thanks and best wishes for the continued success of the Arab cause.

Your private secretary has entered upon the conversations here mentioned in your letter. In accordance with the wish conveyed by him that German policy with request to the Arabs be clarified, I am authorized to inform you as follows:

Germany, which has never possessed Arab territories, has no territorial aims in the Arab area. She is of the opinion that the Arabs, a people with an old civilization, who have demonstrated their competence for administrative activity and their military virtues, are entirely capable of governing themselves. Germany therefore recognizes the complete independence of the Arab states, or where this has not yet been achieved, the claim to win it.

Germany and the Arabs have common enemies in the English and the Jews and are united in the struggle against them. In Germany's traditional friendship for the Arabs and, in accordance with the wish which you had communicated through your private secretary, she is glad to cooperate in a friendly manner with the Arabs and, if they are forced to fight England in order to achieve their national aims, to grant them military and financial assistance in so far as is possible. In order to assist the Arabs in their preparations for a possible struggle against England, Germany is also prepared to supply them with war materials at once, in so far as a route for transporting it can be found.

I would like to suggest that for further discussion of the details of the contemplated friendly collaboration, you send back your private secretary or, should he be prevented from coming, that you send another negotiator here.

Please keep this letter secret. The Italian Government is informed as to its contents and is in agreement.

Your private secretary will, I do not doubt, confirm to you from the impressions he received in Germany that the victory of the Axis Powers is certain and that England's defeat is sealed.

With best wishes for your personal well-being and for further success in your courageous championship of the Arab cause.

Yours, etc.

Weizsacker

Memorandum by an Official of the
Foreign Minister's Secretariat

Berlin, 30 November 1941

RECORD OF THE CONVERSATION BETWEEN THE FUHRER AND THE
GRAND MUFTI OF JERUSALEM ON 28 NOVEMBER 1941, IN THE PRESENCE
OF REICH FOREIGN MINISTER AND MINISTER GROBBA IN BERLIN

The Grand Mufti began by thanking the Fuhrer for the great honor he had bestowed by receiving him. He wished to seize the opportunity to convey to the Fuhrer of the Greater German Reich, admired by the entire Arab world, his thanks for the sympathy which he had always shown for the Arab and especially the Palestinian cause, and to which he had given clear expression in his public speeches. The Arab countries were firmly convinced that Germany would win the war and that the Arab cause would then prosper. The Arabs were Germany's natural friends because they had the same enemies as had Germany, namely the English, the Jews, and the Communists. They were therefore prepared to cooperate with Germany with all their hearts and stood ready to participate in the war, not only negatively by the commission of acts of sabotage and the instigation of revolutions, but also positively by the formation of the Arab Legion. The Arabs could be more useful to Germany as allies than might be apparent at first glance, both for geographical reasons and because of the suffering inflicted upon them by the English and the Jews. Furthermore, they had close relations with all Moslem nations, of which they could make use in behalf of the common cause. The Arab Legion would be quite easy to raise. An appeal by the Mufti to the Arab countries and the prisoners of Arab, Tunisian, and Moroccan nationality in Germany would produce a great number of volunteers eager to fight. Of Germany's victory the

Arab world was firmly convinced, not only because the Reich possessed a large army, brave soldiers, and military leaders of genius, but also because the Almighty could never award the victory to an unjust cause. In this struggle, the Arabs were striving for the independence and unity of Palestine, Syria, and Iraq. They had the fullest confidence in the Fuhrer and looked to his hand for the balm on their wounds which had been inflicted upon them by the enemies of Germany.

The Mufti then mentioned the letter he had received from Germany, which stated that Germany was holding no Arab territories and understood and recognized the aspirations to independence and freedom of the Arabs, just as she supported the elimination of the Jewish national home.

A public declaration in this sense would be very useful for its propagandistic effect on the Arab peoples at this moment. It would rouse the Arabs from their momentary lethargy and give them new courage. It would also ease the Mufti's work of secretly organizing the Arabs against the moment when they could strike. At the same time, he could give the assurance that the Arabs would in strict discipline patiently wait for the right moment and only strike upon an order from Berlin.

With regard to events in Iraq, the Mufti observed that the Arabs in that country certainly have by no means been incited by Germany to attack England, but solely had acted in reaction to a direct English assault upon their honor.

The Turks, he believed, would welcome the establishment of an Arab government in the neighboring territories because they would prefer weaker Arab to strong European governments in the neighboring countries, and, being themselves a nation of 7 millions [Authors' note: It should read "17 millions."], they had moreover nothing to fear from the 1,700,000 Arabs inhabiting Syria, Transjordan, Iraq, and Palestine.

France likewise would have no objections to the unification plans because she had conceded independence to Syria as early as 1936 and had given her approval to the unification of Iraq and Syria under King Faisal as early as 1933.

In these circumstances he was renewing his request that the Fuhrer make a public declaration so that the Arabs would not lose hope, which is so powerful a force in the life of nations. With such hope in their hearts the Arabs, as he has said, were willing to wait. They were not pressing for immediate realization of their aspirations; they could easily wait half a year or a whole year. But if they were not inspired with such a hope by a declaration of this sort, it could be expected that the English would be the gainers from it.

The Fuhrer replied that Germany's fundamental attitude on these questions, as the Mufti himself had already stated, was clear. Germany stood for uncompromising war against the Jews. That naturally included active opposition to the Jewish national home in Palestine, which was nothing other than a center, in the form of a state, for the exercise of destructive influence by Jewish interests. Germany was also aware that the assertion that the Jews were carrying out the functions of economic pioneers in Palestine was a lie. The work there was done only by the Arabs, not by the Jews. Germany was resolved, step by step, to ask one European nation after the other to solve its Jewish problem, and at the proper time direct a similar appeal to non-European nations as well.

Germany was at the present time engaged in a life and death struggle with two citadels of Jewish power: Great Britain and Soviet Russia. Theoretically there was a difference between England's capitalism and Soviet Russia's communism; actually, however, the Jews in both countries were pursuing a common goal. This was the decisive struggle; on the political plane, it presented itself in the main as a conflict between Germany and England, but ideologically it was a battle between National Socialism and the Jews. It went without saying that Germany would furnish positive and practical aid to the Arabs involved in the same struggle, because platonic promises were useless in a war for survival or destruction in which the Jews were able to mobilize all of England's power for their ends.

The aid to the Arabs would have to be material aid. Of how little help sympathies alone were in such a battle had been demonstrated plainly by the operation in Iraq, where circumstances had not permitted the rendering of really effective, practical aid. In spite of all the sympathies, German aid had not been sufficient and Iraq was overcome by the power of Britain, that is, the guardian of the Jews.

The Mufti could not but be aware, however, that the outcome of the struggle going on at present would also decide the fate of the Arab world. The Fuhrer therefore had to think and speak coolly and deliberately, as a rational man and primarily as a soldier, as the leader of the German and allied armies. Everything of a nature to help in this titanic battle for the common cause, and thus also for the Arabs, would have to be done. Anything, however, that might contribute to weakening the military situation must be put aside, no matter how unpopular this move might be.

Germany was now engaged in very severe battles to force the gateway to the northern Caucasus region. The difficulties were mainly with regard to maintaining the supply, which was most difficult as a result of the destruction of railroad and highways as well as of the oncoming winter. If at such a moment, the Fuhrer were to raise the problem of Syria in a declaration, those elements in France which were under de Gaulle's influence would receive new strength. They would interpret the Fuhrer's declaration as an intention to break up France's colonial empire and appeal to their fellow countrymen that they should rather make common cause with the English to try to save what still could be saved. A German declaration regarding Syria would in France be understood to refer to the French colonies in general, and that would at the present time create new troubles in western Europe, which means that a portion of the German armed forces would be immobilized in the west and no longer be available for the campaign in the east.

The Fuhrer then made the following statement to the Mufti, enjoining him to lock it in the uttermost depths of his heart:

1. He (the Fuhrer) would carry on the battle to the total destruction of the Judeo-Communist empire in Europe.

2. At some moment which was impossible to set exactly today but which in any event was not distant, the German armies would in the course of this struggle reach the southern exit of Caucasia.

3. As soon as this had happened, the Fuhrer would on his own give the Arab world the assurance that its hour of liberation had arrived. Germany's objective would then be solely the destruction of the Jewish element residing in the Arab sphere under the protection of the British power. In that hour the Mufti would be the most authoritative spokesman for the Arab world. It would then be his task to set off the Arab operations which he had secretly prepared. When that time had come, Germany would also be indifferent to French reaction to such a declaration.

Once Germany had forced open the road to Iran and Iraq through Rostov, it would be also the beginning of the end of the British world empire. He (the Fuhrer) hoped that the coming year would make it possible for Germany to thrust open the Caucasian gate to the Middle East. For the good of the common cause, it would be better if the Arab proclamation were put off for a few more months than if Germany were to create difficulties for herself without being able thereby to help the Arabs.

He (the Fuhrer) fully appreciated the eagerness of the Arabs for a public declaration of the sort requested by the Grand Mufti. But he would beg him to consider that he (the Fuhrer) himself was the Chief of State of the German Reich for five long years during which he was unable to make to his own homeland the announcement of its liberation. He had to wait with that until the announcement could be made on the basis of a situation brought about by the force of arms that the Anschluss had been carried out.

The moment that Germany's tank divisions and air squadrons had made their appearance south of the Caucasus, the public appeal requested by the Grand Mufti could go out to the Arab world.

The Grand Mufti replied that it was his view that everything would come to pass just as the Fuhrer had indicated. He was fully reassured and satisfied by the work which he heard from the Chief of the German State. He asked, however, whether it would not be possible, secretly, at least, to enter into an agreement with Germany of the kind he had just outlined for the Fuhrer.

The Fuhrer replied that he had just now given the Grand Mufti precisely that confidential declaration.

The Grand Mufti thanked him for it and stated in conclusion that he was taking his leave from the Fuhrer in full confidence and with reiterated thanks for the interest shown in the Arab cause.

Schmidt

The Mufti's Diary on His Meeting with Hitler

Recording in his own handwriting his meeting with Hitler in his diary, Haj Amin al-Husseini says:

The word of the Fuhrer on the 6th of Zul Qaada 1360 of the Hejira (which falls on the 21st of November 1941) [Authors' note: In his diary, the mufti made an error regarding the date. The actual date was November 28, 1941.], Berlin, Friday, from 4:30 p.m. till a few minutes after 6.

The objectives of my fight are clear. Primarily, I am fighting the Jews without respite, and this fight includes the fight against the so-called Jewish National Home in Palestine because the Jews want to establish there a central government for their own pernicious purposes, and to undertake a devastating and ruinous expansion at the expense of the governments of the world and of other peoples.

It is clear that the Jews have accomplished nothing in Palestine and their claims are lies. All the accomplishments in Palestine are due to the Arabs and not to the Jews. I am resolved to find a solution for the Jewish problem, progressing step by step without cessation. With regard to this I am making the necessary and right appeal, first to all the European countries and then to countries outside of Europe.

It is true that our common enemies are Great Britain and the Soviets whose principles are opposed to ours. But behind them stands hidden Jewry which drives them both. Jewry has but one aim in both these countries. We are now in the midst of a life and death struggle against both these nations. This fight will not only determine the outcome of the struggle between National Socialism and Jewry, but the whole conduct of this successful war will be of great and positive help to the Arabs who are engaged in the same struggle.

This is not only an abstract assurance. A mere promise would be of no value whatsoever. But assurance which rests upon a conquering force is the only one which has real value. In the Iraqi campaign, for instance, the sympathy of the whole German people was for Iraq. It was our aim to help Iraq, but circumstances prevented us from furnishing actual help. The German people saw in them (the Iraqis) comrades in suffering because the German people too have suffered as they have. All the help we gave Iraq was not sufficient to save Iraq from the British forces. For this reason it is necessary to underscore one thing: in this struggle which will decide the fate of the Arabs I can now speak as a man dedicated to an ideal and as a military leader and a soldier. Everyone united in this great struggle who helps to bring about its successful outcome serves the common cause and thus serves the Arab cause. Any other view means weakening the military situation and thus offers no help to the Arab cause. Therefore it is necessary for us to decide the steps which can help us against world Jewry, against Communist Russia and England, and which among them can be most useful. Only if we win the war will the hour of deliverance also be the hour of fulfillment of Arab aspirations.

The situation is as follows: we are conducting the great struggle to open the way to the North of the Caucasus. The difficulties involved are more than transportation because of the demolished railways and roads and because of winter weather. And if I venture in these circumstances to issue a declaration with regard to Syria, then the pro–de Gaulle elements in France will be strengthened and this might cause a revolt in France. These men (the French) will be convinced then that joining Britain is more advantageous and the detachment of Syria is a pattern to be followed in the remainder of the French Empire. This will strengthen de Gaulle's stand in the colonies. If the declaration is issued now, difficulties will arise in Western Europe which will cause the diversion of some (German) forces for defensive purposes, thus preventing us from sending all our forces to the East.

Now I am going to tell you something I would like you to keep secret.

First, I will keep up my fight until the complete destruction of the Judeo-Bolshevik rule has been accomplished.

Second, during the struggle (and we don't know when victory will come, but probably not in the far future) we will reach the Southern Caucasus.

Third, then I would like to issue a declaration; for then the hour of the liberation of the Arabs will have arrived. Germany has no ambitions in this area but cares only to annihilate the power which produces the Jews.

Fourth, I am happy that you have escaped and that you are now with the Axis powers. The hour will strike when you will be the lord of the supreme word and not only the conveyor of our declarations. You will be the man to direct the Arab force and at that moment I cannot imagine what would happen to the Western peoples.

Fifth, I think that with this Arab advance begins the dismemberment of the British world. The road from Rostov to Iran and Iraq is shorter than the distance from Berlin to Rostov. We hope next year to smash this barrier. It is better then and not now that a declaration should be issued as (now) we cannot help in anything.

I understand the Arab desire for this [declaration], but His Excellency the Mufti must understand that only five years after I became President of the German government and Fuhrer of the German people, I was able to get such a declaration [the Austrian Union], and this because military forces prevented me from issuing such a declaration. But when the German Panzer tanks and the German air squadrons reach the Southern Caucasus, then will be the time to issue the declaration.

He said (in reply to a request that a secret declaration or a treaty be made) that a declaration known to a number of persons cannot remain secret but will become public. I (Hitler) have made very few declarations in my life, unlike the British who have made many declarations. If I issue a declaration, I will uphold it. Once I promised the Finnish Marshal that I would help his country if the enemy attacks again. This word of mine made a stronger impression than any written declaration.

Recapitulating, I want to state the following to you: When we shall have arrived in the Southern Caucasus, then the time of the liberation of the Arabs will have arrived. And you can rely on my word.

We were troubled about you. I know your life history. I followed with interest your long and dangerous journey. I was very concerned about you. I am happy that you are with us now and that you are now in a position to add your strength to the common cause.

Von Ribbentrop Promises Mufti to Destroy Jewish National Home

Ministry of Foreign Affairs

Berlin, April 28, 1942

Your Eminence:

In response to your letter and to the accompanying communication of His Excellency, Prime Minister Raschid Ali El Gailani, and confirming the terms of our conversation, I have the honour to inform you:

The German Government appreciates fully the confidence of the Arab peoples in the Axis Powers in their aims and in their determination to conduct the fight against the common enemy until victory is achieved. The German Government has the greatest understanding for the national aspirations of the Arab countries as have been expressed by you both and the greatest sympathy for the sufferings of your peoples under British oppression.

I have therefore the honour to assure you, in complete agreement with the Italian Government, that the independence and freedom of the suffering Arab countries presently subjected to British oppression, is also one of the aims of the German Government.

Germany is consequently ready to give all her support to the oppressed Arab countries in their fight against British domination, for the fulfillment of their national aim to independence and sovereignty and for the destruction of the Jewish National Home in Palestine.

As previously agreed, the content of this letter should be maintained absolutely secret until we decide otherwise.

I beg your Eminence to be assured of my highest esteem and consideration.

(Signed) Ribbentrop

To His Eminence
the Grossmufti of Palestine
Amin El Husseini

The Text of Telegrams Sent by
Himmler and von Ribbentrop to the Mufti
on 2 November 1943

The text of telegrams sent by Himmler and von Ribbentrop to the Mufti on 2 November 1943, the twenty-sixth anniversary of the Balfour Declaration. The Mufti's speech and these telegrams were reprinted in a pamphlet entitled "Speech of His Eminence the Grand Mufti at the Protest Rally Against the Balfour Declaration on 2 November 1943." The pamphlet was issued by the Mufti's Islamische Zentralinstitut in Berlin.

The text of Himmler's telegram follows:

The National Socialist Movement has since its inception inscribed the battle against world Jewry on its banners. It has therefore always pursued with sympathy the battle of the freedom loving Arabs against the Jewish intruders. The recognition of this enemy and the common battle against him provides the firm basis for the natural ties between the National Socialist Greater Germany and the freedom loving Mohammedans in the whole world. With this thought I convey to you, on the anniversary of the unholy Balfour Declaration, my deepfelt greetings and wishes for the success of your battle until final victory.

The following is the text of von Ribbentrop's telegram:

I send out my greetings to your Eminence and to those who are today in the capital of the Reich at the gathering under your chairmanship. Germany is tied to the Arab nation by old bonds of friendship and today more than ever we are allies. The removal of the so-called Jewish National Home and freeing all Arab lands from the oppression and the exploitation of the Western powers is an unalterable part of the policy of the Greater German Reich. May the hour not be distant when the Arab nation shall be able to build its future and establish unity in full independence.

Mufti Asks Ban on Jewish Immigration
as Gesture to Arabs

Berlin, 27 July 1944

To the Reichsfuehrer SS and Minister of the Interior
H. Himmler
Berlin

Reichsfuehrer:

In my letter to you of June 5, 1944, I referred back to our conversation in which I reported to you on the inclusion of Jews in the exchange plan of some Egyptians living in Germany.

I asked you, Reichsfuehrer, to take all the measures to prevent the Jews from going. These measures would also be in accordance with German policy in general, especially with the Declaration of the German Government on the occasion of the anniversary of the Balfour Declaration on November 2, 1943, which stated "that the destruction of the so-called Jewish national home in Palestine is an immutable part of the policy of the greater German Reich" and that "the National Socialist movement, since its inception, has inscribed in its banner the battle against world Jewry," as you, Reichsfuehrer, said in your telegram on the same occasion.

In the meantime I have learned that the Jews, nevertheless, did leave on July 2, 1944, and it is to be feared that further Jewish groups may leave Germany and France under the plan for exchanging Palestinian Germans. This exchange of Germans would encourage the Balkan countries to send their Jews to Palestine too. Furthermore, after the Declaration of the German Government, such a step would be incomprehensible to the Arabs and Moslems, and it would create in them a feeling of keen disappointment.

It is for this reason that I ask you, Reichsfuehrer, to do everything necessary to prevent the Jews from emigrating to Palestine, and in this way you would give a new practical example of the policy of the naturally allied and friendly Germany towards the Arab Nation.

Yours, etc.

The Mufti Proposes an Arab Legion to Himmler

Berlin, 3 October 1944

To the Reichsfuehrer and Reichsminister
H. Himmler
Headquarters of the Fuhrer

Reichsfuehrer!

I permit myself to call to your attention the renewal of the dangerous demands of the Jews, with the support of the Allies, for the establishment of a Jewish state in Palestine, as well as the approval given by the British government to the establishment of a Jewish military unit to fight against Germany with a view to thus winning title to such a state. According to the last speech of Churchill in the House of Commons on September 28, 1944, the British government has declared itself ready to establish such a military unit and to provide for its training and arming.

This declaration on the part of the British government has produced the worst possible reaction in all the Arab-Islamic countries. I therefore propose that as a challenge to this act there should be announced the establishment of an Arab-Islamic army in Germany. This army should be established by Arab and Islamic volunteers and should be merged with the Arab-Islamic units already in existence. The German government should declare its readiness to train and arm such an army. This would level a severe blow against the British plan and increase the number of fighters for a greater Germany.

I am convinced that the establishment of such an army and announcement of its purpose would have the most favorable repercussions in the Arab-Islamic countries. I therefore beg you to consider the possibility of making such an announcement on November 2, 1944. It would thus appear on the anniversary of the infamous Balfour Declaration pledging the establishment of the so-called Jewish National Home in 1917, and on the anniversary of the pledge of 1943 by the Foreign Minister of the Reich to destroy the so-called Jewish National Home.

Accept, Reichsfuehrer, the expression of my highest esteem.

Yours,

Affidavit of Dr. Rudolph Kastner at Nuremberg

As a leader of the Jewish Rescue and Relief Committee in Budapest, I requested the competent German authorities to grant the emigration to Palestine of a group of Hungarian Jews.

In the course of these negotiations, which are the subject of my testimony deposed in the minutes of the Nuremberg trial, the high Gestapo official Eichmann declared he would be willing to recommend the emigration of a group of 1,681 Hungarian Jews, on condition that the group should not go to Palestine.

"They may go to any country but Palestine," I was told by Eichmann, who, as leader of the Department IV.B. of the Reichssicherheitshaupant, was personally responsible for the deportation and extermination of the European Jews. At first, his argument for his negative attitude towards the emigration to Palestine was that he did not want to rouse the Arabs against the Reich. At last he said to me literally:

"I am a personal friend of the Grand Mufti. We have promised him that no European Jew would enter Palestine any more. Do you understand now?"

Some days later, SS Hauptsturmfuehrer Dieter Wisliceny, a close collaborator of Eichmann, confidentially confirmed to me the above statement of his chief, and added:

"According to my opinion, the Grand Mufti, who has been in Berlin since 1941, played a role in the decision of the German Government to exterminate the European Jews, the importance of which must not be disregarded. He had repeatedly suggested to the various authorities with whom he has been in contact, above all before Hitler, Ribbentrop and Himmler, the extermination of European Jewry. He considered this as a comfortable solution of the Palestine problem. In his messages broadcast from Berlin, he surpassed us in anti-Jewish attacks. He was one of Eichmann's best friends and has constantly incited him to accelerate the extermination measures. I heard say that, accompanied by Eichmann, he has visited incognito the gas chambers of Auschwitz."

The Record of Collaboration of King Farouk of Egypt with the Nazis and Their Ally, the Mufti

THE OFFICIAL NAZI RECORDS OF THE KING'S ALLIANCE AND OF THE
MUFTI'S PLANS FOR BOMBING JERUSALEM AND TEL AVIV

MEMORANDUM SUBMITTED TO THE UNITED NATIONS JUNE 1948

Mufti Urged Nazis to Bomb Jerusalem and Tel Aviv

While the Jews were helping the Allies, the Mufti was planning with the Axis on the fashion in which Jewish Palestine should be destroyed. His reasons were two:

(1) Personal vindictiveness and hatred of the Jews which had previously caused his active association with the Nazi policy of exterminating the Jews of Europe.

(2) The second purpose was military, namely to destroy an essential military factor which played a role in the subsequent Allied victory in North Africa.

The Mufti was constantly urging attacks on Jerusalem, on the Jewish Agency Headquarters there and on Tel Aviv, the all Jewish city. This is revealed in a number of secret documents found by the Allied Armies in Germany when they entered the country.

Thus, according to one of these documents, a secret report of the German Air Force Command, dated October 29, 1943, revealed that the Mufti for the past six months had been proposing an attack on Jerusalem and the Headquarters of the Jewish Agency by air and an attack on Tel Aviv. According to this report, the Mufti proposed that November 2, the anniversary of the Balfour Declaration should be "celebrated" by such an attack.

At the same time, and again under the Mufti's pressure, the Air Force Command was considering an attack on military objectives along the Palestine coast and expressed the opinion that "even the Grand Mufti, as the Reich Secretary Headquarters has said, would consider this sufficient."

In the same report, the Mufti's efforts to secure an attack on Tel Aviv are described. According to the report, "without doubt Tel Aviv should be considered as the object of counter-attacks against the British and American terrorist attacks. Any attack must be carried out with a very large force in order to have a lasting effect." But Fieldmarshal Goering was obliged to turn down the request on July 17 because no task force in sufficiently large numbers was available.

Apparently the Mufti did not rest, for another report dated March 30, 1944, reveals that the Mufti again urged that the bombing of Tel Aviv again take place on April 1, 1944. Again the Air Force Command reluctantly had to reiterate its refusal to do so.

Notes

CHAPTER 1: RENDEZVOUS WITH DESTINY

1. The definitive study of Nazi foreign policy making and diplomacy on the Wilhelmstrasse, on which Hitler's Foreign Office and Reich Chancellery were both located, can be found in Paul Seabury, *The Wilhelmstrasse: A Study of German Diplomats Under the Nazi Regime* (Berkeley: University of California Press, 1954).

2. Albert Speer, *Inside the Third Reich,* translated from the German by Richard and Clara Winston (New York: Macmillan, 1970), 102.

3. Ibid.

4. Joachim Fest, *Speer: The Final Verdict* (Orlando, FL: Harcourt, 1999), 103.

5. Chuck Morse, *The Nazi Connection to Islamic Terrorism: Adolf Hitler and Haj Amin al-Husseini* (Lincoln, NE: iUniverse, Inc., 2003), 57.

6. "Record of the Conversation Between the Führer and the Grand Mufti of Jerusalem on November 28, 1941, in the Presence of Reichs Foreign Minister and

Minister Grobba in Berlin," *Documents on German Foreign Policy, 1918–1945,* series D, vol. XIII, London, 1964; quoted in Kenneth R. Timmerman, *Preachers of Hate: Islam and the War on America* (New York: Three Rivers Press, 2003), 108.

7. Bernard Lewis, *Semites and Anti-Semites* (New York: W. W. Norton & Co., 1999), 147.

8. Quoted in Alan M. Dershowitz, *The Case for Israel* (Hoboken, NJ: John Wiley & Sons, 2003), 55.

9. Quoted in ibid., 55–56.

CHAPTER 2: THE GENESIS OF MODERN JIHAD

1. Eliyahu Elath, *Haj Muhammad Amin al-Husseini: The Former Mufti of Jerusalem— His Personality and Stages of His Rise to Power* (Jerusalem: Office of the Prime Minister, Bureau of the Advisor of Arab Affairs, 1968), 11.

2. Bernard Lewis, "The British Mandate for Palestine in Historical Perspective," in Bernard Lewis, *From Babel to Dragomans: Interpreting the Middle East* (New York: Oxford University Press, 2004), 152.

3. Elias Cooper, "Forgotten Palestinian: The Nazi Mufti," *American Zionist* LXVIII, no. 4 (March–April 1978): 6.

4. Elath, *Haj Muhammad Amin al-Husseini,* 11.

5. *The Messages and Papers of Woodrow Wilson,* vol. 1 (New York: Review of Reviews Corporation, 1924), 418–419.

6. Martin Gilbert, *Jerusalem in the Twentieth Century* (New York: John Wiley & Sons, 1996), 83.

7. Quoted in ibid., 84.

8. This story is recounted in Michael Bar-Zohar and Eitan Haber, *The Quest for the Red Prince* (New York: William Morrow & Co., 1983), 34–35.

9. Bernard Wasserstein, *Herbert Samuel: A Political Life* (Oxford: Clarendon Press, 1992), 1; and the chapter on Herbert Samuel in Chaim Bermant, *The Cousinhood: The Anglo-Jewish Gentry* (London: Eyre & Spottiswoode, 1971), 329–355.

10. Tom Segev, *One Palestine Complete: Jews and Arabs Under the British Mandate* (New York: Henry Holt & Co., 2000), 148.

11. Ibid.

12. Vivian D. Lipman, "Herbert Louis Samuel," *Encyclopedia Judaica*, vol. 14 (Jerusalem: Keter Publishing House, 1971), 799.

13. Bermant, *The Cousinhood*, 344.

14. Ibid.

15. Martin Gilbert, *Exile and Return: The Struggle for a Jewish Homeland* (Philadelphia: J. B. Lippincott, 1978), 83; and Gilbert, *Jerusalem in the Twentieth Century*, 43.

16. Bermant, *The Cousinhood*, 343.

17. Douglas J. Feith, "Churchill, Palestine and Zionism, 1904–1922," in James W. Muller, ed., *Churchill as Peacemaker* (Washington, D.C.: Woodrow Wilson Center Press and Cambridge University Press, 1997), 217–218.

18. Gilbert, *Exile and Return*, 99.

19. Edwin Montagu letter to Lloyd George, October 4, 1917, quoted in Leonard Stein, *The Balfour Declaration* (New York: Simon & Schuster, 1961), 500; and in Feith, "Churchill, Palestine and Zionism, 1904–1922," 222.

20. Feith, "Churchill, Palestine and Zionism, 1904–1922," 223–224.

21. Stein, *The Balfour Declaration*, 543.

22. Gilbert, *Jerusalem in the Twentieth Century*, 96.

23. Bermant, *The Cousinhood*, 345.

24. Rashid Khalidi. *The Iron Cage: The Story of the Palestinian Struggle for Statehood* (Boston: Beacon Press, 2006), 63.

25. Ibid.

26. Elie Kedourie, "Sir Herbert Samuel and the Government of Palestine," in Elie Kedourie, *The Chatham House Version and Other Middle Eastern Studies* (Chicago: Ivan R. Dee, 1984), 62–63.

27. Philip Matter, *The Mufti of Jerusalem: Hajj-Amin al Husayni and the Palestinian National Movement* (New York: Columbia University Press, 1988), 25.

28. Elie Kedourie, "Sir Herbert Samuel and the Government of Palestine," 64–66.

29. William B. Ziff, *The Rape of Palestine* (New York: Longmans, Green & Co., 1938), 103.

30. Kedourie, "Sir Herbert Samuel and the Government of Palestine," 65.

31. Ibid., 63.

32. Ronald Storrs, *Orientations* (London: Ivor Nicholson and Watson, Limited, 1937), 23–24.

33. Kedourie, "Sir Herbert Samuel and the Government of Palestine," 63.

34. Conor Cruise O'Brien, *The Siege* (New York: Simon & Schuster, 1986), 160.

35. Martin Sieff, *The Politically Incorrect Guide to the Middle East* (Washington, D.C.: Regnery Publishing, 2008).

36. Colonel Richard Meinertzhagen, *Middle East Diary, 1917–1956* (London: Cresset Press, 1959), 97–98 (April 27, 1921, diary entry); also quoted in Feith, "Churchill, Palestine and Zionism, 1904–1922," 245–246.

37. Feith, "Churchill, Palestine and Zionism, 1904–1922," 244–245.

38. As Douglas Feith has noted, "These intrepid officials inconsistently asserted that the Arab community could be appeased after all, if Britain would limit Zionist activity—for example, by restricting Jewish immigration to and settlement of Palestine—and institutionalize Arab political power" by appointing radical Arab Palestinian leaders, such as al-Husseini, to positions of political authority. Ibid., 245.

39. Ibid., 235.

40. Wasserstein, *Herbert Samuel: A Political Life*, 249.

41. As Samuel's biographer Bernard Wasserstein has noted, when His Majesty's government replaced its military government in Palestine with a civilian administration headed by Samuel, "though the chief had changed, the administration's collective frame of mind—its prevailing lack of sympathy with the Balfour Declaration and the pro-Zionist policy of the Lloyd George government—remained intact." Ibid.

42. As Douglas Feith has so aptly described the relationship between Samuel and the anti-Zionist professional military and civilian subordinates on his staff, such

as Ernest Richmond, whose influence Samuel came under: "He [Samuel] supervised, but they led." Feith, "Churchill, Palestine and Zionism, 1904–1922," 235.

43. Ibid.

44. Kedourie, "Sir Herbert Samuel and the Government of Palestine," 53.

45. Feith, "Churchill, Palestine and Zionism, 1904–1922," 243.

46. Cooper, "Forgotten Palestinian," 7.

47. Bermant, *The Cousinhood*, 345.

48. Yossi Melman and Dan Raviv, *Behind the Uprising: Israelis, Jordanians and Palestinians* (Westport, CT: Greenwood Press, 1989), 30.

49. Ibid., 7–8.

50. Wasserstein, *Herbert Samuel: A Political Life*, 256.

51. Ibid., 257.

52. Matter, *The Mufti of Jerusalem*, 33.

53. Ibid., 35.

54. *Palestine: A Study of Jewish, Arab and British Policies* (New Haven: Yale University Press, 1947), 599.

55. Cooper, "Forgotten Palestinian," 8.

56. Gilbert, *Jerusalem in the Twentieth Century*, 120.

57. Maurice Pearlman, *Mufti of Jerusalem: The Story of Haj Amin El Husseini* (London: Victor Gollancz Ltd., 1947), 16.

58. Ibid.

59. *Palestine: A Study of Jewish, Arab and British Policies*, 609.

60. Cooper, "Forgotten Palestinian," 9.

61. Gilbert, *Jerusalem in the Twentieth Century*, 120.

62. Chaim Herzog, *Who Stands Accused?: Israel Answers Its Critics* (New York: Random House, 1978).

63. Cooper, "Forgotten Palestinian," 9.

64. Gilbert, *Jerusalem in the Twentieth Century*, 125.

65. Martin Gilbert, *Israel: A History* (New York: William Morrow & Co., 1998), 64.

66. Maurice Samuel, *What Happened in Palestine* (Boston: Stratford Company, 1929), 88–89.

67. One of the members of the Shaw commission, Lord Harry Snell, dissented from the commission report, submitting a minority statement challenging the report's exoneration of the mufti of responsibility for the 1929 riots. Snell believed that the commission should have been tougher on the mufti. "I therefore attribute to the Mufti," stated Lord Snell, "a greater share in the responsibility for the disturbances than is attributed to him in the report. I am of the opinion that the Mufti must bear the blame for his failure to make any effort to control the character of the agitation conducted in the name of a religion of which in Palestine he was the head." Ibid., 617.

68. Cooper, "Forgotten Palestinian," 9.

69. Gilbert, *Israel: A History*, 80.

70. Howard M. Sachar, *A History of Israel: From the Rise of Zionism to Our Time* (New York: Alfred A. Knopf, 1976), 200.

71. Ibid.

72. Ibid.

73. Cooper, "Forgotten Palestinian," 12.

74. Ibid.

75. Mathew Gutman, "Brothers in Arms," *Jerusalem Post*, November 4, 2004. Quoted in Steven Emerson, *Jihad Incorporated: A Guide to Militant Islam in the United States* (Amherst, NY: Prometheus Books, 2006), 238.

76. Quoted in ibid., 38.

77. Ibid.

78. John Roy Carlson, *Cairo to Damascus* (New York: Alfred A. Knopf, 1951), 92.

79. Ibid., 89–90.

80. Bernard Lewis, *The Crisis of Islam: Holy War and Unholy Terror* (New York: Random House, 2004), 76–77.

81. David Horowitz, *Unholy Alliance: Radical Islam and the American Left* (Washington, D.C.: Regnery Publishing, Inc., 2004), 124.

82. Sayyid Qutb, *Our Struggle with the Jews* (Saudi Arabia, 1970), 7. Quoted in Gabriel Schoenfeld, *The Return of Anti-Semitism* (San Francisco: Encounter Books, 2004), 41.

CHAPTER 3: PARTNERS IN GENOCIDE

1. Lewis, *The Crisis of Islam*, 59–60.

2. *The New York Times*, January 30, 1937; this *New York Times* quote is also cited in Joseph B. Schechtman, *The Mufti and the Fuhrer: The Rise and Fall of Haj-Amin el-Husseini* (New York: Thomas Yoseloff, 1965), 76–77.

3. Lewis, *Semites and Anti-Semites*, 148–149.

4. Quoted in ibid., 147–148.

5. In his response, the führer "took note with great interest of the statements made to him in the name of the King," thanked Farouk "for his confidential disclosures which the Ambassador communicated to him," and told the Egyptian king that he "gladly" anticipated "a closer cooperation with him." Freda Kirchwey et al., *The Record of Collaboration of King Farouk of Egypt with the Nazis and Their Ally, the Mufti: The Official Nazi Records of the King's Alliance and of the Mufti's Plans for Bombing Jerusalem and Tel Aviv—Memorandum Submitted to the United Nations* (New York: Nation Associates, 1948), 3. Sometime later, Farouk "actually promised to join the Axis forces, and gave his blessings to the betrayal of British military dispositions to the German forces engaged in the battle for Egypt." Cooper, "Forgotten Palestinian," 17.

6. Kirchwey et al., *Record of Collaboration*, 5.

7. Ibid., 5–6.

8. Cooper, "Forgotten Palestinian," 15; and David Storobin, "Nazi Roots of Palestinian Nationalism," *Think Israel* (January–February 2005), www.think-israel .org/storobin.nazis.html, 2.

9. Jon Meacham. *Franklin and Winston* (New York: Random House, 2003), 60.

10. George Michael, *The Enemy of My Enemy: The Alarming Convergence of Militant Islam and the Extreme Right* (Lawrence: University Press of Kansas, 2006), 114.

11. John Gunther, *Inside Asia* (New York: Harper & Brothers, 1939), 552; also quoted in Schechtman, *The Mufti and the Führer,* 84.

12. Lukasz Hirszowicz, *The Third Reich and the Arab East* (Toronto: University of Toronto Press, 1966), 109.

13. Ibid.

14. Morse, *The Nazi Connection to Islamic Terrorism,* 51.

15. Saul S. Friedman, *A History of the Holocaust* (London: Valentine Mitchell, 2004), 337.

16. Kenneth R. Timmerman, *The Death Lobby: How the West Armed Iraq* (Boston: Houghton Mifflin, 1991), 1.

17. Morse, *The Nazi Connection to Islamic Terrorism,* 54.

18. Martin Gilbert, *The Churchill War Papers,* vol. 3, 1941: *The Ever-Widening War* (London: William Heinemann, 2000), 1153.

19. Ibid., 1263.

20. Timmerman, *Preachers of Hate,* 106.

21. Michael Bar-Zohar and Eitan Haber, *The Quest for the Red Prince* (New York: William Morrow & Co., 1983), 49.

22. Ibid.

23. Daniel Carpi, *The Axis of Anti-Semitism* (Quebec, Canada: Dawn Publishing Company, Ltd., 1985), 9.

24. Matter, *The Mufti of Jerusalem;* and Carpi, *The Axis of Anti-Semitism,* 9.

25. Carpi, *The Axis of Anti-Semitism,* 9.

26. Bar-Zohar and Haber, *The Quest for the Red Prince,* 48–49.

27. Cooper, "Forgotten Palestinian," 18.

28. Lewis, *Semites and Anti-Semites,* 147.

29. Ronald J. Rychlak, "Hitler's Mufti: The Dark Legacy of Haj Amin al-Husseini," *Crisis* magazine, November 2005, 15.

30. Timmerman, *Preachers of Hate,* 107; Michael, *The Enemy of My Enemy,* 116; and

Norman Cameron and R. H. Steven, trans., *Hitler's Table Talk, 1941–1944* (New York: Enigma Books, 2000), 547.

31. Adolf Hitler, *Secret Conversations, 1941–1944*, 443–444. Quoted in Cooper, "Forgotten Palestinian," 17.

32. Rychlak, "Hitler's Mufti," 15.

33. Michael, *The Enemy of My Enemy*, 330.

34. Cooper, "Forgotten Palestinian," 17–18.

35. Rychlak, "Hitler's Mufti," 15.

36. Michael Bloch, *Ribbentrop* (New York: Crown, 1992), 204.

37. Speeches of His Eminence the Grand Mufti at the Protest Rally Against the Balfour Declaration on November 2, 1943, Islamisches Zentralinstitut, Berlin, Cooper, "Forgotten Palestinian," 23.

38. Freda Kirchwey et al., *The Arab Higher Committee, Its Origins, Personnel, and Purposes: The Documentary Record Submitted to the United Nations* (New York: Nation Associates, 1947).

39. Bloch, *Ribbentrop*, 401–402.

40. Cooper, "Forgotten Palestinian," 22.

41. Ibid., 21–22.

42. Ibid., 21.

43. Ibid.

44. Himmler's role as chief architect of the Final Solution is discussed and analyzed in much substantive detail in Richard Breitman, *Architect of Genocide: Himmler and the Final Solution* (New York: Alfred A. Knopf, 1991).

45. Cooper, "Forgotten Palestinian," 23.

46. Leo Heiman, "Eichmann and the Arabs," *Jewish Digest*, June 1961, 1.

47. Ibid., 160. As Peter Malkin and Harry Stein have documented, "In 1943 and 1944, accompanied by Eichmann, he [the mufti] had secretly inspected Treblinka, Majdanek and Auschwitz, closely questioning the guides on the workings of the facilities." Peter Z. Malkin and Harry Stein, *Eichmann in My Hands* (New York: Warner Books, 1990), 38.

48. Paul Longgrear and Raymond McNemar, "The Arab/Muslim Nazi Connection," *Canadian Friends* (International Christian Embassy, Jerusalem, 2003), www.cdn-friendsicej.ca/medigest/may00/arab.Nazi.html.

49. Cooper, "Forgotten Palestinian," 28.

50. *Jerusalem Post International Edition,* July 9, 1974, 5.

51. Rafael Medoff, "The Mufti's Nazi Years Re-examined," *Journal of Israeli History* 17, no. 3 (1996): 325.

52. Ibid.

53. Pearlman, *Mufti of Jerusalem,* 42–43.

54. Ibid., 43.

55. Ibid.

56. Ibid., 46.

57. Quoted in Richard Bonney, *Jihad: From Qur'an to bin Laden* (New York: Palgrave Macmillan, 2004), 276.

58. Pearlman, *Mufti of Jerusalem,* 49.

59. Cooper, "Forgotten Palestinian," 26; also quoted in Dennis Prager and Joseph Telushkin, *Why the Jews?: The Reason for Anti-Semitism* (New York: Simon & Schuster, 1983), 123; and in Timmerman, *Preachers of Hate,* 109–110.

60. Zvi Elpeleg, *The Grand Mufti: Haj Amin al-Hussaini, Founder of the Palestinian National Movement,* David Harvey, trans. (London: Frank Cass & Co., 1993), 179; this speech of al-Husseini's is also quoted in Timmerman, *Preachers of Hate,* 109; and in Pearlman, *Mufti of Jerusalem,* 51.

61. Timmerman, *Preachers of Hate,* 110.

62. Ibid.

63. Pearlman, *Mufti of Jerusalem,* 48.

64. Lewis, *Semites and Anti-Semites,* 157.

65. Pearlman, *Mufti of Jerusalem,* 68.

66. Ibid.

67. Cooper, "Forgotten Palestinian," 24.

68. Ibid., 21.

69. Michael, *The Enemy of My Enemy*, 117; the history of the Waffen-SS Handschar Division is discussed in much detail in George Lepre, *Himmler's Bosnian Division: The Waffen-SS Handschar Division, 1943–1945* (Arglen, PA: Schiffer Military History, 1997).

70. Quoted in Lepre, *Himmler's Bosnian Division*, 31–32.

71. Carl K. Savich, "Islam Under the Swastika: The Grand Mufti and the Nazi Protectorate of Bosnia-Hercegovina, 1941–1944," (online article, 2001), 9.

72. Cooper, "Forgotten Palestinian."

73. Kermit Roosevelt, "The Puzzle of Jerusalem's Mufti," *Saturday Evening Post*, August 28, 1948, 27.

74. Ibid., 27 and 165.

75. Michael, *The Enemy of My Enemy*, 117.

76. Timmerman, *Preachers of Hate*, 110.

77. Ibid.

78. Ibid., 111.

79. Quoted in Bonney, *Jihad: From Qur'an to bin Laden*, 275–276.

80. Edgar Answel Mowrer, "Official Documents Convict Mufti of Complicity in 6,000,000 Murders," *New York Post*, June 13, 1946, 2. Cited in Medoff, "The Mufti's Nazi Years Re-examined," 329.

81. Medoff, "The Mufti's Nazi Years Re-examined," 329. Eichmann himself, in his testimony at his own trial in 1961, also confirmed that the Nazis had "an agreement with the Grand Mufti" to prevent immigration to Palestine. Eichmann Trial Proceedings, Jerusalem, 1962, Session No. 58, 1053, cited in Medoff, "The Mufti's Nazi Years Re-examined."

82. Raul Hilberg, *The Destruction of the European Jews* (New York: Holmes & Meier, 1985), 504–505; also cited in Medoff, "The Mufti's Nazi Years Re-examined."

83. Lewis, *Semites and Anti-Semites*, 156.

84. Ibid.

85. Daniel Carpi, "The Diplomatic Negotiations over the Transfer of Jewish Children from Croatia to Turkey and Palestine in 1943," *Yad Vashem Studies* 12 (1977): 109–111; also cited in Medoff, "The Mufti's Nazi Years Re-examined," 330.

86. Cooper, "Forgotten Palestinian," 28.

87. Thomas Krumensackeer, "Nazis Planned Holocaust for Palestine Historians," *Washington Post*/Reuters, April 7, 2006.

88. Kirchwey et al., *The Record of Collaboration of King Farouk of Egypt*, 8.

89. Ibid.

90. Ibid.

91. Ibid.

92. Sir Martin Gilbert Archival Collection, the Churchill War Papers (London, England). We would like to thank Sir Martin Gilbert for making this material from his personal archival collection, relating to the Churchill War Papers, available to us.

93. Ibid.

94. Schechtman, *The Mufti and the Fuhrer*, 159.

95. Ibid., 159–160.

96. Ibid., 160.

97. Timmerman, *Preachers of Hate*, 112.

98. Schechtman, *The Mufti and the Fuhrer*, 152.

99. More recently, the Israeli historian Zvi Elpeleg has concluded that "it is impossible to estimate the extent of the consequences of Hajj Amin's efforts to prevent the exit of the Jews from countries under Nazi occupation, nor the number of those whose rescue was foiled and who consequently perished in the Holocaust." Elpeleg, *The Grand Mufti*, 72.

100. Bartley C. Crum, *Behind the Silken Curtain* (New York: Simon & Schuster, 1947), 109.

101. Ibid., 109–110.

102. Schechtman, *The Mufti and the Fuhrer*, 170–172; and Cooper, "Forgotten Palestinian," 30.

103. This was the statement of Hector McNeil, undersecretary for foreign affairs in the Attlee government, which is quoted in Schechtman, *The Mufti and the Fuhrer*, 172; also cited in Cooper, "Forgotten Palestinian."

104. Schechtman, *The Mufti and the Fuhrer*; and Cooper, "Forgotten Palestinian."

105. "Palestine" (editorial), *The Nation*, 165, no. 16 (October 18, 1947): 399.

106. The term *Hitler's Houdini* was first coined by Sir Martin Gilbert in conversation with the authors, in Washington, D.C., on March 22, 2007.

107. Larry Collins and Dominique Lapierre, *O Jerusalem* (New York: Simon & Schuster, 1972), 54.

108. Cooper, "Forgotten Palestinian," 30.

CHAPTER 4: THE MUFTI'S REFLECTION

1. While the mufti's imagined scenario is indeed counterfactual, the footnotes in this section are authentic, establishing the historical basis for all the counterfactual events recounted.

2. William L. Shirer, "If Hitler Had Won World War II," *Look* magazine, December 19, 1961, 30.

3. Ibid.

4. David Fromkin, "Triumph of the Dictators," in Robert Cowley, ed., *What If?: The World's Foremost Military Historians Imagine What Might Have Been* (New York: Berkley Books, 2000), 308.

5. Shirer, "If Hitler Had Won World War II," 30.

6. John Keegan, "How Hitler Could Have Won the War," in Cowley, ed., *What If?*, 297 and 301.

7. Ibid., 295.

8. Fromkin, "Triumph of the Dictators," 308.

9. This is a point made by the military historian David Fromkin in "Triumph of the Dictators."

10. Gilbert, *Jerusalem in the Twentieth Century,* 162.

11. Bevin Alexander, *How Hitler Could Have Won World War II: The Fatal Errors That Led to Nazi Defeat* (New York: Three Rivers Press, 2000), 141.

12. Michael Lee Lanning, "El Alamein," in Michael Lee Lanning, *The Battle 100: The Stories Behind History's Most Influential Battles* (Naperville, IL: Sourcebooks, Inc., 2003), 243.

13. Ibid.

14. This was, of course, a counterfactual scenario imagined by al-Husseini. In fact, Axis losses at El Alamein totaled twenty thousand casualties and thirty thousand prisoners, with all of the Axis tanks and artillery being destroyed or captured. Lanning, *The Battle 100.*

15. This was also a counterfactual account, imagined by al-Husseini, of what Winston Churchill had said. In fact, Churchill had later remarked: "Before Alamein we never had a victory. After Alamein we never had a defeat." (Lanning, *The Battle 100,* 242.) As Wendell L. Willkie said, in his book *One World,* "Had the British lost [the Battle of El Alamein], Rommel would have been in Cairo in a few days." (Wendell Willkie, *One World* [New York: Simon & Schuster, 1943], 5.) And so Rommel was.

16. Peter G. Tsouras, "Operation ORIENT Joint Axis Strategy," in Kenneth Macksey, ed., *The Hitler Options: Alternate Decisions of World War II* (London: Wren's Park Publishing, 2000), 98.

17. Ibid.

18. The mufti actually used this precise quote in a radio address, broadcast over Berlin radio, on March 1, 1944. Elpeleg, *The Grand Mufti,* 179.

19. Ibid.

20. Gilbert, *Jerusalem in the Twentieth Century,* 210.

21. Thomas Krumenacker, "Nazis Planned Holocaust for Palestine," *Washingtonpost.com,* April 7, 2006; Krumenacker's article reports new evidence about the Nazi plans for the extermination of the Jews of Palestine, based on a recent study completed by German historians Klaus-Michael Mallman and Martin Cueppers of Stuttgart University.

22. Ibid.

23. Ibid.

24. In 1922, Beatrice Webb, wife of the British Labor Party leader Lord Passfield, had referred to Mosley, then a Labor Party member of Parliament, as "the perfect politician" and "the most brilliant man in the House of Commons." (Colin Cross, *The Fascists in Britain* [New York: St. Martin's Press, 1963], 17.) Throughout the 1920s, she and many others in England assumed that Mosley would one day become prime minister. This assumption was shared by some, even after Mosley had founded his Union of British Fascists and achieved notoriety as the "Führer of British Fascism." Indeed, the British Labour Party leader Hugh Dalton recalls in his memoirs how Winston Churchill as prime minister in 1940 told his first ministerial meeting that "if the Germans won the war, they would make Britain a slave state under Mosley. . . ." (Cross, *The Fascists in Britain*, 13–14.)

25. Ian Kershaw, *Making Friends with Hitler: Lord Londonderry, the Nazis and the Road to War* (New York: Penguin Books, 2005), xvii.

26. Shirer, "If Hitler Had Won World War II," 29.

27. This is a point noted by William L. Shirer in his article "If Hitler Had Won World War II," 28.

28. Ibid.

29. See, for example, the recent book by the British journalist Melanie Phillips, *Londonistan* (New York: Encounter Books, 2006).

30. The mufti's prediction did, in fact, come true. As British editor and columnist Daniel Johnson has recently noted, in 2006 "London, with over 1000 mosques," was "already Europe's unofficial Muslim capital." (Daniel Johnson, "Allah's England?," *Commentary* 122, no. 4 [November 2006]: 46.)

CHAPTER 5: THE MUFTI'S RETURN TO THE MIDDLE EAST

1. Elpeleg, *The Grand Mufti*, 76.

2. Ibid., 75.

3. Ibid.

4. Roosevelt, "The Puzzle of Jerusalem's Mufti," 26.

5. Elpeleg, *The Grand Mufti*, 77.

6. Ibid., 78.

7. Ibid.

8. Efraim Karsh, *Arafat's War: The Man and His Battle for Israeli Conquest* (New York: Grove Press, 2003), 10.

9. "The Arab Higher Committee of Palestine," 1.

10. Cooper, "Forgotten Palestinian," 30.

11. *Palestine: A Study of Jewish, Arab and British Policies*, 1214.

12. Gilbert, *Jerusalem in the Twentieth Century*, 198.

13. Izzat Tannous, *The Palestinians* (New York: I. G. T. Company, 1988), 656.

14. Melman and Raviv, *Behind the Uprising: Israelis, Jordanians and Palestinians*, 35. King Abdullah wrote to a friend in October 1947, "The Mufti and [Syrian president] Kuwatly want to set up an independent Arab state in Palestine with the Mufti as its head. If that were to happen, I would be encircled on almost all sides by enemies." (Quoted in Melman and Raviv, *Behind the Uprising: Israelis, Jordanians and Palestinians.*)

15. Helena Cobban, *The Palestine Liberation Organization* (Cambridge: Cambridge University Press, 1984), 8.

16. Arnold Forster and Benjamin R. Epstein, *The New Anti-Semitism* (New York: McGraw-Hill Book Company, 1974), 160.

17. Cooper, "Forgotten Palestinian," 36.

18. Anwar Al Sadat, *Revolt on the Nile* (New York: John Day Company, 1957), 51–57.

19. Anwar Al Sadat, "Letter to Hitler," *Al-Mussawar*, no. 1510, September 18, 1953, reprinted in D. F. Green, ed., *Arab Theologians on Jews and Israel* (Geneva: Editions de l'Avenir, 1976), 87. Sadat's letter to Hitler is also cited in Lewis, *The Crisis of Islam*, 60.

20. Anwar Al Sadat, "Speech at the El Hussein Mosque Celebrating the Birthday of the Prophet Muhammad," broadcast on Radio Cairo, April 25, 1972, in Green, ed., *Arab Theologians on Jews and Israel*, 90 and 91.

21. Cooper, "Forgotten Palestinian," 37.

22. Ibid.

23. Ibid.

24. Ibid., 8.

25. Timmerman, *The Death Lobby: How the West Armed Iraq,* 109.

26. Ibid.

27. Ibid.

28. Robert S. Wistrich, "The Old-New Anti-Semitism," in Ron Rosenbaum, ed., *Those Who Forget the Past: The Question of Anti-Semitism* (New York: Random House, 2004), 84.

29. Ibid.

30. Efraim Karsh and Inari Rautsi, *Saddam Hussein: A Political Biography* (London: Brassey's, 1991), 25.

31. Ibid., 34.

32. Ibid., 135–136.

33. Taysir Jbara, *Palestinian Leader Hajj Amin al-Husayni: Mufti of Jerusalem* (Princeton, NJ: Kingston Press, 1985), 191.

34. Yoav Gelber, *Palestine 1948* (Portland, OR: Sussex Academic Press, 2001), 16.

35. Ibid.

36. Collins and Lapierre, *O Jerusalem,* 407.

37. Freda Kirchwey, et al., *The Palestine Problem and Proposals for Its Solution: Memorandum Submitted to the General Assembly of the United Nations* (New York: Nation Associates, April 1947), 54.

38. Ibid., 53–54.

39. Dershowitz, *The Case for Israel,* 76.

40. Benny Morris, *1948 and After: Israel and the Palestinians* (Oxford: Oxford University Press, 1994), 219; also cited in Dershowitz, *The Case for Israel.*

41. Collins and Lapierre, *O Jerusalem,* 340.

42. Dershowitz, *The Case for Israel,* 80.

43. Ibid.

44. Ibid., 81; and Collins and Lapierre, *O Jerusalem*, 408.

45. Ibid.

46. Gilbert, *Israel: A History*, 274.

47. Collins and Lapierre, *O Jerusalem*, 82.

48. Gilbert, *Israel: A History*, 274.

49. Ibid.

50. Elpeleg, *The Grand Mufti*, 125.

51. Gilbert, *Israel: A History*, 274.

52. Elpeleg, *The Grant Mufti*, 126.

53. Lewis, *The Crisis of Islam*, 78–79.

54. Ibid., 79.

55. Yehudit Barsky, *Hamas, Islamic Jihad and the Muslim Brotherhood: Islamic Extremists and the Terrorist Threat to America*, an ADL Special Background Report (New York: Anti-Defamation League of B'nai B'rith, 1993), 5.

56. Dinesh D'Souza, "Osama's Brain: Meet Sayyid Qutb," *Weekly Standard*, April 29, 2002, 16.

57. Timmerman, *Preachers of Hate*, 121.

58. Ibid., 50.

59. Ayatollah Khomeini, "Programme for the Establishment of an Islamic Government," in Ayatollah Khomeini, *Islam and Revolution: Writings and Declarations of Imam Khomeini* (Berkeley: University of California Press, 1981), 127. Quoted in Robert S. Wistrich, *Anti-Semitism: The Longest Hatred* (New York: Schocken Books, 1991), 219; and Phillips, *Londonistan*.

60. The reasons for his move from Cairo to Beirut are discussed in Jbara, *Palestinian Leader Hajj Amin al-Husayni: Mufti of Jerusalem*, 190.

61. Bernard Lewis, *Semites and Anti-Semites*, 157.

62. *The New York Times*, March 28, 1964.

63. Cobban, *The Palestine Liberation Organization*, 31.

64. Elpeleg, *The Grand Mufti*, 151.

65. *Frankfurter Allgemeine Zeitung*, June 15, 1974.

66. Janet and John Wallach, *Arafat* (Secaucus, NJ: Carol Publishing Group, 1997), 280.

67. Elpeleg, *The Grand Mufti*, 162.

68. Ibid.

69. Issa Naklel, *Encyclopedia of the Palestine Problem*, vol. II (New York: Interconti-nental Books, 1991), caption under first photo page.

70. Itamar Marcus, "Nazi Ally, Hajj Amin al-Husseini, Is Arafat's 'Hero,' " *Israel Report*, August 2002.

71. Quoted in Carlson, *Cairo to Damascus*, 413–414.

CHAPTER 6: MANDATE FOR HATE

1. Lewis, *Semites and Anti-Semites*, 256; and quoted in Schoenfeld, *The Return of Anti-Semitism*, 24.

2. As Abraham H. Foxman has put it, "As descendants of those who distorted God's truth and opposed his Prophet, Jews would rightly be humbled before Mus-lims." (Foxman, *Never Again?*, 197.)

3. Timmerman, *Preachers of Hate*, 81.

4. Ibid., 78–79 and 81.

5. Gerber, "Anti-Semitism in the Muslim World," 78.

6. Ibid., 99. As Abraham H. Foxman has noted, while Jews were permitted to live in Muslim lands as *dhimmis*, and were often free to practice their religion, they were always "subject to the humiliation of second-class status." (Foxman, *Never Again?*, 196.)

7. Prager and Telushkin, *Why the Jews?*, 117–118.

8. Foxman, *Never Again?*, 197.

9. Timmerman, *Preachers of Hate*, 100.

10. Wistrich, *Anti-Semitism: The Longest Hatred*, 205.

11. Ibid., 205–206.

12. Timmerman, *Preachers of Hate,* 100.

13. Wistrich, *Anti-Semitism: The Longest Hatred,* 205.

14. Timmerman, *Preachers of Hate,* 101.

15. Ibid.

16. Yehoshafat Harkabi, "On Arab Antisemitism Once More," in Shmuel Almog, ed., *Anti-Semitism Through the Ages* (New York: Pergamon Press, 1988), 231.

17. Bernard Lewis, *The Jews of Islam* (Princeton, NJ: Princeton University Press, 1984), 185; and Lewis, *Semites and Anti-Semites,* 208.

18. Lewis, *Semites and Anti-Semites,* 208.

19. Quoted in Prager and Telushkin, *Why the Jews?,* 125.

20. Gerald Posner, *Secrets of the Kingdom: The Inside Story of the Saudi-U.S. Connection* (New York: Random House, 2005), 45. As Posner has noted, foreign diplomats and titans of industry, whenever they had an audience with the king, "were accustomed to hearing at least a thirty-minute monologue on the evils of Jews and how their Zionist plots were about to destroy the world."

21. Ibid.; and Wistrich, *Anti-Semitism: The Longest Hatred,* 233.

22. Prager and Telushkin, *Why the Jews?,* 125.

23. Alan Dershowitz, *The Case for Israel,* 106, citing Article 32 of the Hamas covenant, which is found in Khaled Haroub, *Hamas: Political Thought and Practice* (Washington, D.C.: Institute for Palestine Studies, 2000), 288.

24. David G. Dalin, *The Myth of Hitler's Pope* (Washington, D.C.: Regnery Publishing, 2005), 142.

25. Alvin H. Rosenfeld, *"Progressive" Jewish Thought and the New Anti-Semitism* (New York: American Jewish Committee, 2006), 2.

26. Ibid., 158–159.

27. Forster and Epstein, *The New Anti-Semitism,* 159.

28. Foxman, *Never Again?,* 198.

29. Forster and Epstein, *The New Anti-Semitism,* 159–160.

30. Ibid., 2.

31. Bernard Lewis, "Muslim Anti-Semitism," in Rosenbaum, ed., *Those Who Forget the Past*, 558.

32. Norman A. Stillman, "Anti-Semitism in the Contemporary Arab World," in Michael Curtis, ed., *Anti-Semitism in the Contemporary World* (Boulder, CO: Westview Press, 1986), 74.

33. Wistrich, *Anti-Semitism: The Longest Hatred*, 235.

34. Prager and Telushkin, *Why the Jews?*, 124.

35. Foxman, *Never Again?*, 213. As the Islamic scholar Norman Stillman has noted, "One of the most disturbing features of the anti-Semitism now current in the Arab world is the ubiquity of the Blood Libel, and of the matter-of-fact discussions of Jewish ritual murder, some of which 'dwell upon it at great length and in morbid detail,' in ostensibly scholarly works by Egyptian and other Muslim writers." (Stillman, "Anti-Semitism in the Contemporary Arab World," 79.)

36. Ibid.; and Wistrich, *Anti-Semitism: The Longest Hatred*, 235.

37. Stillman, "Anti-Semitism in the Contemporary Arab World."

38. Foxman, *Never Again?*, 213.

39. Robert S. Wistrich, "Islamic Judeophobia: An Existential Threat," in David Bukay, ed., *Muhammad's Monsters: A Comprehensive Guide to Radical Islam for Western Audiences* (Green Forest, AZ: Balfour Books, 2004), 202.

40. Wistrich, "Islamic Judeophobia," 202–203.

41. Quoted in Phillips, *Londonistan*, 111.

42. Prager and Telushkin, *Why The Jews?*, 124–125.

43. Foxman, *Never Again?*, 213.

44. Cited in Prager and Telushkin, *Why the Jews?*, 125.

45. Foxman, *Never Again?*, 213.

46. Quoted in Timmerman, *Preachers of Hate*, 71.

47. Foxman, *Never Again?*, 213–214.

48. This conference is discussed in Paul Eidelberg, "A War America Can't Win," *Jewish Press,* October 5, 2001.

49. Green, ed., *Arab Theologians on Jews and Israel.*

50. Eidelberg, "A War America Can't Win."

51. Ibid.

52. Ibid.

53. Hassan Khaled, "Jihad in the Cause of Allah," in Green, ed., *Arab Theologians on Jews and Israel,* 68.

54. Timmerman, *Preachers of Hate,* 88; and Wistrich, "Islamic Judeophobia," 207.

55. Deborah Lipstadt, *Denying the Holocaust* (New York: Plume, 1993), 14; Lipstadt's statement is also quoted in Timmerman, *Preachers of Hate,* 88.

56. Timmerman, *Preachers of Hate.*

57. Lipstadt, *Denying the Holocaust,* 14. Quoted in Timmerman, *Preachers of Hate,* 88–89.

58. *Hitler's Apologists: The Anti-Semitic Propaganda of Holocaust "Revisionism"* (New York: Anti-Defamation League of B'nai B'rith, 1993), 60.

59. Wistrich, *Anti-Semitism: The Longest Hatred,* 233–234.

60. Robert Satloff, *Among the Righteous: Lost Stories from the Holocaust's Long Reach into Arab Lands* (New York: Public Affairs, 2006), 163.

61. Rafael Medoff, "Palestinians May Get a Holocaust Denier as First Prime Minister," *Jewish Bulletin of Northern California,* February 21, 2003, 19.

62. Timmerman, *Preachers of Hate,* 88; and Dalin, *The Myth of Hitler's Pope,* 244–245.

63. Medoff, "Palestinians May Get a Holocaust Denier as First Prime Minister."

64. Satloff, *Among the Righteous,* 164.

65. Quoted in ibid.

66. Ibid., 165.

67. Interview with Mahmoud Abbas by Nahum Barnea and Ronny Shaked in *Yediot Aharonot,* May 30, 2003, as cited in Timmerman, *Preachers of Hate,* 89.

68. In 1982, Issa Nakhleh published an article in *Journal of Historical Review*, a publication devoted to Holocaust denial. (Issa Nakhleh, "Memorandum to the President," *Journal of Historical Review*, 3, no. 3 [Fall 1982].)

69. *A Memorandum Submitted to the Summit Meeting at Camp David by Issa Nakhleh, Chairman of the Palestine Arab Delegation and Permanent Representative of the Arab Higher Committee for Palestine* (New York: Palestine Arab Delegation, 1978), 27.

70. Timmerman, *Preachers of Hate*, 89.

71. Ibid.

72. Muhammad Kheir al-Wadi, "The Plague of the Third Millennium," *Teshreen*, January 31, 2000. Quoted in Timmerman, *Preachers of Hate*, 93.

73. Ibid.

74. Ibid. 90.

75. Ibid., 89–90.

76. Quoted in Wistrich, "Islamic Judeophobia," 209.

77. *The New York Times*, March 26, 2000. Quoted in Wistrich, "Islamic Judeophobia."

78. Dalin. *The Myth of Hitler's Pope*, 154.

79. Ibid. Quoted in Wistrich, "Islamic Judeophobia," 218, footnote 70.

80. Timmerman, *Preachers of Hate*, 94.

81. Ibid.

82. Ibid.

83 Foxman, *Never Again?*, 222–223.

84. Ibid., 223.

85. Ibid.

86. Ibid., 223–224.

87. Ibid., 218, footnote 69.

88. Quoted in the *Jerusalem Post*, April 15, 2001; and in Wistrich, "Islamic Judeophobia," 208–209.

89. *Jerusalem Post,* August 28, 2002.

90. Quoted in Phillips, *Londonistan,* 111.

91. "Holocaust Denial," *Wikipedia,* en.wikipedia.org/wiki/Holocaust_denial, 12.

92. Ibid.

93. Elie Wiesel, "International Community Must Shut Out Ahmadinejad," *Palm Beach Jewish Journal,* December 12, 2006, 25.

94. Ibid.

95. Nazila Fathi, "World's Holocaust Cynics Get Their Chance to Vent: Ex-KKK Leader Duke a Speaker at Caucus in Iran," *San Francisco Chronicle,* December 12, 2006, A19.

96. Matthias Kuntzel, "Iran's Obsession with the Jews: Denying the Holocaust, Desiring Another One," *The Weekly Standard,* February 19, 2007, 18.

97. "Iran Hosts Anti-Semitic Hatefest in Tehran: About the Conference" (New York: Anti-Defamation League of B'nai B'rith, December 21, 2006), 1, www.adl .org/main_International_Affairs/iran_holocaust_conference.htm.

98. Orly Halpern, "Iran Denies Visa to an Arab Shoah Scholar," *Forward,* December 15, 2006, A11.

CHAPTER 7: THE MUFTI'S LEGACY

1. Lewis, *The Crisis of Islam,* 156.

2. Foxman, *Never Again?,* 216.

3. Wistrich, "Islamic Judeophobia," 196.

4. Timmerman, *Preachers of Hate,* 164.

5. Wistrich, "Islamic Judeophobia," 198.

6. Ibid.

7. Ibid., 156–157.

8. Ibid., 198.

9. Ibid.

10. Jonathan Rosen, "The Uncomfortable Question of Anti-Semitism," in Rosenbaum, ed., *Those Who Forget the Past,* 5.

11. Ibid.

12. Wistrich, "Islamic Judeophobia," 199–200.

13. Niall Ferguson, "Clashing Civilizations or Mad Mullahs: The United States Between Informal and Formal Empire," in Strobe Talbott and Nayan Chanda, eds., *The Age of Terror: America and the World After September 11* (New York: Basic Books, 2001), 116.

14. Bonney, *Jihad: From Qur'an to bin Laden,* 272.

15. Ibid., 272–273.

16. Haj Amin al-Husseini, "Summons to a Holy War Against Britain: A 'Fatwa' Issued by Haj Amin al-Husseini, May 1941," reprinted in Joan Peters, *From Time Immemorial: The Origins of the Arab-Israeli Conflict over Palestine* (New York: Harper & Row, 1984), 435–436.

17. Pearlman, *Mufti of Jerusalem,* 49.

18. Quoted in Prager and Telushkin, *Why the Jews?,* 123; and in Timmerman, *Preachers of Hate,* 109–110.

19. Bonney, *Jihad: From Qur'an to bin Laden,* 276.

20. Ibid., xiii.

21. Ibid., 17.

22. These fatwas of bin Laden's are quoted and discussed in more detail in Peter L. Bergen, *Holy War, Inc.: Inside the Secret World of Osama bin Laden* (New York: Simon & Schuster, 2002), 96–99.

23. As Efraim Karsh has pointed out, Arafat's Fatah group was originally established in the late 1950s as the Movement for the Liberation of Palestine (*Harakat Tahrir Filastin*), its Arabic acronym reversed from Hataf ("death") to Fatah to match the Koranic word for "conquest." (Karsh, *Arafat's War,* 23.)

24. Ibid.

25. Benjamin Netanyahu, "Ending the Legacy of Hate," address delivered at a session called "The Question of Palestine" at the Fortieth General Assembly of the United Nations, December 4, 1985, 6.

26. Ibid.

27. Ibid.

28. Ibid.

29. Ibid.

30. Dalin, *The Myth of Hitler's Pope,* 154.

31. Timmerman, *Preachers of Hate,* 213.

32. "PA's Abbas Calls for the Murder of Jews," press release, Zionist Organization of America, January 12, 2007.

33. Ibid.

34. Ibid.

35. Alan Dershowitz, "Arafat Died an Uncontrite Terrorist," *Forward,* November 19, 2004, 9.

36. Hamas covenant, Articles 22 and 7, in Khaled Haroub, *Hamas: Political Thought and Practice* (Washington, D.C.: Institute for Palestine Studies, 2000), 271 and 281–282; and quoted in Phillips, *Londonistan,* 109.

37. Barsky, *Hamas, Islamic Jihad and the Muslim Brotherhood,* 5.

38. Hamas pamphlet quoted in *The Wall Street Journal,* December 18, 1992.

39. Ibid.

40. Albert Speer, *Spandau: The Secret Diaries* (New York: Macmillan, 1976), 80.

Bibliography

Aburish, Said K. *Arafat: From Defender to Dictator*. New York: Bloomsbury, 1998.

Alexander, Bevin. *How Hitler Could Have Won World War II: The Fatal Errors That Led to Nazi Defeat*. New York: Three Rivers Press, 2000.

Alfassa, Shelomo. *Reference Guide to the Nazis and the Arabs During the Holocaust*. New York: International Sephardic Leadership Council, 2006.

Almog, Shmuel, ed. *Anti-Semitism Through the Ages*. New York: Pergamon Press, 1988.

Alon, Dafna. *Arab Radicalism*. Jerusalem: Israeli Economist, 1969.

Alpern, Sara. *Freda Kirchwey: A Woman of the Nation*. Cambridge, MA: Harvard University Press, 1987.

AlRoy, Gil Carl. *Attitudes Toward Jewish Statehood in the Arab World*. New York: American Academic Association for Peace in the Middle East, 1971.

Bar, Shmuel. *Warrant for Terror: The Fatwas of Radical Islam and the Duty of Jihad.*

Stanford, CA: Hoover Institution, Stanford University; and Lanham, MD: Rowman & Littlefield Publishers, 2006.

Barsky, Yehudit. *Hamas, Islamic Jihad and the Muslim Brotherhood: Islamic Extremists and the Terrorist Threat to America,* an ADL Special Background Report. New York: Anti-Defamation League of B'nai B'rith, 1993.

Bar-Zohar, Michael, and Eitan Haber. *The Quest for the Red Prince.* New York: William Morrow & Co., 1983.

Becker, Jillian. *The PLO—The Rise and Fall of the Palestine Liberation Organization.* London: Weidenfeld & Nicolson, 1984.

Ben-Dor, Gabriel, ed. *The Palestinians and the Middle East Conflict.* London: Turtledove Publishing, 1979.

Bergen, Peter L. *Holy War Inc.: Inside the Secret World of Osama bin Laden.* New York: Simon & Schuster, 2002.

Berger, David, ed. *History and Hate: Dimensions of Anti-Semitism.* Philadelphia: Jewish Publication Society, 1986.

Bermant, Chaim. *The Cousinhood: The Anglo-Jewish Gentry.* London: Eyre & Spottiswoode, 1971.

Bloch, Michael. *Ribbentrop: A Biography.* New York: Crown, 1992.

Bonney, Richard. *Jihad: From Qur'an to bin Laden.* New York: Palgrave Macmillan, 2004.

Breitman, Richard. *Architect of Genocide: Himmler and the Final Solution.* New York: Alfred A. Knopf, 1991.

Bukay, David, ed. *Muhammad's Monsters: A Comprehensive Guide to Radical Islam for Western Audiences.* Green Forest, AZ: Balfour Books, 2004.

Cameron, Norman, and R. H. Steven, trans. *Hitler's Table Talk, 1941–1944.* New York: Enigma Books, 2000.

Carlson, John Roy. *Cairo to Damascus.* New York: Alfred A. Knopf, 1951.

Carpi, Daniel. "The Diplomatic Negotiations over the Transfer of Jewish Children from Croatia to Turkey and Palestine in 1943." *Yad Vashem Studies* 12 (1977): 109–121.

———. "The Mufti of Jerusalem, Amin el-Husseini, and His Diplomatic Activity During World War II." *Studies in Zionism* VII (Spring 1983): 101–131.

———. *The Axis of Anti-Semitism.* Quebec, Canada: La Compagnie de Publication Aube Ltée., Dawn Publishing Company, Ltd., 1985.

Catherwood, Christopher. *A Brief History of the Middle East: From Abraham to Arafat.* New York: Carroll & Graf Publishers, 2006.

Cobban, Helen. *The Palestine Liberation Organization.* Cambridge: Cambridge University Press, 1984.

Collins, Larry, and Dominique Lapierre. *O Jerusalem.* New York: Simon & Schuster, 1972.

Cooper, Elias. "Forgotten Palestinian: The Nazi Mufti." *American Zionist* LXVIII, no. 4 (March–April 1978): 5–37.

Cowley, Robert, ed. *What If?: The World's Foremost Military Historians Imagine What Might Have Been.* New York: Berkley Books, 2000.

Cross, Colin. *The Fascists in Britain.* New York: St. Martin's Press, 1963.

Crum, Bartley. *Behind the Silken Curtain.* New York: Simon & Schuster, 1947.

Curtis, Michael, ed. *Anti-Semitism in the Contemporary World.* Boulder, CO: Westview Press, 1986.

Curtis, Michael, Joseph Neyer, Chaim I. Waxman, and Allen Pollack, eds. *The Palestinians: People, History, Politics.* New Brunswick, NJ: Transaction Books, 1975.

D'Souza, Dinesh. "Osama's Brain: Meet Sayyid Qutb." *Weekly Standard,* April 29, 2002.

———. *The Enemy at Home: The Cultural Left and the Responsibility for 9/11.* New York: Doubleday, 2007.

Dalin, David G. "Hitler's Mufti." *First Things* 155 (August–September 2005): 14–16.

———. *The Myth of Hitler's Pope.* Washington, D.C.: Regnery Publishing, 2005.

Dershowitz, Alan M. *Why Terrorism Works.* New Haven: Yale University Press, 2002.

———. *The Case for Israel.* Hoboken, NJ: John Wiley & Sons, 2003.

———. "Arafat Died an Uncontrite Terrorist." *Forward,* November 19, 2004, 9.

———. *The Case for Peace: How the Arab-Israeli Conflict Can Be Resolved.* Hoboken, NJ: John Wiley & Sons, 2005.

Eidelberg, Paul. "A War America Can't Win." *Jewish Press,* October 5, 2001.

Elath, Eliyahu. *Haj Muhammad Amin al-Husseini: The Former Mufti of Jerusalem—His Personality and Stages of His Rise to Power.* Jerusalem: Office of the Prime Minister, Bureau of the Advisor of Arab Affairs, 1968.

Elpeleg, Zvi. *The Grand Mufti: Haj Amin al-Hussaini, Founder of the Palestinian National Movement.* David Harvey, trans. London: Frank Cass & Co., 1993.

El-Sadat, Anwar. *In Search of Identity: An Autobiography.* New York: Harper & Row, 1977.

Emerson, Steven. *Jihad Incorporated: A Guide to Militant Islam in the United States.* Amherst, NY: Prometheus Books, 2006.

Fathi, Nazila. "World's Holocaust Cynics Get Their Chance to Vent: Ex-KKK Leader Duke a Speaker at Caucus in Iran." *San Francisco Chronicle,* December 12, 2006, A19.

Feith, Douglas J. "Churchill, Palestine and Zionism, 1904–1922." In James W. Muller, ed. *Churchill as Peacemaker.* Washington, D.C.: Woodrow Wilson Center Press and Cambridge University Press, 1997.

Ferguson, Niall. "Clashing Civilizations or Mad Mullahs: The United States Between Informal and Formal Empire." In Strobe Talbot and Nayan Chanda, eds. *The Age of Terror: America and the World After September 11.* New York: Basic Books, 2001.

Fest, Joachim. *Speer: The Final Verdict.* Orlando, FL: Harcourt, 1999.

Fischer-Weth, Kurt. *Amin al-Husseini, Grand Mufti of Jerusalem.* Berlin-Friedenau: Walter Titz Publishers, 1943.

Forster, Arnold, and Benjamin R. Epstein. *The New Anti-Semitism.* New York: McGraw-Hill Book Company, 1974.

Foxman, Abraham. *Never Again?: The Threat of the New Anti-Semitism.* New York: HarperCollins Publishers, 2003.

Frangi, Abdallah. *The PLO and Palestine.* London: Zed Books, 1983.

Friedman, Saul S. *A History of the Holocaust.* London: Valentine Mitchell, 2004.

Fromkin, David. *A Peace to End All Peace: The Fall of the Ottoman Empire and the Creation of the Modern Middle East.* New York: Henry Holt & Co., 1989.

——. "Triumph of the Dictators." In Robert Cowley, ed. *What If?: The World's Foremost Military Historians Imagine What Might Have Been.* New York: Berkley Books, 2000.

Gelber, Yoav. *Palestine 1948.* Portland, OR: Sussex Academic Press, 2001.

Gellner, Charles R. *The Palestine Problem: An Analysis Historical and Contemporary.* Washington, D.C.: Library of Congress Legislative Reference Service, Public Affairs Bulletin no. 50, 1947.

Gerber, Jane S. "Anti-Semitism in the Muslim World." In David Berger, ed. *History and Hate: Dimensions of Anti-Semitism.* Philadelphia: Jewish Publication Society, 1986.

Gilbert, Martin. *Exile and Return: The Struggle for a Jewish Homeland.* Philadelphia: J.B. Lippincott, 1978.

——. *Jerusalem in the Twentieth Century.* New York: John Wiley & Sons, 1996.

——. *Israel: A History.* New York: William Morrow & Co., 1998.

——. *The Churchill War Papers*, vol. 3, 1941: *The Ever-Widening War.* London: William Heinemann, 2000.

——. *Churchill and the Jews.* New York: Henry Holt & Co., 2007.

——. Private Archival Collection, the Churchill War Papers.

Gold, Dore. *The Fight for Jerusalem: Radical Islam, the West and the Future of the Holy City.* Washington, D.C.: Regnery Publishing, 2007.

Gowers, Andrew. *Behind the Myth: Yasser Arafat and the Palestinian Revolution.* New York: Olive Branch Press, 1992.

Green, D. F., ed. *Arab Theologians on Jews and Israel.* Geneva: Editions de l'Avenir, 1976.

Gunther, John. *Inside Asia.* New York: Harper & Brothers, 1939.

Gutman, Mathew. "Brothers in Arms." *Jerusalem Post,* November 4, 2004.

Halpern, Orly. "Iran Denies Visa to an Arab Shoah Scholar." *Forward,* December 15, 2006, A11.

Harkabi, Yehoshafat. *Arab Attitudes to Israel.* Jerusalem: KETER Publishing House, 1972.

———. *Palestinians and Israel.* Jerusalem: KETER Publishing, 1974.

———. *Arab Strategies and Israel's Responses.* New York: Free Press, 1977.

———. *The Palestinian Covenant and Its Meaning.* London: Valentine Mitchell, 1979.

———. "On Arab Antisemitism Once More." In Shmuel Almog, ed. *Anti-Semitism Through the Ages.* New York: Pergamon Press, 1988.

Haroub, Khaled. *Hamas: Political Thought and Practice.* Washington, D.C.: Institute for Palestine Studies, 2000.

Heiman, Leo. "Eichmann and the Arabs." *Jewish Digest,* June 1961.

Herzog, Chaim. *Who Stands Accused?: Israel Answers Its Critics.* New York: Random House, 1978.

Hilberg, Raul. *The Destruction of the European Jews.* New York: Holmes & Meier, 1985.

Hirszowicz, Lukasz. *The Third Reich and the Arab East.* Toronto: University of Toronto Press, 1966.

Hitler's Apologists: The Anti-Semitic Propaganda of Holocaust "Revisionism." New York: Anti-Defamation League of B'nai B'rith, 1993.

Horowitz, David. *Unholy Alliance: Radical Islam and the American Left.* Washington, D.C.: Regnery Publishing, 2004.

Huntington, Samuel P. *The Clash of Civilizations and the Remaking of World Order.* New York: Simon & Schuster, 1996.

Hurewitz, J. C. *The Struggle for Palestine.* New York: Schocken Books, 1976.

Jbara, Taysir. *Palestinian Leader Hajj Amin al-Husayni: Mufti of Jerusalem.* Princeton, NJ: Kingston Press, 1985.

Johnson, Daniel. "Allah's England?" *Commentary* 122, no. 4 (November 2006): 41–46.

Karsh, Efraim, and Inari Rautsi. *Saddam Hussein: A Political Biography.* London: Brassey's, 1991.

Karsh, Efraim. *Arafat's War: The Man and His Battle for Israeli Conquest.* New York: Grove Press, 2003.

——. *Islamic Imperialism: A History.* New Haven: Yale University Press, 2006.

Kedourie, Elie. *The Chatham House Version and Other Middle Eastern Studies.* Chicago: Ivan R. Dee, 1984.

Keegan, John. "How Hitler Could Have Won the War." In Robert Cowley, ed. *What If?: The World's Foremost Military Historians Imagine What Might Have Been.* New York: Berkley Books, 2000.

Kepel, Giles. *Muslim Extremism in Egypt: The Prophet and Pharaoh.* Berkeley: University of California Press, 1984.

——. *Jihad: The Trail of Political Islam.* Cambridge, MA: Belknap Press of Harvard University Press, 2002.

Kershaw, Ian. *Making Friends with Hitler: Lord Londonderry, the Nazis and the Road to War.* New York: Penguin Books, 2005.

Khalidi, Rashid. *The Iron Cage: The Story of the Palestinian Struggle for Statehood.* Boston: Beacon Press, 2006.

Khomeini, Ayatollah. "Programme for the Establishment of an Islamic Government." In Ayatollah Khomeini. *Islam and Revolution: Writings and Declarations of Imam Khomeini.* Berkeley: University of California Press, 1981.

Kiernan, Thomas. *Arafat: The Man and the Myth.* New York: W. W. Norton & Co., 1976.

Kirchwey, Freda. *The Palestine Problem and Proposals for Its Solution: Memorandum Submitted to the General Assembly of the United Nations.* New York: Nation Associates, April 1947.

——. *The Arab Higher Committee: Its Origins, Personnel, and Purposes—The Documentary Record Submitted to the United Nations.* New York: Nation Associates, 1947.

—— et al. *The Record of Collaboration of King Farouk of Egypt with the Nazis and Their Ally, the Mufti: The Official Nazi Records of the King's Alliance and of the Mufti's Plans for Bombing Jerusalem and Tel Aviv—Memorandum Submitted to the United Nations.* New York: Nation Associates, 1948.

Krumensackeer, Thomas. "Nazis Planned Holocaust for Palestine." *Washington Post*/Reuters, April 7, 2006.

Küntzel, Matthias. "Iran's Obsession with the Jews: Denying the Holocaust, Desiring Another One." *Weekly Standard* 11, no. 22 (February 19, 2007): 18–22.

———. *Jihad and Jew-Hatred: Islamism, Nazism and the Roots of 9/11.* Translated by Colin Meade. New York: Telos Press Publishing, 2007.

Kurlantzick, Joshua. "The Left and the Islamists." *Commentary* 118, no. 5 (December 2004): 34–37.

Lanning, Michael Lee. *The Battle 100: The Stories Behind History's Most Influential Battles.* Naperville, IL: Sourcebooks, 2003.

Laqueur, Walter, and Barry Rubin, eds. *The Arab-Israeli Reader,* 6th ed. New York: Penguin, 2001.

Laqueur, Walter. *The Changing Face of Anti-Semitism: From Ancient Times to the Present Day.* New York: Oxford University Press, 2006.

Lawrence, Bruce, ed. *Messages to the World: The Statements of Osama bin Laden.* London: Verso, 2005.

Lepre, George. *Himmler's Bosnian Division: The Waffen-SS Handschar Division, 1943–1945.* Arglen, PA: Schiffer Military History, 1997.

Lesch, Ann Mosely. *Arab Politics in Palestine, 1917–1939.* Ithaca and London: Cornell University Press, 1979.

Levitt, Matthew. *Hamas: Politics, Charity, and Terrorism in the Service of Jihad.* New Haven: Yale University Press, 2006.

Lewis, Bernard. *The Jews of Islam.* Princeton, NJ: Princeton University Press, 1984.

———. *The Political Language of Islam.* Chicago: University of Chicago Press, 1991.

———. *The Middle East: A Brief History of the Last 2,000 Years.* New York: Scribner, 1995.

———. "License to Kill: Usama ben Laden's Declaration of Jihad." *Foreign Affairs* (November–December 1998): 14–19.

———. *Semites and Anti-Semites.* New York: W. W. Norton & Co., 1999.

———. "The British Mandate for Palestine in Historical Perspective." In Bernard Lewis. *From Babel to Dragomans: Interpreting the Middle East.* New York: Oxford University Press, 2004.

———. *The Crisis of Islam: Holy War and Unholy Terror.* New York: Random House, 2004.

———. *From Babel to Dragomans: Interpreting the Middle East.* New York: Oxford University Press, 2004.

Lipman, Vivian D. "Herbert Louis Samuel." *Encyclopedia Judaica,* vol. 14, 799. Jerusalem: KETER Publishing House, 1971.

Lipstadt, Deborah. *Denying the Holocaust.* New York: Plume, 1993.

Longgrear, Paul, and Raymond McNemar. "The Arab/Muslim Nazi Connection." *Canadian Friends.* Jerusalem: International Christian Embassy, 2003. www.cdnfriendsicej.ca/medigest/*mayoo*/arab.Natzi.html.

Makovsky, David. *Making Peace with the PLO: The Rabin Government's Road to Oslo.* Boulder, CO: Westview Press, 1996.

Makovsy, Michael. *Churchill's Promised Land: Zionism and Statecraft.* New Haven: Yale University Press, 2007.

Malkin, Peter Z., and Harry Stein. *Eichmann in My Hands.* New York: Warner Books, 1990.

Mandel, Daniel. *H. V. Evatt and the Establishment of Israel.* London: Frank Cass & Co., 2004.

Marcus, Ithamar. *In Their Own Words: Anti-Semitism and Racism as Policy in the Palestinian Authority.* Los Angeles: Snieder Social Action Institute, Simon Wiesenthal Center, 2001.

———. "Nazi Ally, Hajj Amin al-Husseini, Is Arafat's 'Hero.' " *Israel Report,* August 2002.

Matter, Philip. "The Role of the Mufti of Jerusalem in the Political Struggle over the Western Wall, 1928–1929." *Middle Eastern Studies* XIX, no. 1 (January 1983): 104–118.

———. "Amin al-Hysayni and Iraq's Quest for Independence, 1939–1941." *Arab Studies Quarterly* VI, no. 4 (Fall 1984): 267–281

———. *The Mufti of Jerusalem: Al-Hajj Amin al-Husayni and the Palestinian National Movement.* New York: Columbia University Press, 1988.

Meacham, Jon. *Franklin and Winston.* New York: Random House, 2003.

Medoff, Rafael. "The Mufti's Nazi Years Re-examined." *The Journal of Israeli History* 17, no. 3 (1996): 317–333.

———. "Palestinians May Get a Holocaust Denier as First Prime Minister." *Jewish Bulletin of Northern California*, February 21, 2003, 19.

Meinertzhagen, Colonel Richard. *Middle East Diary, 1917–1956*. London: Cresset Press, 1959.

Melman, Yossi, and Dan Raviv. *Behind the Uprising: Israelis, Jordanians and Palestinians*. Westport, CT: Greenwood Press, 1989.

Messages and Papers of Woodrow Wilson, The, vol. 1. New York: Review of Reviews Corporation, 1924.

Michael, George. *The Enemy of My Enemy: The Alarming Convergence of Militant Islam and the Extreme Right*. Lawrence: University Press of Kansas, 2006.

Micosia, Francis R. *The Third Reich and the Palestine Question*. Austin: University of Texas Press, 1985.

Morris, Benny. *1948 and After: Israel and the Palestinians*. Oxford: Oxford University Press, 1994.

———. *Righteous Victims*. New York: Vintage Books, 2001.

Morse, Chuck. *The Nazi Connection to Islamic Terrorism: Adolf Hitler and Haj Amin al-Husseini*. Lincoln, NE: iUniverse, 2003.

Mowrer, Edgar Ansel. "Official Documents Convict Mufti of Complicity in 6,000,000 Murders." *New York Post*, June 13, 1946, 2.

Muller, James W., ed. *Churchill as Peacemaker*. Washington, D.C.: Woodrow Wilson Center Press and Cambridge University Press, 1977.

Nakhleh, Issa. *A Memorandum Submitted to the Summit Meeting at Camp David by Issa Nakhleh, Chairman of the Palestine Arab Delegation and Permanent Representative of the Arab Higher Committee for Palestine*. New York: Palestine Arab Delegation, 1978.

———. "Memorandum to the President." *Journal of Historical Review* 3, no. 3 (Fall 1982).

———. *Encyclopedia of the Palestine Problem*, vol. II. New York: Intercontinental Books, 1991.

Netanyahu, Benjamin. "Ending the Legacy of Hate." Address delivered at a session called "The Question of Palestine" at the Fortieth General Assembly of the United Nations, December 4, 1985.

O'Brien, Conor Cruise. *The Siege.* New York: Simon & Schuster, 1986.

Palestine: A Study of Jewish, Arab and British Policies. New Haven: Yale University Press, 1947.

Pearlman, Maurice. *Mufti of Jerusalem: The Story of Haj Amin El Husseini.* London: Victor Gollancz Ltd., 1947.

Peters, Joan. *From Time Immemorial: The Origins of the Arab-Israeli Conflict over Palestine.* New York: Harper & Row, 1984.

Phillips, Melanie. *Londonistan.* New York: Encounter Books, 2006.

Pipes, Daniel. "The Muslim Claim to Jerusalem." *Middle East Quarterly,* September 2001.

———. *Militant Islam Comes to America.* New York: W. W. Norton & Co., 2003.

———. *Miniatures: Views of Islamic and Middle Eastern Politics.* New Brunswick, NJ: Transaction Publishers, 2004.

Podhoretz, Norman. *World War IV: The Long Struggle Against Islamofascism.* New York: Doubleday, 2007.

Porath, Yehoshua. *The Emergence of the Palestinian-Arab National Movement, 1918–1929.* London: Frank Cass, 1974.

Posner, Gerald. *Secrets of the Kingdom: The Inside Story of the Saudi-U.S. Connection.* New York: Random House, 2005.

Prager, Dennis, and Joseph Telushkin. *Why the Jews?: The Reason for Anti-Semitism.* New York: Simon & Schuster, 1983.

Pryce-Jones, David. "The Islamization of Europe?" *Commentary* 118, no. 5 (December 2004): 29–33.

———. *Betrayal: France, the Arabs and the Jews.* New York: Encounter Books, 2006.

Quandt, William B., Jabber Fuad, and Ann Mosley Lesch. *The Politics of Palestinian Nationalism.* Berkeley: University of California Press, 1974.

Qutb, Sayyid. "Our Struggle with the Jews." Saudi Arabia, 1970.

Roosevelt, Kermit. "The Puzzle of Jerusalem's Mufti." *Saturday Evening Post,* August 28, 1948, 26–27 and 165–166.

———. *Arabs, Oil and History.* New York: Harper & Brothers, 1949.

Rosen, Jonathan. "The Uncomfortable Question of Anti-Semitism." In Ron Rosenbaum, ed. *Those Who Forget the Past: The Question of Anti-Semitism.* New York: Random House, 2004.

Rosenbaum, Ron, ed. *Those Who Forget the Past: The Question of Anti-Semitism.* New York: Random House, 2004.

Rosenfeld, Alvin H. *"Progressive" Jewish Thought and the New Anti-Semitism.* New York: American Jewish Committee, 2006.

Ross, Dennis. *The Missing Peace: The Inside Story of the Fight for Middle East Peace.* New York: Farrar, Straus & Giroux, 2004.

Rubin, Barry. *Revolution Until Victory?: The Politics and History of the PLO.* Cambridge, MA: Harvard University Press, 1994.

Rubin, Barry, and Judith Culp. *Yasir Arafat: A Political Biography.* New York: Oxford University Press, 2003.

Sachar, Howard M. *A History of Israel: From the Rise of Zionism to Our Time.* New York: Alfred A. Knopf, 1976.

Sadat, Anwar El. *Revolt on the Nile.* New York: John Day Company, 1957.

Samuel, Maurice. *What Happened in Palestine.* Boston: Stratford Company, 1929.

Satloff, Robert. *Among the Righteous: Lost Stories from the Holocaust's Long Reach into Arab Lands.* New York: Public Affairs, 2006.

Schechtman, Joseph B. *The Mufti and the Fuhrer: The Rise and Fall of Haj Amin al-Husseini.* New York: Thomas Yoseloff, 1965.

Schoenfeld, Gabriel. *The Return of Anti-Semitism.* San Francisco: Encounter Books, 2004.

Seabury, Paul. *The Wilhelmstrasse: A Study of German Diplomats Under the Nazi Regime.* Berkeley: University of California Press, 1954.

Segev, Tom. *1948: The First Israelis.* New York: Free Press, 1986.

———. *One Palestine Complete: Jews and Arabs Under the British Mandate.* New York: Henry Holt & Co., 2000.

Shirer, William L. "If Hitler Had Won World War II." *Look* magazine, December 19, 1961.

———. *"This Is Berlin": Reporting from Nazi Germany, 1938–1940: A Narrative History.* London: Arrow Books, Random House Group Ltd., 2000.

Shlaim, Avi. *Collusion Across the Jordan: King Abdullah, the Zionist Movement and the Partition of Palestine.* Oxford: Clarendon Press, 1988.

———. *The Iron Wall: Israel and the Arab World.* New York: W. W. Norton & Co., 2001.

Sieff, Martin. *The Politically Incorrect Guide to the Middle East.* Washington, D.C.: Regnery Publishing, 2008.

Speer, Albert. *Inside the Third Reich.* Translated from the German by Richard and Clara Winston. New York: Collier Books, Macmillan, 1970.

———. *Spandau: The Secret Diaries.* New York: Macmillan, 1976.

Stein, Leonard. *The Balfour Declaration.* New York: Simon & Schuster, 1961.

Stillman, Norman A. "Anti-Semitism in the Contemporary Arab World." In Michael Curtis, ed. *Anti-Semitism in the Contemporary World.* Boulder, CO: Westview Press, 1986.

Storobin, David. "Nazi Roots of Palestinian Nationalism." *Think Israel* (January–February 2005): www.think-israel.org/storobin.nazis.html.

Storrs, Sir Ronald. *Orientations.* London: Ivor Nicholson & Watson, Ltd., 1937.

Talbot, Strobe, and Nayan Chanda, eds. *The Age of Terror: America and the World After September 11.* New York: Basic Books, 2001.

Tannous, Izzat. *The Palestinians.* New York: I. G. T. Company, 1988.

Teveth, Shabtai. *David Ben-Gurion and the Palestinian Arabs.* New York: Oxford University Press, 1985.

Timmerman, Kenneth R. *Preachers of Hate: Islam and the War on America.* New York: Three Rivers Press, 2003.

Tsouras, Peter G. "Operation ORIENT Joint Axis Strategy." In Kenneth Macksey, ed. *The Hitler Options: Alternate Decisions of World War II.* London: Wren's Park Publishing, 2000.

Wallach, Janet and John. *Arafat.* Secaucus, NJ: Carol Publishing Group, 1997.

Warner, Geoffrey. *Iraq and Syria, 1941*. Newark: University of Delaware Press, 1974.

Wasserstein, Bernard. *Herbert Samuel: A Political Life*. Oxford: Clarendon Press, 1992.

———. *Divided Jerusalem: The Struggle for the Holy City*. New Haven: Yale University Press, 2002.

Wiesel, Elie. "International Community Must Shut Out Ahmadinejad." *Palm Beach Jewish Journal,* December 12, 2006.

Willkie, Wendell L. *One World*. New York: Simon & Schuster, 1943.

Wistrich, Robert S. *Anti-Semitism: The Longest Hatred*. New York: Pantheon Books, 1991.

———. "The Old-New Anti-Semitism." In Ron Rosenbaum, ed. *Those Who Forget the Past: The Question of Anti-Semitism*. New York: Random House, 2004.

———. "Islamic Judeophobia: An Existential Threat." In David Bukay, ed. *Muhammad's Monsters: A Comprehensive Guide to Radical Islam for Western Audiences*. Green Forest, AZ: Balfour Books, 2004.

Zakheim, Dov S. "The British Reaction to Zionism: 1895 to the 1990s." *The Round Table: The Commonwealth Journal of International Affairs*. 350, (April 1999): pp. 321–332.

Ziff, William B. *The Rape of Palestine*. New York: Longmans, Green & Co., 1938.

Index

A

Abbas, Mahmoud, 118–19, 122, 137, 140
    The Other Side: The Secret Relationship
    Between Nazism and the Zionist
    Movement, 118–19
Abdullah, King of Jordan, 42, 85, 86,
    95–96, 188n.14
    al-Husseini and, 95–96, 99, 101
    assassination of, 95, 99
Abu Dhabi, 124
Achille Lauro, 135
Afghanistan, 37
Afrika Korps, 60, 68–69, 70, 71, 72
Ahmadinejad, Mahmoud, 99, 123, 124–27,
    142
    Holocaust denial, 124–27

al-Agha, Hassan, 121
Al-Ahram, 115
Al-Akhbar, 115
Al-Anwar, 113
Al-Aqsa Mosque, 27, 28, 73, 74, 81, 96,
    102, 129
Al-Arab-al-Yom, 120
Al-'Ashmawy, Muhammad Sa'id, 36–37
Al-Azhar University, 8
al-Bakr, Ahmad Hassan, 90
al-Banna, Hassan, 36–38, 83
al-Baqi, Ahmed Hilmi Abd, 85, 100
Albrecht, Otto, 135
al-Din Jarallah, Sheikh Husain, 19
Al-Dustour, 130
Aleppo, 70, 110

Alexander the Great, 67

Alexandria, 110

al-Gameia, Muhammad, 130

al-Gaylani, Rashid Ali, 43–44, 47, 53,
  88–89, 90, 92, 93

Algeria, 37, 63

al-Hassan, Hani, 135

Al-Hayat-al-Jadida, 120

al-Husseini, Haj Amin, 3–6

  King Abdullah and, 95–96, 99, 101

  academic credentials of, 8

  All-Palestinian government in
    Palestine, 84–88, 100

  appointed mufti of Jerusalem, 14–19,
    21–22, 25

  April 1920 Jerusalem riots, 13–14

  Arab Higher Committee presidency,
    32, 83, 84, 86–87, 95, 99, 100,
    101

  Arab Revolt of 1936–1938, 32–34, 83,
    131

  Arafat and, 82–83, 86–88, 103–104,
    105, 134–38

  assassination threats against, 20

  attitudes toward Jews, 7–11, 18, 22, 46,
    49–64, 74, 91–92, 107–27

  in Beirut, 100–104

  birth of, 7

  blood libel accusation, 114–17

  British appeasement of, 23–26, 40

  in Cairo, 79–88, 94, 99–100

  chronology of his life, 149–52

  correspondence with Hitler, 153–62

  death of, 104–105

  denied burial in Jerusalem, 104–105

  diary on meeting with Hitler, 162–65

  early life of, 7–10

  education of, 7–8

  Eichmann and, 51–52, 62, 80, 100,
    181*n*.47

  emergence as radical Muslim leader,
    11–12, 35–38

  escapes Germany after World War II,
    64–65

  escapes indictment at Nuremberg,
    61–64

  escapes Paris, 79

  exile from Jerusalem, 34–35, 81

  King Farouk and, 80–82, 93, 94, 170–71

  fatwas, 131–34

  in France, 65, 66–67, 79

  in Germany, 3–6, 46–65, 162–65

  Hamas and, 138–41

  high life enjoyed by, 47, 65, 81

  Himmler and, 50–51, 55–59, 62,
    166–68

  Hitler meets with, 3–6, 46–48, 105,
    162–65

  in Iran, 44–45

  in Iraq, 42–44

  Islamization of anti-Semitism, 107–27,
    128–43

  in Italy, 45–46

  later years, 99–104

  legacy of, 88, 105–106, 128–43

  memoirs of, 5–6, 79

  as mufti of Jerusalem, 19–38, 83, 84,
    111, 131

  Muslim Brotherhood and, 35–38, 82,
    96, 97–99

  Muslim Waffen-SS and, 55–59, 63–64

  Mussolini and, 45–46

  name of, 8

  Nazi alliance during World War II, 4–6,
    39–65, 105, 111, 141–43, 153–68,
    183*n*.81

1929 Palestine riots, 26–32

1948 war, 92–94, 133, 136

1967 Six-Day War, 101–103

personality of, 19–20

physical appearance of, 19–20, 47, 81, 138

political base of, 9–10, 22

postwar life and work, 79–104

protégés of, 82–88

Protocols and, 110–14

as public speaker, 20

reflection on "what-if" German victory in Palestine, 66–78

return to Jerusalem, 102

return to the Middle East, 79–106

Sadat and, 87–88

as Supreme Muslim Council president, 23

Khairallah Talfah and, 88–91

temper of, 20

Von Ribbentrop and, 49–50, 165–66

wartime radio broadcasts to Middle East, 52–55, 57, 108, 132, 133

World War I service, 8–9

writings of, 9, 57

al-Husseini, Jamel, 83

al-Husseini, Kamal, 10, 17

al-Husseini, Muheideen, 103

al-Husseini, Musa Abdullah, 96

al-Husseini, Musa Kasim Pasha, 10, 18, 111

al-Husseini, Mustapha, 10

al-Husseini, Sheikh Tahr, 10

al-Husseini family, 10, 17–18, 23

Al-Ikhwan al-Muslimun, 37, 98

al-Jalahma, Umayma Ahmed, 115

al-Jarwan, Seif Ali, 120

al-Kawukji, Fawzi, 33, 92–93

Allenby, Sir Edmund, 12

All-Palestine government, 84–88, 100, 101

Al-Mussawar, 87, 116

al-Nahayan, Zayed bin Sultan, 124

al-Nashashibi, Ragheb Bey, 18

al-Nasser, Shawqi Abd, 111

al-Qaeda, 36, 38, 99, 142

al Rahman, Aisha Abd, *The Enemies of Mankind*, 115

al Rahman, Omar Abd, 133–34, 141, 142

al-Rashid, Harun, 109, 110

Al-Risala, 129

Al-Riyadh, 115

al-Sa'dani, Mustafa, *Illuminations on Zionism*, 114–15

al-Solh, Riad Bey, 95–96

al-Tall, Abdallah, *The Danger of World Jewry to Islam and Christianity*, 114

Al Taqwa Bank, 36

Altern, Erich, 135

Al-Wafd, 129

Amman, 85, 96, 100, 102

Andrews, Lewis, 34

Anglo-American Committee on Palestine, 83

an-Nukrashi, Mahmoud, Pasha, 96

"Anti-Jewish Action Abroad," 49–50

anti-Semitism, 7–8, 16, 21, 40, 87–88, 89–90, 98–99, 142

of al-Husseini, 7–11, 18, 22, 46, 49–64, 74, 91–92, 107–27

April 1920 Jerusalem riots, 13–14

blood libel accusation, 114–17, 193n.35

Holocaust denial, 117–27, 195n.68

Islamization of, 107–27, 128–43

Jews blamed for September 11 attacks, 128–30

literature, 9–10, 25, 31, 40, 47, 70, 94, 103, 107, 110–14, 118 anti-Semitism (*cont'd*):

    Nazi, 5–6, 39–65, 89, 108, 109, 113–14, 117–24, 137, 141–43, 153–68

    1929 Palestine riots, 26–32

    pogroms, 44

    of Qutb, 98–99

    radio broadcasts, 52–55, 57, 108, 132, 133

    roots of, 108–110

appeasement, 23–26, 40

Arab Higher Committee for Palestine, 32, 34, 73, 83, 84–88, 91, 95, 101, 105, 120, 131

    al-Husseini as president of, 32, 83, 84, 86–87, 95, 99, 100, 101

Arab Institute for the Holocaust Research & Education, 127

Arab League, 92, 100–101, 124

Arab Legion, 5

Arab Liberation Army, 92

Arab Revolt (1936–1938), 32–34, 83, 131

Arab Theologians on Jews and Israel (book), 116

Arab War (1848), 92–94, 133, 136

Arafat, Fathi, 117

Arafat, Yasser, 36, 38, 82, 86–88, 91, 94, 108, 113, 117, 121, 141

    al-Husseini and, 82–83, 86–88, 103–104, 105, 134–38

    blood libel accusation, 115–16

    early life of, 82

    Fatah group of, 134–38, 197n.23

    physical appearance of, 138

    as PLO leader, 88, 103–104, 105, 134–37

architecture, Nazi, 4

Argentina, 80, 100

Asquith, Herbert, 8, 15

Atatürk, Kamal, 105

Atta, Mohammed, 142

Attlee, Clement, 62, 79, 80

Auschwitz, 51, 52, 72, 75, 76, 77, 126, 181n.47

Australia, 126

Austria, 42, 67, 122, 123

Azzam, Abdul Rahman Hassan, Pasha, 93

B

Ba'ath Party, 40, 88, 89–90, 120

Baghdad, 42, 44, 71, 74, 90–91

Bahrain, 10, 115

Balfour, Arthur James, 11, 76, 131

Balfour Declaration, 10, 11–12, 16, 21, 23, 24, 32, 49, 50, 51, 54, 60, 76–77, 176n.41

Balkans, 55–59, 67

    Muslim Waffen-SS, 56–59

Balsam, 117

banking, 11, 14, 76

Baruch, Bernard, 77

Battle of Britain, 42, 66, 74

Begin, Menachem, 119

Beirut, 34, 74, 91

    al-Husseini in, 100–104

Belgium, 42, 67, 135

Ben-Gurion, David, 17, 91

Berlin, 3–6, 80, 88

    al-Husseini in, 3–6, 46–65, 162–65

Berliner Illustrierte Zeitung, 56

Bern, 65

Berner, Willy, 135

bin Laden, Osama, 38, 98, 108, 129, 134, 142

Birkenau, 72

Bismarck, Otto von, 4

Blenheim Palace, 76

blood libel accusation, 114–17, 193n.35

Bohemia, 42

Bosnia, 56
  Jews, 56–57, 62, 63–64
  Muslim Waffen-SS, 56–59, 63–64

Buenos Aires, 80, 100

Bulgaria, 58, 59

Bullard, Sir Reader, 45

C

Cairo, 7, 8, 21, 36, 38, 41, 42, 69, 74, 82,
    93, 100, 110, 112, 116
  al-Husseini in, 79–88, 94, 99–100

caliphate, 37

Camp David summit (1978), 119

Canada, 122

Canterbury, archbishop of, 75

Carter, Jimmy, 119

Casablanca, 110

Catholics, 12

Ceauçescu, Nicolae, 135

Central Committee of the Arab Revolt, 132

Chamberlain, H. S., *Foundations of the
    Nineteenth Century,* 40

Chamberlain, Neville, 26, 40

China, 99

Chou En-lai, 99

Churchill, Winston, 13, 22, 42, 45, 66, 69,
    75, 77, 79, 80, 186n.15, 187n.24

Communism, 5

concentration camps, 51, 52, 58–59, 72, 75,
    76, 77, 119, 125, 126, 181n.47

Croatia, 56
  Muslim Waffen-SS, 56–59

Crum, Bartley, 62

Crusades, 12

Cueppers, Martin, 186n.21

Czechoslovakia, 42, 67

D

Dalton, Hugh, 187n.24

Damascus, 34, 42, 71, 74, 100, 110, 112, 115,
    116

de Gaulle, Charles, 65

Denmark, 42, 67

Djerba, 110

Dome of the Rock, 27, 28, 29, 81, 102

Dresden, 57

Duke, David, 126

E

East Bank, 86

Eden, Anthony, 45

Edward VIII, King of England, 74, 75

Egypt, 7, 8, 11, 21, 35, 40–41, 53, 71, 85,
    87–88, 91, 112, 114–15, 120,
    179n.5
  al-Husseini in, 79–88, 94, 99–100
  Battle of El Alamein, 66, 68, 69, 71,
    186nn.14–15
  Jews, 40
  Muslim Brotherhood, 35–38
  Nazi troops in, 42, 66, 67–69
  1948 war, 92–94, 133, 136
  1967 Six-Day War, 94, 101–103, 113

Eichmann, Adolf, 49, 51–52, 55, 58,
    60, 61, 72–73, 74, 76, 77,
    142
  al-Husseini and, 51–52, 62, 80, 100,
    181n.47
  escape to Argentina, 80
  trial of, 51, 52, 100, 183n.81

Einsatzgruppe Egypt, 60, 72

El Alamein, Battle of, 66, 68, 69, 71,
    186nn.14–15

El-Istiqlal, 117

Elpeleg, Zvi, 184n.99

F

Faisal, King of Saudi Arabia, 103, 112, 116,
    192*n*.20

Faris, Habib, *Talmudic Sacrifices,* 114

Farouk, King of Egypt, 41, 65, 80, 86, 94,
    98, 179*n*.5

    al-Husseini and, 80–82, 93, 94, 170–71

Fascism, 45–46, 187*n*.24

Fatah, 115, 134–38, 197*n*.23

fatwas, 131–34

Faurisson, Robert, 119, 126

Fez, 110

Final Solution, 50–52, 54–61, 62, 75–77,
    142

    in Palestine, 59–61, 70–73, 186*n*.21

Finland, 67

First Temple, 27

Five Books of Moses, 27

Ford, Gerald, 88

Fourteen Points, 12–13

Foxman, Abraham H., 191*n*.2, 191*n*.6

France, 8, 10, 112, 122

    al-Husseini in, 65, 66–67, 79

    anti-Semitism, 63, 122, 123

    Holocaust denial in, 122–23

    Jews, 136

    Vichy government, 43, 63, 65, 67

    World War II, 42, 63, 67, 68

Franco, Francisco, 67

Frankfurter, Felix, 77

Franjieh, Suleiman, 104

Free French Forces, 65

Fröhlich, Wolfgang, 122–23, 126

    The Gas Chamber Fraud, 123, 126

G

Garaudy, Roger, 123

    The Founding Myths of Modern Israel, 123

Gaza, 84, 86, 116, 129, 140, 141

George V, King of England, 15

George VI, King of England, 74

Germany, 5, 8

    al-Husseini in, 3–6, 46–65, 162–65

    Nazi ties with radical Islam, 4–6,
        39–65, 105, 111, 141–43, 153–68,
        183*n*.81

    postwar, 79–80

    radio broadcasts to Middle East, 52–55,
        57, 108, 132, 133

    war effort in Palestine, 59–61, 70–73

    World War I, 8, 131

    World War II, 36, 40–46, 53–65,
        66–78, 87, 123

    See also Nazism

Gestapo, 50, 75–76, 135

Ghana, 99

Gilbert, Sir Martin, 185*n*.106

Goebbels, Jospeph, 52, 80

Göring, Hermann, 60–61, 69, 80

Great Britain, 6, 8, 10, 63, 94, 142, 176*n*.38

    al-Husseini's "what-if" reflection on
        German victory over, 66–78

    appeasement policy, 23–26, 40

    Arab Revolt of 1936–1938, 32–34, 83,
        131

    Balfour Declaration, 10, 11–12, 16, 21,
        23, 24, 32, 49, 54, 60, 76–77,
        176*n*.41

    banking, 11, 14, 76

    colonialism, 10–12, 13, 22, 35, 36, 63,
        85, 111

    Eighth Army, 68, 69, 70

    end of British Mandate, 91–92

    fatwas against, 131–34

    Jews, 14–16, 76–77

    1929 Palestine riots and, 26–32

Palestine policy, 6, 9, 10–19, 21–26, 27,
  31–36, 71, 74, 83, 84, 85, 86, 91–92,
  131–33, 176n.41
Parliament, 13, 15, 33, 63, 75, 187n.24
Peel commission, 33–34
postwar, 63, 79
Sykes-Picot Agreement, 10–11, 13
World War II, 42–44, 66–78
Greece, 42, 67
Grimstead, William:
  Anti-Zion, 118
  The Six Million Reconsidered, 118
Gunther, John, 42

H

Haganah, 69, 71
Haifa, 70, 71
Hamas, 36, 38, 99, 112, 118, 125, 129,
  138–41, 142
  ideology, 138–39
"Hatikvah," 29
Hebron, 30–31, 70, 111
Hegazi, Mohammed, 126
Heiden, Luis, 113
Heliopolis, 82
Hertz, Joseph, 76
Herzl, Theodor, 15
Herzog, Chaim, 30
Hezbollah, 36, 38, 99, 125, 142
Hilberg, Raul, 59
Himmler, Heinrich, 49, 50–51, 55, 58, 60,
  61, 73, 74, 80, 142
  al-Husseini and, 50–51, 55–59, 62,
  166–68
  Muslim Waffen-SS and, 55–59
Hitler, Adolf, 3–6, 26, 68, 80, 87, 88, 89,
  105, 106, 107, 122, 123, 125, 141–43,
  179n.5
  al-Husseini meets with, 3–6, 46–48,
  105, 162–65
  Arab-Nazi alliance, 4–6, 39–65, 105,
  111, 141–43, 153–68, 183n.81
  correspondence with al-Husseini,
  153–62
  defeat of, 64–65, 111
  invasion of Soviet Union, 42, 67
  Jewish extermination plan, 5–6,
  50–52, 54–61, 62, 75–77, 142,
  184n.99
  Mein Kampf, 40, 47, 48, 110, 113–14
  rise to power, 39
  in Rome, 45
  suicide of, 80, 111
  working habits, 3
Holland, 42, 67
Holocaust, 58–59, 72, 108, 142, 184n.99
  denial, 108, 117–27, 195n.68
Hungary, 57
  Jews, 57, 59
Hussein, King of Jordan, 96, 101–102,
  104
Hussein, Saddam, 44, 88, 89–91
  al-Husseini and, 89–91
  political development of, 89–91

I

Ibn Saud, King of Saudi Arabia, 5, 42,
  93
immigration, Jewish, 5, 24, 25, 31–34,
  48, 49, 51, 54, 58–59, 111, 167,
  176n.38, 183n.81
  bans on, 25, 32, 167
India, 33, 35, 52, 67, 99, 105
  British rule in, 35, 63
Indonesia, 37
Internet, 108

Iran, 37, 99, 112, 123
  Ahmadinejad regime, 124–27
  al-Husseini in, 44–45
  Holocaust denial, 124–27
  Jews, 44–45
  1979 revolution, 98
Iraq, 10, 11, 33, 37, 42–44, 53, 71, 92,
  100
  al-Husseini in, 42–44
  Ba'ath Party, 88, 89–90
  Hussein regime, 88, 89
  Jews, 44
  1941 coup, 43–44, 88–89, 90, 93, 132
Ireland, 15
Islam, 5, 7, 10, 22, 79, 108. *See also*
  Muslims; radical Islam
Islam and the Jews (al-Husseini), 57
Islamic Jihad, 97–98, 142
Islamische Zentralinstitut, 4–5
Israel, 10, 98, 104, 117, 136, 142
  ancient, 27
  creation of the state of, 84, 85–86,
   91–94
  Hamas vs., 138–41
  Mossad, 130
  1948 war, 92–94, 133, 136
  1967 Six-Day War, 94, 101–103, 113
  terrorist attacks against civilians of,
   135–37
Istanbul, 44
Italy, 59
  al-Husseini in, 45–46
  World War II, 42, 45–46, 67

J

Jaffa, 25, 32, 51, 70
Japan, 52, 67, 68
  attack on Pearl Harbor, 3, 128

Jerusalem, 3, 8–9, 10, 14, 42, 60, 70, 84,
  92, 104–105
  al-Husseini appointed mufti of, 14–19,
   21–22, 25
  al-Husseini exiled from, 34–35, 81
  al-Husseini as mufti of, 19–38, 83, 84,
   111, 131
  al-Husseini returns to, 102
  April 1920 anti-Jewish riots, 13–14, 18
  German war effort in, 60, 70–73
  first intifada, 13–14
  Nashashibi-Husseini rivalry, 17–18,
   20, 23
  Old City, 30, 95
  second intifada, 26–32
  surrendered to British, 12
  Western Wall, 26–31
Jewish Agency, 60
"Jewish Control of the World Media"
  (essay), 120–21
Jews, 4, 5–6
  al-Husseini's attitudes toward, 7–11, 18,
   22, 46, 49–64, 74, 91–92, 107–27
  April 1920 Jerusalem riots, 13–14
  Arab Revolt of 1936–1938, 32–34, 83,
   131
  blood libel accusation, 114–17, 193*n.*35
  Bosnian, 56–57, 62, 63–64
  British, 14–16, 76–77
  extermination of, 5–6, 50–52, 54–61,
   62, 75–77, 142, 184*n.*99
  fatwas against, 131–34
  French, 136
  Hamas terrorism against, 138–41
  Holocaust denial and, 117–27, 195*n.*68
  immigration to Palestine, 5, 24, 25,
   31–34, 48, 49, 51, 54, 58–59, 111,
   167, 176*n.*38, 183*n.*81

Iranian, 44–45

Iraqi, 44

Muslim anti-Semitism and, 107–27,
128–43

Nazi persecution of, 5–6, 39–65, 108,
113–14, 117–24, 137, 141–43,
153–68

1929 Palestine riots, 26–32

Palestinian, extermination of, 59–61,
70–73, 196n.21

Palestinian state issue, 9, 10, 11, 15–16,
21, 54, 82, 91, 131, 133

September 11 attacks blamed on,
128–30

Spanish, 110

yellow badge worn by, 109–110

jihad, 36, 53, 73, 93, 97–99, 109, 128–43

fatwas and, 131–34

Jihad Times, 130

Jobert, Michael, 112

John Paul II, Pope, 122, 135

Johnson, Daniel, 187n.30

Jordan, 10, 42, 85, 86, 95–96, 101–102,
115, 120, 130

assassination of King Abdullah, 96, 99

Journal of Historical Review, 195n.68

K

Karsh, Efraim, 197n.23

Kastner, Dr. Rudolf, 61, 169

Khaled, Hassan, 117

Khomeini, Ayatollah, 38, 98, 99, 112, 124,
133

Kissinger, Henry, 112

Klinghoffer, Leon, 135

Knights Without a Horse (TV show), 113

Koran, 27, 36, 37, 38, 54, 65, 70, 87, 108,
109, 132, 133

Koubbeh Palace, Cairo, 82

Krumenacker, Thomas, 186n.21

Kuwait, 10, 115, 130

L

Lake, Veronica, 126

Lawrence, T. E., 11

League of Nations, 14

Lebanon, 10, 34, 37, 53, 85, 91, 92, 95, 113,
117

al-Husseini in, 100–104

Liberal Party, 14, 16

Libya, 68, 92

literature, 133

anti-Semitic, 9–10, 25, 31, 40, 47, 70,
94, 103, 107, 110–14, 118

Holocaust denial, 118, 122, 123

Liverpool, 14

Lloyd George, David, 14–16, 24, 176n.41

London, 11, 31, 75, 76–77, 78, 187n.30

World War II, 42

Londonderry, Marquess of, 75

Lovett, Robert A., 85

Luxembourg, 42, 67

M

Mahameed, Khaled Kasab, 127

Majdanek, 181n.47

Mallman, Klaus-Michael, 186n.21

Masada, 71–72

Mashaal, Khaled, 125, 140

McNeil, Hector, 185n.103

Mecca, 65

pilgrimage to, 8

Medina, 108

Meinertzhagen, Richard, 22, 24

Mein Kampf (Hitler), 40, 47, 48, 110,
113–14

Mizrachi, Abraham, 30

Montagu, Edwin, 16

Montagu family, 14

Montgomery, Bernard L., 68, 69

Moravia, 42

Morocco, 37, 40, 63, 110

Mosley, Sir Oswald, 74–75, 187*n*.24

Mossad, 130

Mosul, 71

Mowrer, Edgar Ansel, 58, 65, 106

Muhammad, Prophet, 7–8, 10, 37, 55, 87,
    108–109, 140

Munich, 26
    1972 Olympics, 135

Muslim Brotherhood, 35–38, 82, 87, 96,
    97–99, 112, 129, 136
    founding of, 35–37

Muslim Religious Trust, 23

Muslims, 7–8, 27
    anti-Semitism, 107–27, 128–43
    clergy, 8
    media, 108, 114, 115–16, 117, 120, 124,
        129–30
    Waffen-SS, 55–59, 63–64
    women, 34

Mussolini, Benito, 42
    al-Husseini and, 45–46

N

Nablus, 84

Nada, Youssef, 36

Nakhleh, Issa, 100, 105, 119–20,
    195*n*.68

Napoleon Bonaparte, 45–46, 67

Nashashibi family, 17–18, 19, 20, 23

Nasser, Gamal Abdel, 35, 40, 87, 91, 94,
    98, 99, 101–103, 112, 114, 118, 134

Nation, The, 64

Nazism, 4–6, 40–65, 82, 87, 88, 89, 92,
    108, 109, 113–14, 117–24, 134, 135,
    137, 141–43
    al-Husseini and, 4–6, 39–65, 105, 111,
        141–43, 153–68, 183*n*.81
    Arab alliance with, 4–6, 39–65, 105,
        111, 141–43, 153–68, 183*n*.81
    architecture, 4
    defeat of, 64–65
    Final Solution, 50–52, 54–61, 62,
        75–77, 142
    führer-mufti meeting, 3–6, 46–48,
        105, 162–65
    Holocaust denial and, 117–27
    propaganda, 40, 43, 52–55, 113
    radio broadcasts to Middle East, 52–55,
        57, 108, 132, 133

Nebi Musa festival, 13

Nehru, Jawaharlal, 99, 105

neo-Nazis, 134–35

nepotism, 23

Netanyahu, Benjamin, 197*n*.25

Neve Yaakov, 92

New York Post, 58, 65

New York Times, The, 39, 101, 121

New Zealand, 122

Nietzsche, Friedrich Wilhelm, 40

niqab, 34

Nkrumah, Kwame, 99

Noel, Cleo A., 135

North Africa, 55, 63
    World War II in, 66–68

Norway, 42, 67

Nuremberg Laws, 40

Nuremberg trials, 50, 51, 61–64, 65,
    169

al-Husseini escapes indictment at,
61–64

O

oil, 43, 69
Olympics, 1972 Munich, 135
Operation Barbarossa, 42, 67
Ottoman Turkish Empire, 8, 10–13, 15, 27,
109–110, 131
division of, 10–11, 12

P

Pahlavi, Shah Reza, 44–45
Pakistan, 37, 107, 108, 118, 130
Palestine, 5, 6, 9, 11, 37, 40, 53, 69, 114
al-Husseini's "what-if" reflection on
German victory in, 66–78
All-Palestinian government in, 84–88,
100, 101
appeasement, 23–26, 40
Arab Revolt of 1936–1938, 32–34, 83,
131
British mandatory government, 6, 9,
10–19, 21–26, 27, 31–36, 71, 74, 83,
84, 85, 86, 91–92, 131–33, 176n.41
demographics, 24
end of British Mandate, 91–92
German war effort in, 59–61, 70–73,
186n.21
Jewish immigration to, 5, 24, 25,
31–34, 48, 49, 51, 54, 58–59, 111,
167, 176n.38, 183n.81
Jewish state issue, 9, 10, 11, 15–16, 21,
54, 82, 91, 131, 133
Nazi alliance, 5–6, 39–65, 105, 111,
141–43, 153–68, 183n.81
1929 riots, 26–32

1948 war, 92–94, 133, 136
political elite of, 10
Palestine Arab Congress, 85
Palestine Liberation Organization (PLO),
88, 93, 101, 102, 103, 117, 118,
134–38, 142
Palestine National Movement, 9, 81, 104,
134, 137, 142
Palestinian National Authority, 113,
118–19, 121, 122, 129, 136, 140
Palestinian Red Cross Society, 117
Paris, 65, 126
al-Husseini in, 65, 66–67, 79
Paris Peace Conference, 11
Passfield, Lord, 187n.24
Passover, 114–16
Paul II, Pope, 45
Pearl, Daniel, 107, 108, 142
Pearl Harbor, Japanese attack on, 3, 128
Pearlman, Moshe, 55
Peel, Lord Robert, 33
Peel commission, 33–34
pogroms, 44
Poland, 42, 58, 67, 68, 119
Portugal, 67
Posner, Gerald, 192n.20
press, Arab, 108, 114, 115–16, 117, 120, 124,
129–30
Protection of the Mosque Al-Asqa
Association, 29
Protocols of the Elders of Zion, The, 9–10, 25,
31, 70, 94, 103, 107, 110–13, 124,
128, 140

Q

Qasim, Abd al-Karim, 100
Qatar, 115

Qutb, Mohammad, 98
Qutb, Sayyid, 38, 82, 91, 94, 97–99, 141
  Signposts, 98
  violent ideology of, 97–99

R
Rabin, Yitzhak, 96
radical Islam, 5–6
  al-Husseini's emergence as leader of,
    11–12, 35–38
  al-Husseini's postwar support for,
    79–104
  anti-Semitism, 107–27, 128–43
  April 1920 Jerusalem riots, 13–14
  Arab Revolt of 1936–1938, 32–34, 83,
    131
  attitudes about America, 97–98
  blood libel accusation, 114–17,
    193*n*.35
  British appeasement of, 23–26, 40
  Fatah, 134–38
  fatwas, 131–34
  Hamas, 138–41
  Holocaust denial, 117–27, 195*n*.68
  Jews blamed for September 11 attacks
    by, 128–30
  jihad and terror, 128–43
  media, 108
  Muslim Brotherhood, 35–38, 82, 96,
    97–99
  Nazi alliance, 5–6, 39–65, 105, 111,
    141–43, 153–68, 183*n*.81
  1929 Palestine riots, 26–32
  protégés of al-Husseini in, 82–88
  rise of, 10, 11, 35–38
radio, 52, 108
  Fatah, 115–16

Nazi broadcasts to Middle East, 52–55,
  57, 108, 132, 133
Tehran, 123
Rafsanjani, Ali Akbar Hashemi, 123
Ramadan, 113
Rauff, Walther, 60, 72
Reich Chancellery, Berlin, 3–6, 46–48
Richmond, Ernest, 21–23
  al-Husseini and, 21–23
Rida, Sheikh Rashid, 7
Romania, 58, 59, 135
Romans, 27, 71
Rome, al-Husseini in, 45–46
Rommel, Erwin, 42, 60, 67, 68–69, 70, 71,
  72, 73
Roosevelt, Eleanor, 77
Roosevelt, Franklin D., 77
Roosevelt, Kermit, 57
Roosevelt, Theodore, 57
Rothschild, Anthony Gustav de, 76
Rothschild, James de, 76, 77
Rothschild, Nathaniel Mayer Victor, 76
Rothschild, Lord Walter, 11
Rothschild family, 11, 76
Rumbold, Sir Horace, 33
Rushdie, Salman, *The Satanic Verses*, 133
Russia, czarist, 110

S
Sa'ada, Anton, 40
Sabri, Sheikh Ikrima, 121–22, 129
Sadat, Anwar Al, 35, 40, 87–88, 91, 94, 119
  al-Husseini and, 87–88
  anti-Semitism of, 87–88
  assassination of, 97, 134
  In Search of Identity, 87
  as president of Egypt, 88

Saeed Sheikh, Ahmed Omar, 108, 142

Said, Nuri, Pasha, 43

Saladin, 12

Samuel, Sir Herbert, 14–19, 20, 76,
    176nn.41–42
    al-Husseini appointed mufti by, 16–19,
        21–22, 25
    appeasement policy, 23–26
    as high commissioner of Palestine,
        14–19, 23–26
    Memoirs, 24
    personality of, 24

Sarajevo, 56, 57

Saudi Arabia, 5, 10, 37, 42, 65, 92, 93,
    102–103, 112, 113, 115, 116,
    192n.20
    Holocaust denial, 117–18

Schindler's List (film), 114, 116

Schuller, Johann, 135

Second Palestine Arab Congress, 86

Second Temple, 27

September 11 terrorist attacks, 98, 113,
    128–30, 141
    Jews blamed for, 128–30

Shakespeare, William, *The Merchant of
    Venice*, 121

Sharia, 8

Sharon, Ariel, 122

Shaw, George Bernard, 15

Shaw commission, 31, 111, 178n.67

Shuqairy, Ahmad, 93, 101, 103

Singapore, 68

Six-Day War (1967), 94, 101–103, 113

Slovakia, 58

Smith, Bradley R., 126

Snell, Lord Harry, 178n.67

South Africa, 130

Soviet Union, 42, 67, 118, 137
    Nazi invasion of, 42, 67
    World War II, 42, 44

Spain, 67
    Jews, 110

Spandau Prison, 80, 141

Speer, Albert, 4, 80, 141

SS, 50, 60
    Einsatzgruppe Egypt, 60
    Muslim Waffen-SS, 55–59, 63–64

Stillman, Norman, 193n.35

Storrs, Sir Ronald, 21–22

Sudan, 37

Suez Canal, 68, 69

Supreme Muslim Council, 22–23, 28–29,
    104

Sweden, 67

Switzerland, 65, 67, 122

Sykes-Picot Agreement, 10–11, 13

Syria, 10, 33, 34, 37, 40, 43, 53, 71, 85, 92,
    99, 101, 102, 114, 120, 130

Syrian Popular Party, 40

Syrian Socialist Nationalist Party, 40

T

Talfah, Khairallah, 44, 88, 104
    al-Husseini and, 88–91

Talmud, 114, 115

Tehran, 41, 44–45, 74, 112, 125, 130
    2006 Holocaust denial conference,
        125–27

Tehran Times, 120, 124

Tel Aviv, 25, 32, 51, 60, 70, 92
    German war effort in, 60–61,
        70–73

television, 108, 113, 121

Temple Mount, 26–27, 28

Temple of Solomon, 27, 28, 29, 31
terrorism, 36, 82, 98–99, 107, 125,
     128–43
  Fatah, 134–38
  fathers of modern Islamic, 134–38
  Hamas, 138–41
  September 11 attacks, 98, 113, 128–30,
     141
  See also specific groups
Teshreen, 120
Third UN World Conference Against
     Racism (2001), 130
Three God Should Not Have Made: Persians,
     Jews, and Flies (pamphlet), 89
Tikrit, 90
Tireault, Jean, 135
Tito, Marshal, 63–64, 79, 99
Tlass, Mustafa, *The Matzah of Zion,* 116
Tobruk, 68
Torah, 27
Transjordan, 11, 37, 92
Treblinka, 181n.47
Truman, Harry, 94
Tunis, 37, 110
Tunisia, 63, 110
Turkey, 8, 10, 35, 37, 105, 113
  Parliament, 10
  World War I, 8

U
ul-Islam, Sheikh, 131, 133
Union of British Fascists, 187n.24
United Arab Emirates, 11, 124
United Nations, 84, 100, 105, 106, 120
  General Assembly, 88, 91, 197n.25
  Palestine partition vote, 91
  Security Council, 92

United States, 12–13, 94, 112, 142
  Camp David summit (1978), 119
  Congress, 118
  fatwas against, 131–34
  Holocaust denial, 126
  Middle East policy, 53–54, 85–86,
     87–88, 94, 119
  postwar, 94
  radical Islamic attitudes about,
     97–98
  September 11 terrorist attacks, 98,
     113, 128–30, 141

V
van der Put, Karl, 135
Versailles, 4
Von Ribbentrop, Joachim, 47, 49–50, 61,
     69
  al-Husseini and, 49–50, 165–66
  Nuremberg trial, 50

W
Waffen-SS, 50, 56
  Muslim, 55–59, 63–64
Wall Street Journal, 107
Wannsee Conference (1941), 62
Waqf, 23, 26
Webb, Beatrice, 187n.24
Weizmann, Chaim, 24, 76–77, 111
Wertheim, Georg, 4
West Bank, 86
Western Wall, 26–31
White Paper, 31–32
Wiener Illustrierte, 57
Wilhelm II, Kaiser, 131
Wilson, Woodrow, 12
  Fourteen Points of, 12–13

Windsor, Duke of, 74, 75

Wisliceny, Dieter, 51, 52, 58, 61–62

Wolff, Heinrich, 39

World Islamic Conference, 35, 91, 99, 118

World Trade Center attacks:
  of 1993, 134, 141–42
  of 2001, 98, 113, 128–30, 141

World War I, 8–9, 10, 15, 16, 27, 33, 131, 133
  end of, 11, 23

World War II, 26, 36, 40–65, 87, 108, 109, 119, 120, 123
  Arab-Nazi alliance, 4–6, 39–65, 105, 111, 141–43, 153–68, 183n.81
  end of, 61, 64–65
  North African campaign, 66–68

World Zionist Congress (1921), 17

Y

Yassin, Sheikh Ahmad, 139–40, 141

Yediot Aharonot, 119

Yemen, 10, 37, 92

Yom Kippur, 27–28

Young Egypt Society, 40

Yousef, Ramzi, 141–42

Yugoslavia, 42, 56, 67, 79, 99, 119
  postwar, 63–64

Z

Zayed Center for Coordination and Follow-Up, 124

Zionism, 14, 15, 16, 17, 21, 22, 24, 29, 31, 35, 39, 46, 70, 76, 85, 88, 89, 91, 94, 103, 111, 116, 119, 129, 130, 176n.38

Zulficar, Said, Pasha, 41

About the Authors

DAVID G. DALIN is the Taube Research Fellow in American History at the Hoover Institution at Stanford University. He is the author, co-author, or editor of nine books, including *Religion and State in the American Jewish Experience* (with Jonathan D. Sarna), *The Presidents of the United States and the Jews,* and *The Myth of Hitler's Pope.* His numerous articles and book reviews have appeared in *American Jewish History, Commentary, First Things, The Weekly Standard,* and the *American Jewish Year Book.*

JOHN F. ROTHMANN serves on the faculty of the Fromm Institute at the University of San Francisco. He is an author, teacher, archivist, political consultant, and talk show host on the ABC-affiliated KGO 810-AM Newstalk Radio in San Francisco. He has lectured on American politics and the presidency and the Middle East throughout the United States, Canada, and Israel.